CRIMINAL LAW AND SOCIETY IN
LATE MEDIEVAL AND TUDOR ENGLAND

CRIMINAL LAW AND SOCIETY IN LATE MEDIEVAL AND TUDOR ENGLAND

John G. Bellamy

ALAN SUTTON · Gloucester

ST MARTIN'S PRESS · New York
1984

First published 1984
Alan Sutton Publishing Limited
Brunswick Road
Gloucester

British Library Cataloguing in Publication Data

Bellamy, John, *1930–*
    Criminal law and society in late Medieval and Tudor England.
    1. Criminal law—England—History
    I. Title   344.205′09   KD7850

ISBN 0-86299-127-7

First published in the United States of America in 1984
St. Martin's Press, Inc.
175 Fifth Avenue
New York, NY 10010

Library of Congress Cataloging in Publication Data

Bellamy, John G., 1930–
    Criminal law and society in late medieval and Tudor England.

    Includes bibliographical references and index.
    1. Criminal law—England—History. 2. Criminal procedure—
    England—History. I. Title.
    KD7850.B45 1984   345.42′009   83-40623
    ISBN 0-312-17215-X   344.205009

Typesetting and origination by
Alan Sutton Publishing Limited
Photoset Goudy Roman 10/11
Printed in Great Britain

CONTENTS

ACKNOWLEDGEMENT

This book has been published with the help of a grant from the Social Science Federation of Canada, using funds provided by the Social Sciences and Humanities Research Council of Canada.

1

INTRODUCTION

If we look back between fifty and a hundred years to when the history of English law was beginning to capture the interest of lawyers and historians in a way it had not done for centuries if ever before, we find that the criminal law of the later middle ages and the early modern period was viewed with considerable desdain. It was thought of as lacking the exciting developments of earlier and later periods. Thus what progress there was in the fourteenth and fifteenth centuries was reckoned to lie in the 'detailed working out of the principles which had been laid down in the reign of Edward I', not in novel concepts or devices, for 'the great outlines of criminal law . . . seem to have been regarded as fixed for all time'.[1]

In holding these view Holdsworth and Maitland were not alone. Earlier Stephen had argued that between the thirteenth and sixteenth centuries 'the substantive part of the criminal law . . . varied very little'. One area where he saw little sign of progress was procedure. Drawing on the Corone section of Fitzherbert's *Abridgement*, which he regarded as good a source as existed, Stephen noted with obvious disappointment that he found only information relating to 'matters of practice' and these were to play little part in the future development of the criminal law.[2] This viewpoint was not substantially different from that of Holdsworth, who found the criminal law 'cumbered with decadent survivals' namely appeals, benefit of clergy, sanctuary and the like, together with 'intricacies of process' which hampered its proper administration.[3]

The small amount of progress they allowed to have been made in the development of the criminal law Stephen, Maitland, and Holdsworth, found in different places and promoted by different agencies. Stephen noted the creation by parliament of about a score of new felonies and a similar number of misdemeanours. The defining of the latter he attributed to the work of the 'Court of the Star Chamber'.[4] Maitland's interpretation was more complex. The statutes of the fourteenth and fifteenth centuries were largely concerned with trade offences. Indeed parliament had 'abandoned the idea of controlling the development of the common law' and limited its actions to spasmodic remedies for specific evils as for example by trying to 'circumvent the circumventors of a

1

statute'.[5] For Maitland what progress there was was the work of the judges and the lawyers, presumably through their interpretations and exploitations of the law. Only in the Tudor period did matters change: from Henry VIII's time onwards statute was sovereign and the judges were 'expected to attend very closely to the words that Parliament utters, to weigh and obey every letter of the law'. Holdsworth assessment was not dissimilar to Stephen's. The criminal law was developed in the fourteenth and fifteenth centuries at least by statutes rather than any other agency; and it was through parliament also that the common law was able to retain total control of offences involving life and limb, which prevented the council 'exercising a liberal influence upon the doctrines of the common law'.[6]

This dismal assessment of the development of English criminal law from Bracton's time to the Tudor age was primarily the result of the paucity of sources available to legal historians in the late nineteenth and early twentieth centuries. Stephen used the writings of Bracton, Britton, Fitzherbert, Staunford, Lambarde, Coke, and Hale, the *State Trials*, the statute rolls, and the rolls of parliament but lamented the fact that save for Fortescue there was no treatise writer on the subject from the late medieval period.[7] Although he seems to have made more use of the Year Books Holdsworth relied on a collection of sources which were not dissimilar, while Maitland was making general statements about a period of legal history he never studied in any depth and utilised sources which were only traditional ones.

Significant progress in unravelling the history of the late medieval criminal law was in fact only achieved in the 1930s. In 1938 there appeared Bertha Putnam's *Proceedings before the Justices of the Peace in the Fourteenth and Fifteenth Centuries* wherein were included indictments covering all types of offences and a masterly index by T.F.T. Plucknett analyzing the word forms used. Here, generally *in extenso* were the records of courts of the first instance and this made the volume more important in many ways than even the valuable contributions to be found in contemporary volumes of the Selden society.[8] Putnam and Plucknett wrote as professional historians whose interest was the English medieval criminal law, not as lawyers with a historical bent like for example Stephen, whose main intent was tracing the roots of those institutions still existing in his own day. They were therefore more cognizant of the social background and wider in their interests than earlier investigators. Plucknett in addition had the ability to focus attention on important topics which had not been studied in depth in the past as for example the notoriety of certain offences and offenders, trials of a summary nature, pardons, witnesses and evidence, examination, crimes in the nature of larceny, and the variable terminology used by accusing juries.[9]

After this seminal research there followed a period of relative quiescence and then another, in the 1970s, when the subject began to attract renewed attention, quite often from younger scholars.[10] As a result there have appeared a fair number of studies on particular topics which through their depth have revealed the period from the end of the thirteenth to the late sixteenth century as one of greater change than suspected, even as a time of relative enlightenment. Thus despite a contrary opinion that in these centuries 'nothing worthwhile was created' and there is 'no achievement to trace' a recent writer on the law of the early sixteenth century has concluded that at that time at least criminal justice was thought of as having an importance equal to that governing private cases. Furthermore 'it would be misleading to deduce . . . that criminal jurisprudence was undeveloped or lightly regarded in the dark days before Staundford'. There was little that was 'vague and imprecise' in it. The writings left by the lawyers of the early sixteenth century, he notes, give the impression of 'conscientious men who were anxious to see justice done to all concerned and to see the law developed in a humane fashion'.[11] There were several ways such development could occur: through questions of law arising at actual trials from indictments or the evidence, through indictments moved by writ of *certiorari* into the king's bench, through adjournment of difficult questions into the exchequer chamber or Serjeants' Inn where the judges of the two benches and the exchequer might be consulted, and through readings on criminal law, with subsequent debates in the inns of court. Since in all likelihood all of these procedures were in existence as early as the beginning of the fifteenth century, perhaps even in the fourteenth, the extent to which the late medieval period had been underestimated is now becoming clear.

In examining developments in the criminal law from roughly *circa* 1300 to *circa* 1600 in the pages which follow I have not sought to cover the entire field but have directed my attention to what seem to be obvious problem areas. The topics are, I think, important ones but they are not alone in this quality; there are others similar which I have not investigated the reason for my choice being that those chosen demonstrate procedure, usually trial procedure and sometimes procedure which was not at all to do with appeal or indictment and trial by juries of peers, the traditional way of doing criminal justice. Despite the dearth of published work on the operation of the criminal law in the period under review I cannot claim to be the first to examine the areas selected. Indeed some were first studied a good while back. Stephen, who with Plucknett amongst the older scholars mentioned, was gifted with perhaps the best eye for significant development in criminal law, had something to say about riot statutes, criminal informations, witnesses, examination, benefit of clergy, and was the first to notice the importance of the statute of labourers to procedure.[12] Maitland paid some attention to the parliamentary statutes designed to control the private wars of the upper classes. Holdsworth noted the medieval beginnings of the laws against vagrancy even if he not draw out their relevance to special process.[13] Plucknett had useful things to say on this matter of unusual accusations and trials, as well as about examination, benefit of clergy. More recently there has appeared a short but interesting commentary on the criminal law of the period which has brought out the development of alternative methods of prosecuting offences as well as illustrating the legal fa tors involved in the feuds and unruliness of the *generosi* of the fourteenth and fifteenth centuries.[14]

The sources of which I have made use below are a mixture. Legal treatises, statute and parliamentary rolls, law reports, have been used by virtually all previous investigators although we have by no means exhausted what they can be made to tell. Particularly is this true of the statute rolls. Too often it has been the practice to draw on a single statute or a small number so as to demonstrate a particular theme or answer a problem without considering these laws in relation to the general tenor of parliamentary legislation over the previous twenty, thirty, years or so. Because of this the development of more general legal notions has sometimes gone unnoticed, the interelationship between preventative measures in regard to different types of crime has been missed and the continuous development and alteration in parliamentary vocabulary has caused bemusement and mistaken emphasis. The statutes in fact are basic fare in what follows below. The diet, readers should be warned, is of necessity a fairly severe one since often it is quite futile merely to sum-marize the general drift of a single or a group of statutes without paying attention to the exact wording.

Recent invesigators of the English criminal law in the period under review because of their reliance on the records of gaol delivery have been compelled to concentrate almost entirely on the felonies. No one can deny the import-ance of these enquiries, yet a great deal is missed by this emphasis. The later middle ages saw the appearance of a fairly large number of criminal trespasses, or misdemeanours as they later came to be called. These are not to be categorized as of only minor importance in either criminal law or the general history of society. For example riot and forcible entry, and offences against the labour laws were not only representative of great forces and stresses operating in the bowels of English society but were responsible for legal procedures for the handling of their manifestations which were quite novel, being of a summary nature and often involving the examination of suspects or witnesses. These inventions were very soon adopted for dealing with commercial and trade offences and it was probably in that sphere that they had their greatest impact and longest life.[15] The administration of these summary or shortened procedures was put largely into the hands of the justices of the peace. This was probably because on the one hand of the shortage of professional judges to deal with offences not carrying the death penalty and on the other because of the desire to have that authority on the part of the classes which provided the J.P.'s and were so strongly represented in parliament. These were the employers of late medieval England and it is significant that the first time authority was given to them to make use of the new procedure was under the ordinance of labourers of 1349. Perhaps because they were abusing it and utilizing the machinery of justice to further their private ends, the king by the fifteenth century may have regretted allowing them this authority since we notice, for example, that in certain circumstances those accused of riot could be cited before the king's council or into the king's bench.

The use of truncated procedure may have been prompted in the first place by the failure of juries to present the perpetrators of particular types of crime. In behaving in this way they were probably influenced by attitudes in their communities as well as by fears for their own safety. The government's distrust of presenting jurors manifested itself not only in the use of summary procedure and examination but also in the encouragement of the delation of offences by private individuals and a favouring of private prosecution. This is studied below in the chapter *Information and the Penal Laws*. Since the laying of information was often used in the place of presentment by a jury it can be regarded as another and probably the earliest type of truncated procedure, but early in its development it was married by means of statutes to the practice by which the informer was given a right to part of the forfeiture resulting from the conviction of the offender. The reason for this was that the informer was considered to be complaining on the king's behalf as much as his own. The extensive use made of these truncated procedures shows quite clearly governmental dissatisfaction with the traditional methods of accusation and trial in criminal cases, and its determination where crimes were involved which did not have to be dealt with the traditional fashion to construct a different system, one which seems eventually to have developed the jurisdiction of the council as a controlling agent.

The decline of the institution commonly known as benefit of clergy is another topic selected. The intention is to clarify earlier writings such as the pioneer work of Leona Gabel and then examine how the privilege operated up to the end of the sixteenth century.[16] Where the later fifteenth century had seen a determined attempt by the clergy to preserve their rights, the early years of Henry VIII produced, over the issue of who was entitled to benefit, as fierce a battle between laity and clergy as had been seen for centuries and one which caused the questioning of several fundamental tenets of the church. The Tudor period in general saw benefit no longer permitted for an increasing number of traditional felonies and newly created ones, although there were occasions when for the moment the tide seemed to be flowing in the other direction. Radical changes in the system occurred in the last quarter of the century and the suspicion has arisen that at that time also the judges took it upon themselves to allow or disallow the privilege as they saw fit which gave them the opportunity to 'plea bargain' with the accused and moderate the anomalies of the common law. The thesis has been offered that before the end of the sixteenth century they dared to ignore a recent and important statute on clerical benefit and even the technical distinction between clergyable and non-clergyable felonies.[17] All this calls for careful consideration.

One interesting feature of the English criminal law which will emerge below is the degree to which Tudor devices and practices were anticipated in preceding centuries. It would, of course, be unnatural if the institutions of a later age did not develop from an earlier but there is undoubtedly good cause to remark how the sixteenth century criminal law owed so much to developments of the fourteenth and the period of the Lancastrians and Yorkists. Thus truncated procedure utilizing examination was well established by 1485, as was the laying of information and the operation of the penal laws, while riots and forcible entries were being handled a great deal by institutions which were not primarily concerned with the common law. Significant changes in the areas under review that can be attributed on the other hand to the Tudors include the wider use of summary or truncated procedure (even its extension to take in one or two felonies) radical alteration to benefit of clergy, a growth in the role of witnesses, a clarification of the rules of evidence, and some intriguing amalgamations of secular and ecclesiastical legal process. The overall impression of the English criminal law which will emerge below is of anything but an obsolete system neglected by the lawyers. The Tudor age was full of new development but these were by no means sparse in the two preceding centuries, which should remind us that to judge progress from the evidence of *Year Books* is extremely hazardous. Change and experimentation were fairly frequent and we must therefore add to the recent suggestion that the English system was 'comparatively enlightened and humane' and endowed with judges 'conscientious and keen the law should develop in a humane fashion'[18] the conclusion that there was also clear progress at a more mundane level in the form of a continuous and successful drive to achieve greater efficiency in the operation of that law.

NOTES

1. W.S. Holdsworth, A History of English Law (Boston, 1923), iii, 276; F.W. Maitland, Collected Papers (Cambridge, 1911), ii, 478.
2. J.F. Stephen, A History of the Criminal Law of England (London, 1883), ii, 202–3.
3. History of English Law, iii, 276–7.
4. History of the Criminal Law, ii, 219.
5. Maitland, Collected Papers, ii, 478–80.
6. History of English Law, iii, 277.
7. History of the Criminal Law, ii, 202.
8. Appearing at about the same time were the first three volumes of G.O. Sayles' important work Select Cases in the Court of King's Bench (Selden Soc., 55, 57, 58, 1936–9).
9. See T.F.T. Plucknett, A Concise History of the Common Law (London, 1956), pp. 429–33, 435–41. For a balanced appreciation of Plucknett's interests and scholarship see the obituary by S.F.C. Milsom in Proceedings of the British Academy, li (1966), 505–19.
10. I am thinking of those who have given relevant papers at the series of Legal History Conferences held from 1972 onwards, as well as a number of North American scholars. In recent times however there has been no detailed examination of the field of English criminal law as a whole for the period under review.
11. S.F.C. Milsom, Historical Foundations of the Common Law (London, 1969), p. 353; The Reports of Sir John Spelman, ed. J.H. Baker (Selden Soc., 98–4, 1977–8), ii, 299–300, 303.

12. *History of the Criminal Law*, i, 122, 201–2, 217–20, 263, 294–5, 350, 459–62.
13. Maitland, *Collected Papers*, ii, 479; *History of Enlish Law*, ii, 460, iii, 276, iv, 394.
14. T.F.T. Plucknett, 'The Origins of Impeachment', *Trans. Roy. Hist. Soc.* 4th Series, xxii (1942), 50–68; A. Harding, *The Law Courts of Medieval England* (London, 1973), pp. 88–90, 92–4, 110.
15. See chapters two and four.
16. See L.C. Gabel, *Benefit of Clergy in England in the Later Middle Ages.* (Northampton, Mass., 1928–9).
17. J.S. Cockburn, 'Trial by the Book? Fact and Theory in the Criminal Process, 1558–1625', *Legal Records and the Historian*, ed. J.H. Baker (London, 1978), pp. 72–9; J.S. Cockburn, *A History of English Assizes, 1558–1714* (Cambridge, 1972), p. 128.
18. *Reports of Sir John Spelman*, ii, 299–300.

2

SUMMARY PROCESS AND EXAMINATION

Our first theme must be a double one: the examination of suspects and alongside it the abridgement of normal common law judicial process. The two are closely linked, being if not essentially alien then antagonistic to the concept of law envisaged by Magna Carta and subsequent judicial development. There the emphasis was on due process in the form of no judgment without the accused being put to answer to a presentment brought forward by a jury or to the direct accusation of an appellor. Examinatioñ and the truncation of judicial procedure often approached close to doing justice summarily. The evidence concerning these important yet strangely neglected legal processes is extensive and the best way to approach it is to proceed chronologically from the fourteenth century to the sixteenth by reigns but within the reigns and sometimes in adjacent ones to pursue particular themes and lines of development.

Both examination and the powers to do summary justice possessed by common law justices seem to have stemmed largely from the labour legislation passed in 1349 and 1351. The Ordinance of Labourers' of 1349 (23 Edward III cc. 1–7) in dealing with labourers, artificers, workmen, or sellers of victuals, who when offered employment at the wages current in their occupation in 20 Edward III or reasonable price for their food, refused to serve or sell, ordered they should go to gaol until they found sureties they should so serve or (if victuallers) pay damages. For our purposes the important section is the one referring to how refusal should be proven in law. It was to be done by the statements of two 'true men', probably eye-witnesses, before the sheriff, constable of the vill or royal bailiff. What the judicial procedure was is not entirely clear. The wording of the ordinance suggests that from the time the eye-witnesses gave their statements the person refusing service or reasonable sale was held convicted. It is, however, possible that if the accused party made an objection, perhaps on the grounds that he was not available for the service offered, a personal action between him and the employer resulted and proper trial followed.[1] The statute of 1351, which, as Miss Putnam pointed out, 'supplemented' rather than re-enacted the first piece of legislation, differed substantially in regard to the judicial procedure envisaged.[2] Servants, labourers

8

and artificers were to take an oath twice a year to obey the rules fixing wage rates. If they would not, or if they broke their oath by refusing to work, they could be put in the stocks or imprisoned until they 'justified' themselves. If they took more than the proper rates of pay, information was to reach officialdom through enquiry on the part of stewards, bailiffs or constables. These were to conduct their investigation 'diligently, by all the good ways they may' and certify the names to justices of labourers. The justices were then to attach the culprits to answer and 'so make fine and ransom to the king': they were to be imprisoned until they gave sureties they would actually perform their work.

The 1351 statute therefore retained summary justice for refusing work properly offered, although it made the stocks the alternative penalty to gaol. In regard to the newly-created offence of taking more than the proper rate of pay the procedure was much more formal and regular. The crime was to be enquired into by officials, not reported by 'true men', and the justices were to put the miscreants to answer, that is to say put them on trial in the proper manner. The surviving plea rolls relating to cases dealt with by the justices of labourers show that this was in fact done.[3] The only cause for comment is how, at their trials, the accused usually admitted their guilt, which suggests the evidence was difficult to refute. The pattern contrasts distinctly with the incidence of conviction in regard to other crimes.

For our purpose a most important clause is the one which ordered enquiry by officials. They were not simply to 'enquire' *tout court*, meaning they should use a jury of local men to ascertain the facts. They were to enquire 'diligently by all good ways', a novel phrase which suggests that they themselves were to take the major role, probably by interviewing and questioning persons supposed to have knowledge of the misdeed. They would be conducting, in fact, what in the fifteenth and sixteenth centuries would be called an examination. However, these examinations did not serve in place of an indictment but seem to have been used merely to provide material for the charges eventually brought by the presenting jurors. Procedure had moved from conviction on the report of two witnesses in 1349, to trial on information gathered by the authorities and made available to jurors in 1351. No examples of these examinations under the statute of 1351 survive today, but then no others from the fourteenth or early fifteenth centuries for common law purposes do either.

The reasons for the truncated process for dealing with offenders against the ordinance and statute of labourers are not difficult surmize. Both in 1349 and 1351 presenting juries were regarded by the upper classes with suspicion. It was probably felt that out of sympathy with the would-be employee they might refuse to report offences. Whether one man had in fact offered service and the other had refused it would have beeen hard for the offerer to prove to the presenting jurors without the evidence of the two 'true men', since very probably it would have been one man's word against another's. Class ties had hardened and it was this situation which saw the birth of summary justice of an every-day nature under the common law.

In the remainder of Edward III's reign after 1351 there were no other statutory introductions of examination or truncated judicial procedure, but the reigns of Richard II and Henry IV showed several, even if none were concerned specifically with labourers, servants or artificers. A statute, 2 Richard II st.1 c.6, cancelled remarkably enough by the very parliament which had just passed it, allowed members of the upper classes, as soon as they were 'credibly certified' to arrest rioters and other illicit assemblers causing general terror without waiting for indictment.[4] A parallel to this can only be discovered in 1336, when the like was permitted temporarily in regard to notorious malefactors and their maintainers.[5] From the parliament of October 1383 examination emerged again and in a much clearer form. By the act 7 Richard II c.5 justices of assize, sheriffs, justices of the peace and those with judicial authority in towns were given the power to enquire of vagabonds, who at that time were abundant, and 'feitors'. If these persons could not find sureties for good behaviour they were to be sent to gaol until the next delivery, when the justices would do 'as seems best'. The enquiry could be made either by jurors or by direct and diligent examination of the suspects on the part of the justices. If the former was the method chosen, then presumably an indictment resulted. If it was the latter then possibly there was no indictment and the examination took its place; or maybe, as in the statute of labourers of 1351, it provided material for charges later on, the evidence is by no means clear. The reason for permitting examination was very likely that the suspects were strangers to the region where they were stoppped, and thus the members of a presenting jury would know little about their background.

So far the normal process of accusation and trial had been abbreviated only in regard to offences by the lower classes, but from 1391 this changed. The statute 15 Richard II c.2 confirming the statutes and ordinances on forcible entries, riots, routs and assemblies in disturbance of the peace, gave authority for justices of the peace, when they received a complaint about a forcible entry, to go with a posse to the place where the offence had been committed, and, if they found an entry by force had indeed been effected, then to put any persons still holding the property into gaol 'there to abide convict by the record of the justices of the peace' until they made a fine. In other words there was to be no normal trial for those arrested: the recital of the mere written word of the justices of the peace as to what they had found and done was to be sufficient for conviction. This form of procedure was not entirely new, it had been used to convict traitors taken in arms against the king and the 'record' had been the king's own word. What was novel in 1391 was the category of offence for which it was used and the low rank of the justices who were given the power of doing such summary justice.

This summary procedure was next extended to deal with the connected problem of livery giving. This was by the statute 2 Henry IV c.21 which, confirming 1 Henry IV c.7, whereby no lay or ecclesiastical lord was to give livery of cloth to any man save members of his household or his legal advisers, gave power to justices of assize and justices of the peace to hear and determine such offences either by enquiry or by record in their presence. 'Enquiry' here again meant the usual procedure of inquest by jury, the jury then presenting a charge if an offence was found to have occurred. 'Record in their presence', which was intended to stand in contrast, seems to have meant a statement or certificate of by some official (justice of the peace, sheriff, royal bailiff or constable perhaps) that he had seen the offence of wearing livery committed, and thus caught the delinquent red-handed. This statement would serve in place of a presentment or indictment. Whether it obviated the need for a normal arraignment, as had been the fashion in the treason cases mentioned above, is unclear.[6]

A much more explicit demonstration of what 'record' could mean was provided by the next extension of shortened judicial process. This occurred in the very significant statute 13 Henry c.7, which was concerned with riot, an offence frequently occurring alongside forcible entry and the giving of livery. The act stated that where riots, routs and illicit assemblies were reported, two justices of the peace with the sheriff or under-sheriff should go with a posse and arrest the miscreants. The three officials were authorized to make a record of what happened in their presence, and by this record the offenders were to be convicted in 'the manner as is contained in the statute of forcible entries'. This was probably a reference to the act 15 Richard II c.2 which we have met above, and thus the intent was that there should be no normal trial but simply a recital of the officials' record with a judgment, the sentence to be a period in gaol until a fine was made with the king. Confirmation that this was what the laconic statute intended is provided by other procedures laid down for use if the offenders had dispersed before the justices of the peace and the sheriff arrived and therefore, since they had not seen the incident, could not record. In that case they were to enquire within a month about those involved, which meant utilizing local juries of presentment, and then were to hear and determine the matter according to the law of the land. This emphasis on normal trial procedure stands in sharp contrast with the summary process envisaged in the previous clause. The government had no great expectation that these normal methods of enquiry and indictment and trial would be successful, so it allowed that if truth could not be discovered thereby, the justices of the peace and the sheriff should certify what had happened to the king and his council 'which certificate shall have the force of a presentment of twelve'. Upon this the offenders should be put to answer and, if he admitted his guilt, be punished according to the discretion of the council. However, if the accused denied the facts as given in the presentment then the certificate and the denial were to be sent into the king's bench for trial. Should the accused fail to appear after proclamation had been made he was to be held forthwith as convicted of riot.

This remarkable statute, the influence of which was seminal in the development of English criminal law, demonstrated the desire of the government to supplement the usual methods of accusation and trial in regard to the endemic offence of riot. It provided for conviction by record where the justices of the peace and sheriffs were witnesses to the misdeed, but where they were not it did not dare introduce the device. The investigation to be made if the trouble makers had dispersed before the justices' arrival was to be of the traditional sort: but on what the certificate to be sent to the council should the first method fail was to be based is not clear. It might have been on the enquiries of jurors: it might have been on the justices' own conclusions concocted from common report and those to whom they had talked. Obviously the latter would have had much in common with examination of suspects and interested parties, which became normal practice in the sixteenth century. Although the act was of great importance in novelty of procedure, it was not put into immediate execution. The statute 2 Henry V st.1 c.8 tells us just that and demonstrates that the fault at that point lay with the justices of the peace and sheriffs, who were negligent. Therefore it allowed the injured party to bring the matter to the attention of the chancellor, who in turn would order the justices of the peace to do their duty in the proper summary manner.

So far we have been concerned with the summary doing of justice by way of record. The next development was for the government to achieve the same type of procedural truncation by means of the process of examination. This happened in the reign of Henry V and the early years of Henry VI, and the first statute to use the method was significantly one dealing with the wages of labourers and servants (2 Henry V st.1 c.4).[7] The justices of the peace were given power to examine these employees, and also their masters, on oath so as to discover if and how they had broken the statutes of 1349 and 1351 through taking or giving excessive wages. Gone was the report of the two 'true men' of 1349 and the diligent enquiry 'by all good means' on the part of stewards, bailiffs and constables of 1351. This is the first time we find the phrase 'examine on oath' in the statutes; it is one which suggests a formalization of the justices' enquiry, giving the procedure a new respectability and putting the examinee on the same plane as a juror of presentment as an attestor.[8] The act did not go as far towards setting up summary justice as did the one touching riot and record (13 Henry IV c.7), since the justices of the peace were only allowed to give punishment on confession of guilt. If the suspects denied the offence, then no doubt they were arraigned in the normal manner. Whether the examination might be offered by the crown in evidence we have no way of telling.

The statute 2 Henry VI c.18 was a supplement to 2 Henry V st.1 c.4 and said so. Whereas the latter had permitted the examination of masters as well as labourers and servants so as to discover if they had broken the statutes of labourers through excessive wages, and had awarded automatic punishment if they confessed, they could now on examination be sent summarily to gaol for a month, regardless of whether they admitted it, if the justices considered them guilty. The act also extended this rule to all labourers, masons, carpenters, tilers, thatchers and daubers, although in regard to receiving, not giving, wages.[9] In addition it ordered justices of the peace to set the sale price of all products and food, and if any artificer or victualler should sell them for more to examine them. If the justices should discover the suspects to be guilty they were to imprison them for a month likewise. Another act of the same parliament, 2 Henry VI c.7, introduced such 'attaint . . . by examination', as one contemporary description had it, for use by justices who had to investigate malpractices by cordwainers and tanners. It was to be an option to the normal enquiry and determination by jurors. In 1433 (11 Henry VI c.12) the same power was given to justices of the peace in regard to the exactions of waxchandlers: they were to enquire by examination and search 'and punish them that by such examination and search shall be found guilty'.

The growth of examination and resulting summary conviction was therefore directly related to the ordinance and statute of labourers, and especially to the taking and giving of excessive wages on the part of masters, labourers, artificers and servants. If the hand of the parliamentary lords and commons can be seen in such legislation, annoyed as they must have been at the demands for more in wages by the lower classes and by the willingness of some of their own members to pay, it is less in evidence in regard to other offences to which examination and summary conviction now spread.

The first statute concerned with the rising problem of livery giving, 1 Richard II c.7, was aimed at preventing maintenance in quarrels and provided for justices of assize to enquire in the normal manner and to punish. A second act, 13 Richard II st.3, which was concerned with the illegal giving of livery and the presence of maintainers, barrators and embracers in lords' retinues, failed to give a clear indication as to how the offences dealt with should be investigated and tried, but a third, 20 Richard II c.2, which stopped any man under the rank of esquire from bearing livery unless he was a household servant or 'continual' officer of the lord, gave justices of the peace the power to enquire of offenders and punish them at their discretion. It is not clear if this meant inquiry by jurors but then summary punishment with no normal trial, or whether there was to be usual common law procedure throughout. The act 1 Henry IV c.7 extended the restriction of the Richardian act from esquires to lords, while the statute 7 Henry IV c.14 confirmed the two previous livery acts but transferred the job of enquiry to justices of assize who were to enquire by jurors but then certify their proceedings to the king's bench. The reason for the change was likely the establishment of procedure which gave to any man who would sue the offender half of the fines which the statutes imposed on those convicted.

In 1429 the way livery offences were to be enquired into and tried was again altered. Because of maintenance and failure to indict, the two earlier statutes on livery were not being kept. Therefore by the act 8 Henry VI c.4 justices of assize and justices of the peace, instead of having to await presentment, were given authority to take suspects as if they had actually been indicted for trepass *vi et armis*, examine them and if they were considered guilty to fine them as the statute provided. Once more examination and summary conviction was the judicial method preferred. The problem of enforcement, however, still remained forty years later, for livery giving offences were as common as ever. Thus the government in the act 8 Edward IV c.2 increased the penalties on recipients and made provision for the encouragement of informers. The giving of information, was combined with what later became known as *qui tam* procedure. The informer was admitted to sue both on his own behalf and the king's, his information which was on oath serving in place of a bill of indictment or original writ.[10] If the accused was convicted the informer was to receive a half of any forteiture. The judges, who were intended to be justices of the king's bench, the common pleas, oyer and terminer or justices of the peace, were given power to examine those accused and 'to judge . . . them convicted or attainted as well by such examination as by trial' at their discretion. In other words they could hold a trial before a petty jury or they could convict summarily with no trial at all.

Other crimes were considered in this period to merit the same handling. They included manufacturing and trading offences and deeds contrary to the acts of apparel. By the statute 3 Edward IV c.1 justices of the peace were given authority to examine those illegally exporting wool and do justice on them in the usual manner or summarily. The defaults of cloth workers and the non-payment of their wages led to the passing of the act 4 Edward IV c.1, which allowed examination of accused employees and their masters by justices of the peace, mayors and bailiffs with similar judicial authority, and even stewards of wapentakes and leets. Justice was to be done by the normal trial process or summarily on the revelations of the examination. In another part of the act, on the other hand, it was provided that keepers of cloth seals who were negligent, or who refused to show their seals when asked, might be convicted by examination on the testimony of sufficient persons of good reputation before the treasurer and barons of the exchequer. Later in the same reign the act 17 Edward IV c.4, which set down rules for the making of tiles, entrusted jurisdiction over defaulters to justices of the peace. They could proceed by calling in 'searchers' to look at the various technical processes utilized and the accusations of these experts would have the same weight as presentment by twelve jurors. They could alternatively determine the matter themselves either by normal procedure or summarily, subsequent to their own examination. The statutes which dealt with rules about apparel were 3 Edward IV c.5 and 22 Edward IV c.1. Both gave justices of the peace the power to enquire into infractions of the law by normal procedure or to use examination and 'determine by like process'; the rules about the seizure of suspects and their punishment were to be as for trespass *vi et armis*.

If we consider why these laws on apparel, trade, manufacturing and livery, which after all were only minor part of the criminal law legislation of the period, took the shape they did in allowing examination of suspects and summary conviction as a result of the information thereby discovered, certain common elements soon become apparent. All the laws had a close connection with the master-servant relationship, whether it was economic or social, and also, though a less proximate one, with service and reward and keeping to one's proper place in society. Perhaps more important was the fact that these crimes, when committed, became and difficult to conceal. Apparel and livery were manifest on the persons of their wearers: defective cloth or tile making left behind an examinable product. The offences, as fourteenth century lawyers might have said, were thus notorious.[11] It could therefore be argued there was no need for enquiry by presenting jurors with their knowledge of the locality, nor even for trial by petty jury. Equally persuasive in making the crown resort to these methods was probably a belief that jurors were not likely to accuse men of their own class or occupation, nor convict them: nor should we forget that the relative mildness of the penalties, which were only fines or imprisonment and never touched life or limb, was some form of inducement.

On the face of it summary conviction by justices as a result of what they discovered by examination was less arbitrary than the procedure set down for forcible entry by 15 Richard II c.2 and for riot by 13 Henry IV c.7, both of which allowed a man to be put in gaol as convicted simply on the justices' own certificates that they had found such offences to have been committed. Here the justices were also the witnesses, whereas by examination, as used for other types of offence, the testimony came from either the accused or from men at the scene. The reason was probably a practical one: armed rioters and entrants were not likely to offer themselves willingly for examination by a justice of the peace. They would have to be seized by force first, and bloodshed or at the very least cracked heads were the likely preliminary.[12] That the offences where examination superseded presentment and the normal process of trial were the ones which needed special rules of accusation and arraignment there can be little doubt, although it is debateable whether in the fifteenth century these were properly used. A statute of 1495 stated explicitly that the acts dealing with riots, unlawful assemblies, retaining and giving and receiving excessive wages, were not being executed because of embracery, maintenance and the corruption of inquests,[13] which suggests that summary procedure, was not being utilized in regard to these crimes to the exclusion of normal judicial procedure.

The practice of summary judicial procedure under the common law, including the use of examination either as a form of indictment or actual trial, seems to have reached new heights in popularity in the reign of Henry VII. No fewer than ten statutes made use of these procedures in some way, three using more than one of them. In four statutes examination was merely an alternative to presentment or indictment, in one it took their place, in five (if we include 'record' as well) it served as an alternative to trial by petty jury and in three it replaced such trial entirely. The first of the four statutes which allowed the use of examination as an alternative to presentment was 11 Henry VII c.2. It moderated the severities of the act 7 Richard II c.5 touching vagabonds and permitted householders, who let their homes be used by apprentices and servants for playing illegal games, to be discovered by examination before justices of the peace as well as by other means. The other three statutes in this category were all from the parliament of 1504 and each of them, we may notice, made use also of examination as a method of trial. 19 Henry VIII c.12 re-enacted the provisions just mentioned of 11 Henry VII c.2, but then added that later process was to be of the type usual in trespass cases: examination was not allowed to stand in place of trial. 19 Henry VII c.13 dealt with cases where an indicting or presenting jury would not find forcible entry because of maintenance or embracery while 19 Henry VII c.14, the purpose of which was to handle the problems of livery and retaining, permitted two justices of the peace (one being of the *quorum*) to examine those suspected of retaining or being retained illegally and then certify their names to the king's bench, the certificates being 'as good as an indictment'. The crime which was the subject of the act 11 Henry VII c.15 was, in contrast, a new one to be associated with examination, namely the practising of deceitful extortion in county courts by sheriffs, undersheriffs and shire clerks. The statute ordered one or more justices of the peace to enquire into these offences by examination only, although since the deceits were practised against defendants in actions of debt, covenant and the like, the justices of the peace first received intimation by complaint of a private party. Furthermore, since the examination was to serve in place of trial as well, it was unique in two different ways. We may surmise that the reason for the lack of alternatives lay in the nature of the persons suspected: the sheriff and his deputy were those whose job it was to produce panels of grand and petty jurors, and it must have been reckoned that they would have been able to obtain men ready to refuse charges or force their acquittal. No doubt, also, it was not thought fitting to have jurors enquire into what was an abuse of court procedure and a technical matter of law.

In the category of laws which offered examination as an alternative to normal trial is to be found the act 11 Henry VII c.4, which empowered two justices of the peace, being of the *quorum*, to enquire and determine by examination or otherwise complaints that mayors and bailiffs had failed to inspect weights and measures, and offences by buyers and sellers. A second act, 11 Henry VII c.17, allowed examination before justices of the peace as an alternative mode of trial when the offence was the taking or killing of hawks. Another relevant statute from the same parliament, the one to produce more legislation providing for exams than any other, was 11 Henry VII c.22; the crime, violation of wage rates, was one with which examination had been connected before. Quite novel was the provision of two different types of examination. Those indicted for breaking the laws on wages by paying above the fixed rate were to be convicted by normal procedure, or by examination by justices of the peace at the sessions, or by examination of two justices of the peace out of sessions, the last suggesting a large amount of work to be got through and considerable urgency.

The act 19 Henry VII c.13, which rehearsed and confirmed 13 Henry IV c.7, the first riot act, and made an addition to it, utilized 'record', not examination, just as had the parent statute. When two justices of the peace and the sheriff went to a riot or illicit assembly their record that it had occurred was sufficient to convict the miscreants. Furthermore if they found the troublemakers had dispersed they were to enquire what had happened by means of a jury, and hear and determine the case in the normal manner. All of this was common to both statutes. The new act however provided that if the jury could not indict the offenders because of maintenance or embracery on someone's part then the sheriff might certify who the maintainers were, and this certification had the effect of instant conviction. This was a measure more severe than any part of the parent statute of Henry IV and displaced a similar certificate to the king and council which was only to have the effect of a presentment. Thus the council was now deprived of jurisdiction in favour of automatic conviction at a lower level, although we should notice that it was expected the cases going to council would be those where the suspect admitted guilt. Where he contested the charge he was to be tried originally in the king's bench, which therefore lost custom also. Maintenance and embracery, especially in regard to riot and forcible entry, were at the very heart of upper class inspired disorder. The parliament of 1504 recognized this and was willing to legislate even more drastically than its precursor of 1412. It was no doubt thought that the sheriff, being the official who had most to do with jurors and therefore most knowledgeable in the matter of their corruption, was the man to be entrusted with summary power rather than the justices of the peace.

The same parliament which enacted this remarkable promotion of summary justice also dealt once more with illicit liveries and retaining. The act in question, 19 Henry VIII c.14, was not the first Tudor one to do so. There had been one in 1495 (11 Henry VII c.3), but it did not mention examination; it simply allowed the giving of information to take the place of presentment.[14] The 1504 act, observing that the king had called to mind how previous statutes about retaining, being retained and the giving and receiving of livery, were ignored, arranged for examinations, informations or suits concerning these offences to go to the council attendant on the king, the justices of the king's bench or the chancellor or the keeper of the great seal in the Star Chamber. Each of these tribunals was given authority to examine the accused 'as well by oth as oderwyse' and to convict them 'by such examynacion as otherwyse'. Should no examination, information or suit be forthcoming the chancellor and the keeper, the council, and the justices of the king's bench, were to have the power to send for any suspect by writ of subpoena, privy seal warrant or otherwise, to examine them on oath and adjudge them 'by verdict, confession, examination proves or otherwise as if they had been condemned at common law'. Since the council and probably the chancellor and keeper of the privy seal already convicted men as a result of their examinations, the novelty in the act was the enabling of the king's bench to do likewise.

There were also in this reign three statutes which ordered examination as a mandatory replacement for trial, rather than as an alternative. One, 11 Henry VII c.15, the act which dealt with sheriffs and others using deceitful practices to extort in cases in county court, also provided for examination to supersede presentment as we have seen. A statute from the first parliament of the reign, 1 Henry VII c.7, is even more arresting in its detail. It condemned those who went hunting, wearing disguises. The procedure laid down was for justices of the peace to take those against whom information was brought and examine them. If a suspect, presumably one whose guilt became clear, would not admit to his nefarious activities or reveal the names of his confederates, the crime which was no more than trespass was to become a felony. If, on examination, the suspect confessed his offence then he was to be fined for trespass at the next general sessions, the examination serving as the trial. When, because of refusal to admit guilt, the crime became a felony, procedure followed the normal course of the common law with perhaps the examination serving as evidence. The third statute relying on examination to take the place of trial was 19 Henry VII c.12, which dealt with gaming and vagabonds. Those found on examination to be vagabonds or beggars were no longer to be put in gaol as under 7 Richard II c.2, but were to be set in the stocks for a day and a night and then sent to their place of birth: if they were caught defaulting they were to suffer a threefold penalty. Local officials suspected of failing to enforce the act might be examined before the chancellor, the two chief justices and the chief baron of the exchequer or by the justices of assize on their circuits. If by such examination the suspects were reckoned to be guilty they were to be punished 'as if convicted by due process and course of the king's laws'. Such mandatory use of summary procedure again shows the determination to suppress laxity and corruption amongst local office holders by the most efficient methods possible.

The statutes of Henry VII which provided for examination or in some way shortened the normal form of criminal trial under the common law show a number of other shared elements. All except 19 Henry VII c.13, which allowed a sheriff's certificate to take the place of a jury verdict when maintenance and embracery prevented the finding of a forcible entry, put the operating of the examination into the hands of justices of the peace. Two of the statutes, namely 11 Henry VII c.3 and 11 Henry VII c.22, had a direct connection with the labour laws of 1349 and 1351 and two others (11 Henry VII c.2 and 19 Henry VII c.12), which dealt with the examination and imprisonment of vagabonds, had a similar link with the act 7 Richard II c.2. A third, 11 Henry VII c.15, which was concerned with weights and measures, followed the statutes of 1429 and 1433 (8 Henry VI c.5 and 11 Henry VI c.8), although it also allowed enquiry and determination by examination in regard to failure by urban officials to inspect deceitful practices in the same field. Each of the statutes except the one which dealt with hunting in disguise was a product of the fifth or seventh parliament of the reign and six of them came from the session of 1495. It would, however, be wrong to argue that in the latter parliament the king, lords or commons were eager to introduce into the common law much greater use of examination and summary procedure because of an aroused interest in legal process as such. The fact that the vagabond problem had recently grown to greater proportions must have been relevant, as must have the degree of success of truncated procedural methods in the same or similar fields. None of the crimes involved, we should notice, were felonies; all were trespasses or, as the new term was, misdemeanours. None were truly ancient crimes; they had originated largely in the late fourteenth and the fifteenth centuries. Hence in ordering them to be dealt with in some sort of summary fashion parliament was making no alteration to the handling of the fundamental offences of the common law. The crimes of excessive wages, vagabondage, riot, forcible entry, illegal giving of livery, and illegal retaining first appeared on the statute book only after 1349, and summary or shortened procedure, if it did not appear in the first act dealing with each, came in the next. Areas of crime to which the new procedure was introduced for the first time in the reign of Henry VII were the hunting and poaching of game, failure by civic authorities to inspect weights and measures, extortion and corrupt behaviour of officials in county courts and illegal gaming in private houses. What these offences had in common is not immediately evident. Hunting and poaching and illegal gaming may have been likely to create riots, and so might the discovery in an urban market that customers were being defrauded by false weighing practices. We might also argue that the offences to which summary process was extended in this reign were, for the most part, those usually committed by the lower classes. But a much more plausible argument is the one already suggested, namely that the offences were close in their nature to other offences which were already being handled in the summary manner, and the extension was therefore a logical one.

Mention must also be made of a feature to be found in the first and the last of Henry VII's 'summary' statutes. This was a reference which each contained to the king's council. The act 1 Henry VII c.7 referred to information concerning disguised hunters being given to council as well as the justices of the peace, although it left process entirely with the latter. The act 19 Henry VII c.14, on the other hand, in its setting up of a complete judicial system to deal with illegal retaining, made the justice of the peace the centre figure, but also allowed for those who sued or complained before the chancellor and keeper of the great seal in the Star Chamber, or in the king's bench or before the king in council. It permitted the defendant to be examined there on oath and to be convicted on the examination as if condemned according to the common law. The tribunals mentioned could furthermore summon suspects before them at their discretion. Through this general application of summary procedure and examination, although admittedly in regard to only one type of offence, this statute came closer than any other to uniting common law procedure with that which derived from the council.

The reign of Henry VIII showed almost the same number of new acts which stipulated examination and summary procedure in handling criminal offences as the previous one. If we omit those whose basic concern was with religious misdeeds and sought to put authority primarily in the hands of the bishop there were, in fact, eleven.[15] There were five (1 Henry VIII c.7, 3 Henry VIII c.3, 3 Henry VIII c.9, 6 Henry VIII c.3 and 25 Henry VIII c.15) whereby examination was to serve as an alternative to presentment, and one which set up examination as a mandatory replacement for it. In regard to trial three statutes (1 Henry VIII c.7, 3 Henry VIII c.9 and 32 Henry VIII c.13) made examination an alternative to normal procedure whereas four (22 Henry VIII c.12, 25 Henry VIII cc.15 and 17 and 33 Henry VIII c.1) ordered it as the only method to be used. There was also one statute (34/5 Henry VIII c.1), concerned with 'contrary' books on religion, which laid it down that two justices of the peace should sit with the bishop when it was being executed and should join in both the examining of the suspects and witnesses and the final determination. Here, howerever, process and trial were really under the law ecclesiastical and are not germane to our argument.

Of the relevant statutes providing for alternative forms of accusation 1 Henry VIII c.7 was intended to be operated by justices of assize and justices of the peace against coroners who extorted a fee for doing their office. They were to enquire and determine the matter 'aswell by examination as by presentment'. The act 3 Henry VIII c.3 had as its main objective making sure all the male adult population was in possession of long bows. Justices of assize, of gaol delivery and of the peace as well as stewards of leets were given power to discover failure to have bows by either examination or enquiry. The act 3 Henry VIII c.9, which was directed against those who in disguise or wearing visors attempted to break into houses or assaulted travellers on the highway, stipulated that the sellers of the 'visours' should be enquired into by examination as well as by inquisition in the normal common law manner. 6 Henry VIII c.3, which was an act for the setting of wages of labourers and artificers, provided that those who refused to work at the proper rates should be charged by means of examination or presentment. The statute 25 Henry VIII c.15 instructed that any two of the lord chancellor, lord treasurer and the two chief justices could enquire into the unreasonable pricing of books by either the oaths of twelve honest persons or by 'due examynacion by theire discreacions'. The only act making examination a compulsory replacement for presentment was 25 Henry VIII c.17, which laid down that persons offending by illegally shooting crossbows and handguns should be taken before the next justice of the peace for an examination which would serve as both presentment and trial.

Of the acts which seem to provide examination as an alternative form of trial 1 Henry VIII c.7 and 3 Henry VIII c.9 we have just met. 32 Henry VIII c.13, concerned with the weeding out of stoned horses and the failure of officials to achieve this, rather oddly allowed justices of the peace in quarter sessions to hear and determine the case, after presentment had taken place, by examination or otherwise.[16] Quite possibly the statute 3 Henry VIII c.3 should be placed in this category in addition to being in the first since the justices were seemingly empowered to take fines as a direct result of their findings by examination as well as after trial.

The first, chronologically speaking, of the statutes which made examination the only form of trial was 22 Henry VIII c.12, which dealt largely with those who begged without a licence. It ordered in one subsidiary section that wanderers claiming to be scholars of Oxford and Cambridge, sailors, proctors, pardoners or tellers of fortunes, should be examined by two justices of the peace, one being of the county *quorum*, and if proven guilty by a witness to be whipped and pilloried. Here for the first time some hint is given as to how the trial by examination was conducted. The justices were not merely to cross-question the suspect but seek out and listen to those who knew something of his behaviour. Two other acts were passed in the parliamentary session of early 1534; 25 Henry VIII c.15, which as we have seen dealt with inflating the prices of books, ordered the chancellor, treasurer and two chief justices to convict by examination offending printers, binders and sellers; 25 Henry VIII c.17 provided that when anyone contravening the 'crossbow and shotgun' act had been taken before a justice of the peace he should upon due examination and proof 'before hym had or made by hys discression' commit the offender to gaol till he paid a fine. The fourth act in this category was 33 Henry VIII c.1, whose target was the deceitful use of counterfeit letters and 'privy tokens' whereby men obtained money and chattels from their friends. To achieve its end it stipulated that suspects should be tried 'by witness' before the chancellor and by 'exam of witness' before council, justices of assize on circuit or justices of the peace in their sessions. It is the only sixteenth century statute which gives the impression of seeking to introduce the procedures of council and chancery into common law practice directly. There is perhaps one other act which deserves mention here since it involved summary procedure, even if neither examination nor trial was actually mentioned. One part of the statute 3 Henry VIII c.3 dealt not with long-bows but with those who were involved in the playing of unlawful games. It ordered that justices of the peace and mayors, who were 'knowing of' unlawful games such as tennis, bowls and 'closshe', might commit the participators to gaol until they gave surety they would not play in future.

The statutes of Henry VIII which introduced examination and summary procedure to new areas of the criminal law were few; furthermore those areas seem to have had little in common. There was, on the other hand, some connection with the acts of Henry VII in this category. At the minimal level there was some similarity between the method of handling the sellers of visors (in 3 Henry VIII c.9), who might henceforth be convicted by examination, and the summary procedure to be used against hunters in disguise in 1 Henry VII c.7. The act 3 Henry VIII c.3 had something in common with both 11 Henry VII c.2 and 19 Henry VII c.12 in that all three dealt in part with the illegal playing of games or permitting the same. Whereas the second and third of these statutes allowed examination to serve as one form of presentment, 3 Henry VIII c.3 stipulated that justices of the peace could send offenders to gaol for a term without any trial. The two statutes of Henry VII were also directed against vagabonds and beggars and were thus connected in essence with 22 Henry VIII c.12, which added whipping to the punishments to be inflicted. The closest connection between the 'examination' and 'summary' statutes of Henry VIII and those of his father is to be found in the remedies they introduced for dealing with negligent officials. There were two such acts from the reign of the first Tudor king, namely 11 Henry VII c.4, which was concerned with mayors and bailiffs failing to inspect weights and measures, and a vagabond act we have just met, 19 Henry VII c.12, which arranged for the punishment of sheriffs and other officials who failed to enforce it. There were also two acts of this type passed in the parliaments of Henry VIII. One, 32 Henry VIII c.13, whereby *inter alia* justices of the peace were given the power to discover negligence of stewards of leets by examination, had no other connection with the statutes of Henry VII previously mentioned; 1 Henry VIII c.7, on the other hand, allowed coroners suspected of extortion to be enquired of and convicted by examination and thus in the matter of determining the offence had a close relationship with 11 Henry VII c.4 and 19 Henry VII c.12. Finally we should notice the act 6 Henry VIII c.3, designed to alter the levels of wages paid to labourers and artificers, which in its enforcement sections copied the rules set down in 11 Henry VII c.22.

In part the paucity of new statutory provision of examination and summary procedure under Henry VIII must have been because it had already been established in all the most profitable areas during the reign of the previous king, and the acts concerned were, unlike some, continued after the new monarch's accession. Nonetheless it is odd that no new statute of the type in question should appear during the period of Wolsey's ascendancy, for there was a clear gap, save for 6 Henry VIII c.3, between 3 Henry VIII c.9 and 22 Henry VIII c.12. If we omit the latter act, and two in 25 Henry VIII, there was no relevant statute passed between the third parliament of Henry VIII and 1540, when 32 Henry VIII c.13, concerning 'stoned' horses, appeared.

There were seven statutes passed in the reign of Edward VI which had a connection with examination and summary procedure, yet it is quite apparent that examination was usually not the examination of the Henrician and medieval statutes and that the summariness of procedure was of a much less marked degree than hitherto. Three acts may be said to have offered examination as an alternative form of accusation and one as a mandatory, though supplementary, method. One statute made examination an alternate type of trial and another made it an obligatory one. A seventh provided something similar to examination as a supplement to presentment rather than as an alternative.

The act in question was the very first statute of Edward's reign (1 Edward VI c.1), one concerned with non-conforming preachers, and it declared an intent to examine witnesses rather than suspects. [17] It ordered three justices of the peace, one being of the *quorum*, to take information and accusations about the offence by oath and deposition from two 'able' witnesses. Their charges and supporting data were then to be submitted to a jury of presentment which, if it approved, would return them as an indictment. In a later section the act gave the justices of the peace authority to 'examine' (this was the word used) the accused as to the identities of any other witnesses present at the offence. Accuser and witnesses were then to be bound to appear at the trial. Clearly the suspect himself was not being questioned for the purpose of getting a present-ment, as had been the previous way of things. Perhaps there was at this point in time a fear that examination of the suspect came close to getting him to incriminate himself. It was now the examination of two witnesses which provided the material for the formal charge, the examination of the accused being, in this case at least, merely for the minor and incidental purpose of finding out who had observed the commission of the crime. How in 1547 the justices elicited statements from the witnesses is not clear, though some form of leading, if not actual questioning, was surely inevitable even if it did not amount to the usual common law exam. [18] Whatever the nature of the deposing, it was not really an alternative to presentment but rather a supplement to it. Furthermore the examination of the suspect in regard to persons who had witnessed the offence neither superseded nor stood as an alternative to any part of the accusatory process.

Of the Edwardian acts which undeniably offered examination as an alterna-tive form of accusation only one featured it in the old manner. This statute, 2/3 Edward VI c.9, was concerned with the 'true currienge' of leather. Justices of assize, of gaol delivery, of the peace, as well as stewards of leets and the head officers of cities, boroughs and towns, were empowered to hear and determine offences against the act in the normal common law way, but also to examine all supposed offenders at their sessions at their discretion, presumably as an alternative way of raising charges. A second act offering examination as an alternative form of accusation was 5/6 Edward VI c.14, dealing with forestalling, engrossing and regrating, which allowed justices of the peace in quarter sessions to enquire of such offences by inquest, presentment, bill (i.e. of indictment), information or by examination of two lawful witnesses. Then the normal trial process was to follow as if the accused had been 'indicted by twelve men'. All acts previous to the reign of Edward VI touching examination were concerned with something quite different. For them the person to be examined was apparently the suspect, but now the examination was of those who could give evidence about the miscreant and the doing of the misdeed. The act is also important because it alone of Edwardian acts, when referring to the use of witnesses for purposes of accusation, actually states they shall be examined. Other statutes could be construed, though wrongly, as allowing the witnesses to testify and give depositions, not as being strictly questioned. A third act in this category, 2/3 Edward VI c.10, which was concerned with the making of malt, gave power to justices of the peace in their sessions and stewards in leets to enquire, hear and determine offences 'as well by presentment of twelve men as by accusacion or information of two honest witnesses'. This statute was by no means so obviously involved with examination as the two preceding, since the word itself is missing, as in 1 Edward VI c.1. However, unlike the latter, the words of the witnesses did not merely supplement presentment but could stand in its place. It is best seen as a stage in the development towards the formula 'examination of witnesses' which came three years later. Examination was implied by the act, even if not specifically stated. The same is true of the other two relevant statutes of the reign. The act 5/6 Edward VI c.4 offered this examination as an alternative form of trial for those accused of armed assault or threatened assault in a church or churchyard. The miscreants were to be convicted before justices of assize or justices of the peace by verdict of twelve jurors, by their own confessions or by two witnesses. The statute which stipulated this form of examination as the only method of trial was 1 Edward VI c.3, where it dealt with vagabonds. Such persons, if they refused work when it was offered them or agreed to work but then fled, might be branded and made a slave. If, later on, he ran away, he might be branded a second time on proof given before two justices of the peace by two 'sufficient witnesses'. The same act in another section set mayors to examine impotent beggars and ensure they were, if found such, conveyed to their place of birth or residence. It ordered justices of the peace, if they saw an idle person, to examine him to discover if he was a vagabond: if the examination revealed that he was then they must have him branded.

From where, it may be asked, did this new-found popularity of witnesses and their depositions derive? The answer seems to be that it originated in those statutes of Henry VIII concerned with the king's ecclesiastical supremacy and religious doctrine. The act 28 Henry VIII c.10 against papal authority had set bishops to enquire of suspect ecclesiastical persons by means of presentment, accusation, and also examination 'by witnes or confession'. The examination here was obviously different from the type taken hitherto by the common law justices. The act of 'six articles' (31 Henry VIII c.14), which talked of bishops taking information and accusation of offences under the act by means of the oaths and depositions of two able and lawful persons 'at least', said also that those before whom presentments, informations and accusations were made (and they included justices of the peace and stewards of leets as well as bishops) should examine the accusers as to what other witnesses to the misdeed there were. The arrangements here, as can be seen, were very similar to those in 1 Edward VI c.1, save that the latter did not envisage ecclesiastics acting as judges or enquirers. The use of witnesses who deposed or were questioned as found in the Edwardian statutes listed above therefore derived in part at least from the practices of the ecclesiastical law. How far the appearance in the common law of this new type of examination was because of a general dislike of Henrician investigative procedure and how far to a protestant preference for biblical practice is unclear. The legal writers of the period have nothing to say about this striking change.

There were only two statutes passed in the reign of Queen Mary which fell within the four general categories used above; one made examination a compulsory replacement for the usual accusatory method of presentment, while the other stipulated that examination should be the only method of trial. The first of these acts, 1/2 Philip and Mary c.5 restricted the carrying of corn, victuals and wool overseas. Enquiries into offences against the statute were to be carried out by justices of the peace, who were also to hear and examine the sailors and passengers aboard the vessels which transported the goods. There was no reference to witnesses or depositions, or, as in 1 Edward VI c.1, to confirmation of the charges elicited through examination by means of a jury of presentment. Trial was to be in the manner usual for 'other trespasses and offences'. The return to pre-Edwardian practice was quite complete. The second Marian statute to be considered is 1 Mary st.2 c.3, which was concerned with those interrupting or disturbing ministers or preachers in church. It ordered the miscreants should be arrested by constables or churchwardens who should take them before a justice of the peace, and there accuse them of their fault. Within six days the justice of the peace in concert with another, was to examine the offence. Then, by means of the examination and through either his confession or the use of two 'sufficient' witnesses, the accused was to be adjudged by the justices of the peace. Although two witnesses secured mention, the examination was not of them specifically. It was concerned with the offence, which meant, no doubt, the misdoer and the pertinent circumstances. The law was passed in 1553 and, as the mention of witnesses shows, the ideas of the Edwardian lawyers still had some influence.

There were two Marian statutes giving examination considerable attention which do not fit into any of our categories; these were 1/2 Philip and Mary c.13 and 2/3 Philip and Mary c.10. The former said that two justices of the peace, or one of them if he was of the *quorum*, when a prisoner was brought before them on suspicion of manslaughter or felony, before he was bailed or mainperned, should examine him and take information from those who brought him concerning the circumstances of the alleged offence. This, or as much as was thought necessary to prove the felony, was to be put in writing to be certified to the justices at the next general gaol delivery. The intent was presumably that the justices of gaol delivery should, if the suspect failed to appear at those sessions, have record of the evidence against him which could be used to construct an indictment and support a presentment or bill of indictment for dereliction of duty against the justices of the peace. Here, both in regard to the suspect or the negligent justices of the peace, the examination was quite definitely not being used as an alternative to presentment, nor was it taking the place of trial. It was serving as evidence pure and simple, as will be shown at greater length below. The act 2/3 Philip and Mary c.10, 'An Act to take the examination of Prisoners suspected of Manslaughter or Felony', can be interpreted in a similar manner. In places it follows the wording of 1/2 Philip and Mary c.13 closely. When someone suspected of manslaughter or felony was brought before one or more justices of the peace they should examine him, as well as take information from those who had brought him. The information gained, which in this case was to be put into writing within two days, was to be certified as in the earlier statute. Witnesses against the suspect were to be bound to appear at the next gaol delivery to give their evidence.

Interesting as these acts are, they have only a distant connection with examination as a part of summary procedure. Their importance was that they brought 'examination' into the statute book when it was a part of normal procedure, that is to say when it served as a supplement to presentment or indictment and, as evidence, helped the jury and the judges at the actual trial. Examination must have been the practice in virtually all criminal cases for more than an hundred years, but no king had dared to put it formally into a statute except where a new crime was being created and he had felt he could use it to cut short normal process.[19] These offences were nearly all trespasses, the essential shape and scope of the basic felonies having been decided long ago. The old felonies were at last linked with examination in 1/2 Philip and Mary c.13 but not, as we have seen, in an act aimed simply at providing statutory sanction for examination. The reason given for its promulgation was the deceitful practices of bailing by individual justices of the peace; if something sensible was to be done about these, reference to examination could not be avoided. Of course it is quite possible the crown's lawyers recognized that here was also a good chance to introduce the word into the statutes dealing with felony, and took advantage of it. The second act supports this 'casual' interpretation. It ordered the examination to be certified when the prisoner was sent to gaol, whereas by the earlier act the examination was to be sent in if he was not put in custody, a piece of clarification necessary because of the previous law covering the exceptional rather than the general.[20]

The statutes providing for examination promulgated in the reign of Elizabeth touched suspects rather than witnesses.[21] There were seven which were obviously relevant. Four stipulated examination as an alternative to presentment, one made it a mandatory replacement for the same, while in two acts examination was to serve as the form of trial. Two other acts, we should notice, provided for summary trial. Of those in the first category 5 Elizabeth c.9, which was concerned with the suborning of witnesses to commit perjury in cases involving land and its title, seems to have permitted accusation by means of examination, although that word is not actually mentioned. Justices of assize, of gaol delivery and of the peace, as well as judges of the courts where the perjury had occurred, were instructed to enquire by means of inquest, presentment, bill, information 'or otherwise lawfully' and then to hear and determine the matter. The statute 23 Elizabeth c.10 was directed against those who took or killed pheasants or partridges by night. It gave authority to justices of the peace to examine offenders and bind them over to appear at their general sessions, although trial could also be before justices of assize or the stewards of leets or lawdays. It is less clear whether the act 5 Elizabeth c.8, which was concerned with the working of leather, fits in this division. Jurisdiction to enquire, hear and determine the offences named in the act was entrusted to justices of assize, gaol delivery, and of the peace as well as stewards of franchises, leets and lawdays and the head officers of cities, boroughs and towns. They were ordered to 'examyne all persons suspected toffende this Acte' 'by their discretyons'. As with 23 Elizabeth c.10 the examination was probably intended to serve as an alternative to the usual presentment. Much more obvious is the design behind 5 Elizabeth c.12, an act for the licensing of badgers of corn and drovers of cattle. There can be no doubt that in this case examination was to operate as a method of accusation alongside inquest, presentment, bill of indictment and information. It was distinct from the other three acts in this category in that examination was to be of two lawful witnesses rather than the suspect. The reason for this may have been that the act was in essence aimed at strengthening an earlier one, 5/6 Edward VI c.14, which had been passed in the high period of witness examination.

The only Elizabethan statute making examination the sole method of providing an accusation for the courts was one which also allowed the doing of summary justice subsequently. This was 18 Elizabeth c.3 which, being designed to improve the act 14 Elizabeth c.5, gave authority to two justices of the peace where one was a member of the *quorum* to examine the mother and reputed father of bastard offspring as to the circumstances of the birth, to punish them at discretion, and take order for the child's keeping. Since it was the first secular law to touch bastardy there were no obvious precedents to follow. The reasoning which allowed such summary procedure probably developed from the premise that illegitimate children might be as much a burden on the parish as vagabonds, the laws against whom were similar. Knowledge of former ecclesiastical practice in the sphere may have also played a part. On the practical side it may have been felt that the examination of the mother by a magistrate would get at the truth far more easily than the deliberations of a jury.

The two Elizabethan statutes which made trial by examination the only method of doing justice were 5 Elizabeth c.4, the so-called statute of artificers, and 43 Elizabeth c.7, which dealt with the taking away of produce from corn fields, orchards and gardens. By the first justices of the peace, chief officers of cities, boroughs or towns and the councils of the North and of Wales were empowered to examine servants reported as quitting service or refusing to serve. Guilt was to be established 'upon suche Proofes and good Matter as to their discretions shall be thought sufficient'. This meant conviction or acquittal could follow from what happened at the examination, that is to say how the suspect answered the questions which were put to him. Since the statute, where it dealt with servants leaving service without leave, was following a succession of earlier statutes dating from the labour laws of 1349 and 1351, the introduction of trial by examination was not novel but following in a long tradition. The second act in this section, 43 Elizabeth c.7, ordered trial of the suspected produce thieves and also their procurers and receivers before a single justice of the peace or chief officer of a town. He was authorized to convict them through their confession or by the testimony of 'one sufficient witness upon oath'. Although not strictly essential, it is likely that the confession was gained by examination and that the witness and suspect were questioned in a methodical way. Even allowing for a wave of this type of crime as mentioned in the statute's preamble, the use of a single witness for purpose of conviction is unexpectedly severe for so late in the Tudor era. Presumably the fear that the offences were 'great causes of the maintaining of idleness' and thereby no doubt promoted vagabondage and begging as well as ordinary crime, allowed the act to be regarded as having a connection with the laws against vagabonds and so excused its peremptoriness. Very possibly it was modelled on 14 Elizabeth c.5, which was also to do with vagabonds, whereby justices of the peace could convict by inquest or by two credible witnesses on oath those who refused to enter service. The reason for 43 Elizabeth c.7 demanding a witness may also have lain in the authority given to the justices of the peace to award damages to the injured party, and the fear of spurious charges for the purpose of gaining these. Thirdly there is the possibility it may have sprung from the procedure authorized in an act of four years earlier. This statute, 39 Elizabeth c.11, which was directed against the illicit use of logwood in the dyeing of cloth, ordered reported miscreants to be examined 'by their oath or otherwise' by head officers of cities and towns who were justices of the peace. The names and examinations of those who were found to have behaved suspiciously, together with the depositions of those who had reported it, were to be certified to the next quarter or gaol delivery sessions where justices of assize or justices of the peace were to indict and try the offenders 'by the usuall course of Indictment and Trialls in like cases'. Here examinations of suspects and the examinations or depositions of witnesses were to be used to formulate the indictment, and were thus a supplement rather than a replacement for the normal procedure of charge construction and trial, a device which had only occurred previously in legislation in the act 1 Edward VI c.1. The same is true of the act 39 Elizabeth c.20, which was even closer to the testimony of one sufficient witness of 43 Elizabeth c.7. It concerned those who were deceitfully stretching or 'taintering' northern cloth. It set justices of the peace in quarter sessions to enquire, hear and determine offences contrary to the act. The charges were to be made by presentment, information, bill or on proof by the testimony of 'two sufficient witnesses openley geven to the Jurye and thereuppon Presentment made by the Jurye'. The normal form of arraignment then followed.

At the end of Elizabeth's reign it was thus becoming increasingly frequent for examination of suspects to be supplemented by the examination and depositions of witnesses for the purposes of serving as an alternative to presentment, and also as a way of providing the presenting and indicting jurors with accurate information in order to construct their charges. The abbreviated procedure in which examination of suspect served as a method of summary trial was in retreat, (at least it figured in fewer new statutes than earlier in the century), as was that where it supplanted presentment, indictment and information and acted as the only form of accusation permissible before normal trial. Overall there was no thrust towards noticeably greater use of examination, if we judge by the number of acts which introduced it during the last Tudor reign.

If we take the Tudor period as a whole, or better still set the Tudor period alongside the preceding one and a half centuries and look at the incidence of relevant acts in regard to the different categories of offence where examination and summary procedure was used, some interesting patterns emerge. The most salient point is that few types of crime show a succession of acts across the whole period. The exceptions were the persistent problems of wages for labourers and artificers and the burden of vagabonds, the former providing at least nine relevant acts and the latter five. These were of course intractable problems, and continuous experiment and improvement of judicial techniques on the part of the government was to be expected. In contrast there were a number of offences which drew forth a number of statutes for a time, but then new laws ceased, although we know the amount of that sort of crime continued largely undiminished. Thus the illegal giving of livery led to six statutes between 1397 and 1504, but then nothing further. In the reign of Edward IV there were two acts against the wearing of illicit apparel which stipulated examination but none later, despite other laws in the same field. The three acts 2 Henry V c.9, 31 Henry VI c.2 and 33 Henry VI c.1 which decreed that those who failed to appear in answer to a summons from the chancellor should stand automatically convicted of their offences were followed by no others. The reason why these important areas produced no new laws introducing additional shortened process was probably the judicial activity of the Tudor council and court of the Star Chamber, both of which made examination the key feature of their judicial procedure. It was, furthermore, procedure which, as long as life or limb were not endangered, need not follow the rule of any statute since it was based on the very wide authority enjoyed by the king's counsellors in medieval England. As the Tudor era progressed the handling of offences like the giving of livery, retaining, riot and the malfeasance of officials, which were in fact those most likely to cause grave disturbance of public order, passed increasingly to the council and the Star Chamber, leaving to the common law the less dangerous. Quite clearly the offences which might be investigated or judged by means of examination in the sixteenth century were, as in the later middle ages, those which from the government's point of view were less suited to enquiry and trial by jury. The refusal to work for a certain level of wages, being a vagabond, wearing the wrong apparel, using forbidden practices in manufacture or construction, the playing of illegal games and poaching, were obviously dealt with more efficiently by a magistrate's examination since there was likely to be some doubt as to the unbiasedness of the investigating and the trial juries in what were often master-versus-servant confrontations. The fear was that the jurors would favour the suspect too much.

Excluding acts which entrusted examination to commissions made up of a mixture of laity and ecclesiastics there were but ten pieces of new legislation which made examination the sole form of trial, and only two where it was to serve as the one method of accusation. It is quite clear that most Tudor statutes offering examination made it an alternative to the normal processes of the common law. This may have reduced the number of cases where examination was utilized very considerably, although on the other hand the attractions for justices of summary procedure can be imagined. Unfortunately, summary process by its very nature tends to leave few records behind and since furthermore from *circa* 1450 to the reign of Elizabeth records of all but the courts at Westminster are very sparse, it seems unlikely that historians will ever be in a position to judge accurately in what percentage of these cases examination was the method of accusation or trial used.

The most important single fact in regard to Tudor use of examination for whatever purpose was its limitation to trespass, or misdemeanour as it came to be called, and its persistent exclusion from felony. Thus, whereas the statute 11 Henry VII c.17 allowed the taking or killing of hawks, a trespass, to be tried by means of examination, the act 31 Henry VIII c.12 which added to it and made failing to return to its owner any falcon, goshawk, laneret or such a felony, laid it down that judicial process should be according to the laws of the realm, that is to say entirely normal. There were only two exceptions to this rule, the statutes 31 Henry VIII c.14 and 5/6 Edward VI c.4.[22] The first concerned what were really errors of religious belief, being the notorious act of 'six articles'. Enforcement was entrusted primarily to the bishops, who were to examine suspects and witnesses, and only secondarily to justices of the peace, who were merely instructed to enquire by jury. The second act also had a religious connection, being concerned with persons who struck others with weapons either in church or churchyard. The trespasses or misdemeanours which involved examination as part of the legal process for dealing with them were, as we have already noticed, largely crimes which were appearing among the statutes for the first time, the government being keen to associate them from the outset with what may be called the 'new process'. The more frequent use of examination was perhaps prompted by the rising popularity of conciliar method, an examinatory process which was adopted as the *modus operandi* of virtually every new court which emerged in the Tudor period.[23] It was a method essentially sympathetic to authority but hostile to the popular judicial method of the common law of the thirteenth and early fourteenth century. It was not a Tudor invention; it had been developing slowly since 1349. The Tudors extended its operation a great deal but were clearly unable to achieve a break-through into the area of felony, the offences which carried the death penalty. There was a future for examination in the field of felony, but not as a method of indictment or trial. It was as a form of evidence to be put to the presenting jurors and perhaps to be offered in court at the arraignment.

As to the greater phenomenon, the truncated forms of accusation and trial of which examination was often a part, we have seen they made frequent appearances in the statutes of the period under review. They recur often enough to make a powerful argument for their relative efficency in contrast with what may be designated as the traditional forms of doing justice. They must also have been popular with the class which operated them as well as with the crown. No doubt they enabled the gentry as justices of the peace to discipline without fear of interference from the puisne justices those who broke the labour laws, entered lands illicitly, poached, took or gave livery illegally, interfered with jurors and the doing of justice, or became vagabonds. Doing summary justice in regard to matters which closely affected their own daily lives must have been some consolation for their loss as justices of the peace, from the late fourteenth century onwards, of the right to try felonies. We can see that truncated process spread in the later fifteenth century and the sixteenth from primary areas to others such as commerce and religion. It was still expanding if at a less rapid rate than previously in the reign of Elizabeth. How it fared in the seventeenth century has still to be investigated.

NOTES

1. For a commission under the ordinance of 1349 see *Foedera* ed. T. Rymer (The Hague, 1740), III, Pt. i, 61–2.
2. B.H. Putnam, *The Enforcement of the Statute of Labourers* (New York, 1908), pp. 249–50.
3. *Ibid.*, pp. 142–254.
4. This parliament also renewed the ordinance of 1349.
5. The statute was 10 Edward III st.2 c.3.
6. There are no cases in the peace rolls which remain. If in fact it was summary justice no records can be expected.
7. T.F.T. Plucknett implied that 'summary trial' started only with this statute: *Concise History of the Common Law* p. 438. J.F. Stephen, even more erroneously, thought there was no summary jurisdiction of criminal offences before the mid-eighteenth century, only the punishment of offenders against 'rules laid down for some administrative purpose' (which belonged to administrative law rather than criminal). He said nothing further: *History of the Criminal Law*, i, 122.
8. Examination on oath does not reappear in later statutes until 39 Elizabeth c.11: *vide infra*.
9. The act 23 Henry VI c.12 extended this to servants.
10. See chapter five.

11. See Plucknett, 'Origin of Impeachment'.
12. See chapter four.
13. The statute was 11 Henry VII c.3.
14. The act also extended to maintenance, embracery and excessive wages. Plucknett, probably through following Holdsworth too closely, seems to have believed the statute was particularly significant. He did not comment on the several other statutes of the reign which also promoted summary procedure: see *Concise History of the Common Law*, p. 438.
15. The total might in fact be twelve: 24 Henry VIII c.4, concerned with the sowing of flax and hemp, instructed justices of the peace to enquire of offences against the act by the oaths of twelve men (i.e. by jury) 'as otherwise by information by their discretions'. When arranging for the division of any forfeitures the act stipulated half should go to the king and half to the informer 'if any be convicte by confession or otherwise by examynacion upon any informacion made by any persone'. What examination means in this context is not at all clear.
16. 'Oddly' because instead of the common arrangement, whereby examination took the place of presentment but was coupled with the normal method of trial (i.e. by jury), here the standard form of the accusatory process was retained, but the manner of trial was to be of the new type.
17. Obviously there was a new consciousness of the difference between witnesses and suspects, accompanied by a recognition they should be treated differently in legal process. Previously, so it seems, examination had been of both, with little distinction drawn between them. The desire to distinguish roles probably derived from a dislike of examinees being made to accuse themselves.
18. In the case of a crime which seemed to threaten public order dangerously the council might send interrogatories, which were a set of carefully contrived questions, for the use of the examiners. See J.G. Bellamy, *The Tudor Law of Treason: An Introduction* (London and Toronto 1979), pp. 104–5.
19. For some earlier cases see J.G. Bellamy, *Crime and Public Order in England in the Later Middle Ages* (London and Toronto, 1973), pp. 136–7.
20. For an interpretation of the two Marian acts as a watershed in the prosecution of crime see J.H. Langbein, *Prosecuting Crime in the Renaissance* (Cambridge, Mass., 1974), chapters two and three.
21. There were three acts where examination was of witnesses: 5 Elizabeth c.12, 23 Elizabeth c.1 and 43 Elizabeth c.7.
22. The act 28 Henry VIII c.10, which was directed against the authority of the pope, was another such act, but only if we include treason in the category of felony.
23. The court of admiralty however in 1535 changed to common law procedure.

3

WITNESSES AND EVIDENCE

Alongside the rising popularity of examination and summary procedure came a growing awareness of the value of witnesses. It would be quite wrong to say they were unknown before the Tudor period, yet their role in the later middle ages was undoubtedly slight in regard to criminal offences. They were first mentioned in legal writings in Bracton's *De Legibus et Consuetudinibus Angliae* in the mid-thirteenth century but both there and in the *Mirror of Justices* of a few years later it was in relation to personal actions, not actions on the king's suit. Not, in fact, until Fortescue's *De Laudibus Legum Anglie* does a legal writer refer to witnesses in connection with the criminal law. Fortescue was so keen to demonstrate that the English common law had all the advantages but none of the disadvantages of the continental civil law that in certain sections of his treatise he claimed the jurors, from their own knowledge of the suspect, the offence and the characters of those who gave evidence about it, were witnesses themselves. Thus what he has to say is somewhat clouded by his eccentric terminology. He never, in fact, deals directly with the vital issues of the use of witnesses at indictment and arraignment but only incidentally in regard to matters which may seem to us to be of minor importance. They are discussed in connection with a suspect who tries to establish an alibi and then only as to how many are necessary. Fortescue eventually makes the more substantial statement that the English laws allow the truth to be proven by two witnesses when it would not otherwise be known, but there is no admission, doubtless because of the tenor of his main argument, that witnesses were appearing regularly in criminal cases in common law courts in the mid-fifteenth century.[1] No light is thrown by the court records themselves, since the presence of witnesses was never noted even when, in the sixteenth century for example, we know from other sources that they must have been present. Not only would they have been present at indictment and trial, they must also have been in attendance on various occasions when justices examined suspects under those fourteenth and fifteenth century laws which laid down examination as an alternative or replacement for the normal judicial procedure. Even if the intent was to examine the suspect alone, there must have been many instances when only by examining several persons was the suspect's identity revealed. Although the word 'witness' is almost entirely absent from the statutes which stipulated examination, the operation of a system of summary procedure by means of an examinatory process must have relied partly on the use of witnesses for the purpose of identifying where the main blame should lie, and under a smaller number of statutes actually proving the suspect's guilt.

With this connection with summary procedure in mind, it is of considerable interest to find that the first clear reference to witnesses in legislation occurred in 1349 (23 Edward III cc.1–7) in the so-called 'ordinance of labourers'. This ordered that men without land, craft or business of their own, a variety of artificers who refused to serve those who required their services at the 1346–7 wage level, together with sellers of food who refused to sell at reasonable prices, were to be put in gaol until they obeyed. Refusal was to be proven before 'the sheriff, bailiff, lord, or constable of the town' by two 'true men' and it carried automatic conviction. From where this device of the two witnesses originated is not at all clear. It may have been borrowed from ecclesiastical court procedure: in canon law the concordance of two witnesses was proof enough. The idea may have derived from legal notions brought back from the military expeditions to France: from such stimuli the court of chivalry had just been born and some continental ideas about the scope of treason may have begun to circulate.[2] Most likely the Black Death's catastrophic effect on agricultural labour and the natural reluctance of the lower classes to accept wages and prices of pre-plague times which resulted, persuaded the upper classes that to rely on conviction of offenders by the usual juries was useless, and to put their faith instead in a pair of 'true men' who were likely to prove more sympathetic to the employers' viewpoint. Whether this judicial device, so much at odds with the normal processes, would have ever, in its original form, been passed as a statute we can only speculate.[3]

If the summary procedure established by the ordinance of labourers resulted in the erection of similar process in regard to other crimes, it did not result, except in its own confirmations, in further references to witnesses in legislation until the second half of the fifteenth century. Significantly, in the three 'labour' statutes 2 Henry V st.1 c.4, 2 Henry VI c.18 and 23 Henry VI c.12, infraction of the laws of 1349 and 1351 was to be proven by the examination of the suspect parties by justices of the peace, although the second of these acts, as if remembering the original arrangement of 1349, spoke of the justices discovering the taking of illegal wages 'by examination or in any other manner'. Possibly the two 'true men' of 1349 had soon got themselves such undesirable notoriety among the lower classes that the king and parliament feared to make use of them in other ways. A change only came about in the reign of Edward IV in an act (4 Edward IV c.1) concerned partly with the defaults of cloth workers and the non-payment of their wages which allowed justices of the peace or chief officers of towns to call the accused before them and to fine them, should they be found guilty by examination or 'other due proof'. The latter alternative gives the impression that here witnesses may have been looked for, since it was stipulated that keepers of cloth seals who were negligent or who refused to show their seals when required could be convicted by examination before the treasurer and barons of the exchequer on the testimony of 'sufficient persons of good reputation'. Another act of the same parliament (4 Edward IV c.2), which was concerned with merchants failing to report their exports to the exchequer, was the first to use the actual term 'witness'. In that section of the statute dealing with how the merchants should proceed if the goods were lost at sea it was decreed such loss must be proven in the exchequer by examination of the merchant or 'two credible witnesses sworn' or by 'other witnesses and proofs'. This reference to evidence by witnessses is quite unequivocal, but obviously the procedure envisaged, since it was in the exchequer, was only on the fringe of the criminal law and did not concern justices of gaol delivery or of the peace. As regards the criminal justice dispensed by the latter, fifteenth century statutes said very little about the status of witnesses there, even if their actual and frequent use cannot be in doubt. Apparently it was customary as early as the reign of Henry IV when, at an arraignment, evidence against an offender was lacking or insufficient, for proclamation to be made that anyone who would give relevant information to the justices and the jurors on the king's behalf should come and be heard.[4] Thomas Marowe, in his reading *De Pace Terre*, which dates from about 1503, mentions witnesses hardly at all and then only in regard to personal actions, but his omission is quite understandable. He was chiefly concerned, like nearly all the authors of Tudor legal tracts, with how the statutes and the common law defined and dealt with different crimes and the powers they gave to the various types of justices for their determination, not with what happened at indictment or trial.

The role of witnesses in common criminal process received clear recognition in statutes only towards the end of the reign of Henry VII. The parliament of 1504 produced two acts which, although they did not use the actual word witness, talked unequivocally of the giving of evidence, which itself was a new word in the official vocabulary of the English criminal law.[5] The act 19 Henry VII c.4 stated that anyone who saw a men of less than a certain degree of wealth using a crossbow for the purpose of killing the king's deer was allowed to seize the weapon and give 'open evidence' concerning the offence at the next assizes or sessions of the peace. Whether this meant that the informer was expected to give evidence to a grand jury or only to the petty jury at the trial is not clear. Obviously he had to tell the justices what he had seen and done, otherwise the case would never have come to court. The statute also said that if the evidence of the man who had seized the bow led to a conviction he was to receive ten shillings, which suggests that the evidence-giver was viewed as much as an informer as he was a witness. The act appeared at a time when the king's advisers were seeking, to the dislike of many, to enforce the so-called penal statutes more effectively. These were operated through informers, or 'promoters' as they were sometimes called, and the fact that neither word appeared in the crossbow act may indicate an effort to avoid controversy, opposition in parliament, or even an actual compromise during the passage of the bill. Emphasis was placed on the evidence-giver having actually seen the cross-bow being used and having seized it. The other relevant act of the parliament of 1504, 19 Henry VII c.14, was concerned with the perennial problem of illegal retaining and giving of livery. In one section it ordered the chief constables and bailiffs of hundreds, and constables of towns, in attendance at the sessions should be instructed by the justices of the peace to give evidence on oath to the grand jurors concerning these offences. The issues of livery and illicit retaining were quite crucial to the government and there is every indication the king was bent on obtaining the best procedural and judicial devices to get the act to work effectively. Enquiry was vested in the justices of the peace, but trial was to be in the king's bench where, it was no doubt thought, local influence would be less potent. An alternative method of obtaining charges was also established. Men (they were called 'plaintiffs or informers') could complain to the king's bench direct or to the chancellor or keeper of the seal in the Star Chamber or to the council attendant on the king. These tribunals were given authority to summon the accused, examine them on oath and 'adjudge all persons found guilty by verdict, confession, examination, proves or otherwise'. The 'plaintiffs or informers', if the case resulted in the conviction of the accused, were to get their costs and a 'reasonable' reward. Evidence at this point in time was obviously as much connected with plaintiffs and informers, that is to say with accusers, as it was with witnesses in the modern sense. The actual word 'witness', we may note, had not yet appeared in statutes dealing with criminal offences.

The double-barrelled system of the act 19 Henry VII c.14 for obtaining accusations and supporting evidence should cause us to ask if setting the justices of the peace to command the appearance of chief constables and bailiffs of hundreds and constables of towns so they should give evidence on oath may not have derived in some measure from the conciliar measures found elsewhere in the act.[6] That the giving of evidence was stipulated also in the statute 19 Henry VII c.4 is no unanswerable argument against such a thesis, since so complex a statute as 19 Henry VII c.14 may have originated in parliament first but taken a longer time in the subsequent fashioning, it is impossible to be sure. If in fact this was the case then the relevant section of the crossbow act may have derived from the legistic ideas which found form in the livery and retaining act. The livery statute also provided for punishing any grand jury which failed to find as true charges of illegal retaining about which its members had knowledge or credible evidence had been given. Such a regulation was quite novel and one wonders whom the legislators intended should decide whether the jury had failed in its duty. Of most interest, however, is the clear demonstration that the grand jurors of this time drew their knowledge of the misdeed from both their own enquiries and the witnesses who came before them, a fact we may easily surmize but which is nowhere else set down. The last point to be made in regard to these statutes of Henry VII concerns the role of the witnesses within the judicial process. Under the ordinance of 1349 the witnesses were used for the purpose of trial. Their testimony worked the conviction of the suspect, for there was to be no normal procedure of arraignment. Under the two Henrician acts, on the other hand, the evidence given by the witnesses merely provided material which could be used by grand jurors for presentments, supplementing the facts they possessed of their own knowledge. Procedure under the two Tudor acts might be called normal, whereas under the fourteenth century law it was most definitely summary.

The next stage in the history of witnesses was a most distinct one. It lasted from the early days of the Reformation Parliament to the death of Henry VIII. It was not a period when the criminal side of the common law deveoped according to its own principles and logic unmolested. There were strong pressures from outside and the prevailing influence was undoubtedly that of the ecclesiastical law. There were, however, three statutes of these years concerned with witnesses which did not show this effect, including the earliest, 22 Henry VIII c.12, which was directed against those begging in an illicit manner, 27 Henry VIII c.25, concerned with the illegal quitting of service by youths, and 33 Henry VIII c.1 which dealt with those obtaining money from friends by means of counterfeit letters. One section of the first of these acts ordered that constables of townships and inhabitants who failed to arrest both strong and impotent beggars should be tried for their default by justices of the peace on presentment or 'bill of information'. If the accusation was made by the second method and was denied by the suspect, then it was to be proved against him by 'suffycyent witnes'. Another part of the same act decreed that other types of beggars, including scholars of Oxford and Cambridge and fortune tellers, should be punished by whipping or whipping plus the pillory if, on examination by two justices of the peace, 'by provable Wytnes' they should be found guilty. By the second act, 27 Henry VIII c.25, youths who refused to serve their master might be found guilty by confession or sufficient testimony. Under the third 33 Henry VIII c.1, suspects were to be convicted either by witness before the lord chancellor or by examination of witnesses before the council, justices of assize on circuit or justices of the peace in general sessions. In each of these instances, so it seems, witnesses were being used as the method of determining guilt. They did not give evidence to a jury; their testimony decided the justices directly on their verdict. Procedure was thus by common law standard summary, probably because the statute was in the tradition of several earlier ones dealing with vagabondage,[7] although it was not quite as summary as some other methods of conviction since the justices did not give the verdict simply from what they saw themselves or heard at second hand: they had also to get the report of those who had actually seen the offence committed.

The other five relevant statutes of the period were concerned with ecclesiastical matters, matters with which the government felt it must interfere for reasons of security, following the breach with Rome. What the acts had in common was that they were to be administered by ecclesiastics and laity together, although only two set out more or less the same judicial process. These two were the heresy act, 25 Henry VIII c.14, and the act of 'six articles' (31 Henry VIII c.14). According to both, enquiry into offences was to be undertaken by lay authorities as well as by bishops. The bishops were to obtain their accusations through detection by two lawful witnesses 'at the leest' under the heresy act, and by 'two able and lawful persons at least' under the 'six article' act. Both stipulated that charges should also be obtained by presentment of twelve men in the common law fashion. Another similarity between the two statutes was vesting the power to try offences in the ordinary. The act against those upholding the authority of Rome (28 Henry VIII c.10) had several things in common with these two statutes. The lay authorities, justices of assize and of the peace, might enquire of offences by means of presentments, the ecclesiastical by witness or confession. The difference lay in the form of the trial envisaged: here, probably because of the very important nature of the offence, it was to be by the council.

The other two statutes in this group show considerable differences from the three already considered. The act concerning those who printed or sold prohibited books (34/5 Henry VIII c.1) relied on accusation by private persons, and trial by 'sufficient' witness, provided seemingly by both accuser and accused, before either two members of the king's council or the ordinary in conjunction with two justices of the peace. The strong ecclesiastical penchant of this statute was further demonstrated by its provision that 'in trial by witness' (it was the only act of the five using witnesses for purpose of trial for in the others witnesses only assisted in accusation) the defendant should be allowed to purge his innocence by his own witnesses 'as manye or moo in number and of as good honestie and credence' as those which deposed against him. The remaining statute, 35 Henry VIII c.5, intended to amend the act of 'six articles', provided new machinery for its operation and enforcement. It is one of the most informative statutes of the whole century about the role and value of witnesses in judicial process in this period. Trial was to be before three 'assigned commissioners', or three or more justices of the peace, or three justices of oyer and terminer, but not before the bishops or their officers, as in the act of 'six articles', unless such men were appointed as 'assigned commissioners'. Accusation, unless it was against a preacher contravening the act when it could be by a single person with two supporting witnesses, was to be by means of presentment only, not as in the parent act by presentment or two witnesses. Any other type of accusation was to be void, although it might be used 'as an evidence to be yeoven and declared to th'enquest of inquire and dellyverye', that is to say, told to the grand and petty juries.

This was victory for common law process against that of the ecclesiastical courts. Accusation by witness, even if there were two or more of these, was no longer acceptable in 1544, whereas ten years earlier it had been introduced into the new heresy act, 25 Henry VIII c.14, seemingly as a precaution against the peremptory seizure and examination of a heresy suspect by the ordinary on 'capcious interrogatories' without proper process of accusation and witness or presentment, verdict and outlawry.[8] Most important for our purpose is the clear demonstration of enforced co-operation between secular and ecclesiastical justices and the inter-connection of the two laws which developed in this period. The advantages and disadvantages of the use of witnesses must have been brought to the notice of a good number of secular justices. Of course the move towards using common law rather than ecclesiastical processs which is apparent in the statute 35 Henry VIII c.5 may well have been promoted as much by popular resentment at the latter as by the government's belief in the judicial efficacy of the former.

Of the five Henrician statutes dating from 1534 onwards which have been discussed above, four made use of witnesses for purpose of enquiry and accusation while one allowed them to serve as a method of trial. Out of six criminal law statutes, including two dealing with treason, from the reign of Edward VI which mentioned witnesses, four made use of them for giving evidence to the grand or petty jury or both, while two gave witnesses the power by their evidence to convict the suspect without the involvement of a jury. These two statutes were concerned respectively with vagabonds and those who with weapons assaulted or threatened others in churches or churchyards. The vagabond act, 1 Edward VI c.3, was obviously in the mould of the 1349 ordinance of labourers: a master taking an idle man before the authorities and proving by two witnesses his refusal to accept work. The church assault act (5/6 Edward VI c.4) said strikers with weapons could be convicted before justices of assize, of the peace or oyer and terminer, by means of jury, confession or two witnesses. The offence was a new one in the statute book following in none of its established traditions; probably it drew some inspiration from the acts which had combined ecclesiastical and secular legal practice in the previous reign. This is certainly true about one of the other four statutes, 1 Edward VI c.1, which in providing for the examination by justices of the peace of those who accused non-conforming preachers ordered the former to discover who were the witnesses and bind them over to appear at the trial. Clearly it was modelled closely on the 'six article' act in this respect, while in allowing the accused to clear himself by producing more witnesses than had deposed against him the act was borrowing a device which had been used in 34/5 Henry VIII c.1 against those who published or sold contrary books on religion.

Of the other three Edwardian statutes under discussion, 5/6 Edward VI c.14, which was directed against forestallers, regrators and engrossers, allowed the testimony of two 'lawful' witnesses as an alternative to 'inquisition, present-ment, bill or information' as a method of providing charges. The remaining two acts, 1 Edward VI c.12 and 5/6 Edward VI c.11, which dealt in fact with treason, provided for a pair of witnesses to testify at both the indictment and the arraignment. For neither commodity speculation or treason had there been any previous provision of witnesses by statutes, although there had been plenty of the latter. Since these classes of criminal offence had nothing in common with the ecclesiastical group of misdeeds of Henry VIII's reign, we may assume that the king's legal advisers, when drafting the statutes, gave consideration to a general feeling that witnesses were now an important concomitant in the laying of many criminal charges and their subsequent determination.

There were three criminal law statutes, excluding those on treason, promulgated in Mary's reign which were directly concerned with witnesses. One, 1 Mary st.2 c.3, which dealt with those who offended preachers and ministers in church, provided that the miscreants should be arrested by constables or churchwardens who would take them to a justice of the peace and make an accusation. Then two J.P.'s were to examine those involved in the incident and if they confessed or there were two 'sufficient' witnesses as to their guilt they were to be declared convicted and punishment was to follow. This statute was clearly modelled on 5/6 Edward VI c.4, which had provided the same type of judicial procedure for those who made assaults with weapons in churches or churchyards. The Marian act was the only one of the reign to use witnesses in place of trial by jury. The other two statutes of the reign which were concerned with witnesses and their evidence dealt not with just one type of offence, as had other 'witness' statutes, but serious crime in general. The more important of the two, from our view-point, was the act 2/3 Philip and Mary c.10 which stipulated that justices of the peace, when a person suspected of manslaughter or felony was brought before them, should examine him and take information from the bringers, put what appeared to be good proof into writing within two days, and bind over those who had something material to say to appear at the next sessions of gaol delivery whither, in fact, the 'good proof' was supposed to have been certified.

The chief purpose of this statute, one writer has suggested, was to 'institute systematic questioning of the accused and the witnesses'. This demanded the justice of the peace should make investigations as soon as he received the prisoner or heard of the crime. His enquiries would provide a written summary of the case which could be sent to the assize judges as advance information about the crime and the persons involved. If we place the emphasis within the phrase 'institute systematic questioning' on the second word, namely 'systematic', rather than elsewhere, then this seems to be an accurate description of what the statute was intended to accomplish. On the other hand, to suggest that thorough questioning of the accused and witnesses in cases of felony had not been common before this time would be quite implausible.[9] Thomas More tells us that in his day examination was much used in crimes of felony and treason, since without it indictments would never have been found.[10] It would also be incorrect to argue that the 'book' of examinations and depositions, with comments upon them, which the justices of the peace compiled, were not frequently sent in advance to those who were to conduct the next gaol delivery sessions. What was happening was that common judicial practice was now being given proper sanction by means of statute.

What factors made the government in 1555 decide on systematization is not certain, but there are several probabilities. It may have been one particular and embarrassing case which is now lost to us.[11] It may have been simply a desire to rationalize, to extend the provisions of a limited number of statutes so they should take in the whole field of felonies. The statutes utilizing witnesses for the purpose of giving evidence and proving guilt passed since the beginning of the Reformation Parliament had in general dealt with offences which were being put into the statute book for the first time. The vast majority of serious crimes were unaffected; indeed, only two of the 'witness' statutes of the reigns of Henry VIII and his son, excluding those dealing with treason, related to felonies.[12] Nonetheless these may have been the connecting link. One of them, 5/6 Edward VI c.4, dated from late enough in the previous reign to be still clearly remembered in 1555.

That the 'committal' statute of 1555 borrowed procedural details from previous acts seems quite clear. A strong case can be made that the act in some parts followed closely another Marian statute which touched on witnesses and evidence, namely the 'bail' statute 1/2 Philip and Mary c.13. This act laid it down that when justices of the peace received a prisoner suspected of manslaughter or felony they should, before granting bail, examine the prisoner, take 'information' about the offence from those who had brought him, put this in writing and certify it to the next general sessions of gaol delivery. The connection of these provisos with the 'committal' act is obvious. The rule that the facts elicited in the examination of the accused and the witnesses should be put into writing within two days may have derived something from experience with the stipulation in the statute 1 Mary st.2 c.3 that the offence must be examined by the justices of the peace within six days of the accusation. The 'committal' act put considerable emphasis on the binding over to appear and give evidence at the next gaol delivery sessions of all those who could 'declare anything material to prove the said manslaughter or felony'. Similar provisions for the binding over of witnesses to testify at the trial had occurred in a Henrician act and an Edwardian one. The 'six articles' act had told justices of the peace and bishops to discover from the accusers what other witnesses there were and who also 'had knowledge' of the offence; these were to be bound by recognizances to appear before the commissioners at the trial. The Edwardian act against preachers who spoke irreverently against the sacrament (1 Edward VI c.1) demanded similarly that justices of the peace should take information from the accusers and examine the accused to find out the names of witnesses and bind over such persons to appear when the offender was tried.[13]

The certification, by justices of the peace to trial court, of evidence in the form of the examinations of the accused, their apprehenders and the witnesses, also figured in statutes before the reign of Mary. The origins seem to have been as far back as the act 13 Henry IV c.7 which commanded that two justices of the peace and a sheriff who failed to get accusations against rioters by the normal procedure of jury inquest should certify all they knew about the miscreants and misdeed to the king and council, the certificate serving then as a presentment. Not until the reign of Henry VIII did the next mention occur. In the act against those who upheld the jurisdiction of the bishop of Rome (28 Henry VIII c.10), authority was given to bishops and their officers to enquire of and examine suspected members of the clergy using presentments and witnesses. Those 'presented, suspected, accused or found culpable' were to be committed to gaol on surety taken to appear before the council, whither the bishops were to certify the examination or accusation. The third example of certification of evidence occurred in the act of 'six articles' of 1539 which ordered that examinations of suspects were to be certified by the takers within twenty days to those commissioned to hear and determine the offences.

The designers of the 1555 'committal' act must also have been influenced by the recent development of the law of treason. Three acts promulgated since 1547 had clearly defined the role which witnesses were to play under them. None of the acts contained references to taking the examinations of apprehenders, discovering those who had anything material to say or binding over both or either to appear at the sessions where the offenders were to be tried. What they did, in contrast, was to state simply that witnesses were necessary at indictment and arraignment. The first Edwardian act of treason, 1 Edward VI c.12, stipulated that no person should be indicted, arraigned or convicted for high treason unless accused by two sufficient, lawful and willing witnesses. The second general Edwardian act (5/6 Edward VI c.11) demanded two 'accusers' in attendance at those same parts of the judicial process and, in addition, thought fit to order that they should, if alive, appear in person before the accused and avow the charges in the bill of indictment. The use here of the word 'accuser' probably reflects some difficulty common lawyers were discovering in legal terminology. Hitherto the word 'witness' had only been used in statutes which divided jurisdiction between ecclesiastical and lay judges or which allowed the supercession of trial by jury in favour of conviction by witness, originally an ecclesiastical device. It may have been argued at the time of the second Edwardian act that at common law those bringing a bill of indictment were technically accusers and not witnesses, as those who levied charges in ecclesiastical courts were. The third treason statute which made reference to witnesses was 1/2 Philip and Mary c.10. It declared that any person arraigned under it should have the right to have brought before him at least two persons who had confessed or deposed matter against him. They were to repeat their accusations to his face, so to speak. There was, however, no suggestion in this act that these witnesses were necessary adjuncts at the indictment. No statute treats the issue of whether witnesses had to be present at felony trials. Yet since they were bound over to appear at the sessions where the accused was to be tried, they must surely have been available for both indictment and arraignment, which usually occurred on the same day. What is important to our investigation is that these contemporary treason statutes must have been in the minds of those who drafted the Marian 'committal' act and the 'bail' act of the previous session. There was also one other influence which very likely affected the designers, namely the notoriety which witnesses and their testimony had acquired in treason trials, such as those of Sir Nicholas Throckmorton and William Thomas in the first year of Mary's reign.[14] There was, it is true, no reference to the recording of evidence by the examiners, or binding over of witnesses or certifying of relevant material for use in prosecution, but clearly the subject of witnesses, for as well as against the accused, their depositions or lack of them, their appearance in court and the validity of their testimony, were all matters of concern.

We may, therefore, conclude with some confidence that the crown and its legal advisers felt that in establishing rules by means of the act 2/3 Philip and Mary c.10 about witnesses and evidence in felony cases, it was keeping in step with similar provisions existing in regard to treason. There can have been no apprehension on account of novelty since, as we have seen, the arrangements of the 'committal' act in regard to taking examinations, binding over witnesses and certifying evidence had been anticipated in some fashion in statutes of the previous two reigns. It would be going too far, therefore, to regard this act and its forerunner the bail statute as being a watershed or turning point in the history of the development of English criminal law. It simply made standard and solemnized judicial procedure which already existed and was probably in everyday use. What this, or rather the trend it blessed, meant in practicalities to the efficiency of the everyday operation of the criminal law is not completely clear, but it can only have benefited the effective prosecution of offences. Witnesses would not dare fail to appear at the arraignment. The examination of the suspect and those who brought him to the justices of the peace, the insistence that the examining magistrate should make a record of his findings, the certification of the evidence to the next sessions of gaol delivery, meant that examinations would be efficiently conducted and that they would be available as material for indictments and as proof at trials. Quite clearly the influence of justices of the peace in trial procedure was increased, while that of the jury of presentment, because it no longer drew all the information it needed from among its own members, was necessarily diminished.[15]

In the reign of Elizabeth there were passed a further eight statutes which referred to witnesses or the giving of evidence. All of them except one stipulated the use of summary procedure and examination in some form. Three allowed witnesses' testimony to serve in place of a petty jury, for purposes of conviction. In the other four the witnesses' depositions were to be used merely for the purpose of fabricating indictments or to stand in their place. Of those in the first category two had a long pedigree. The act 14 Elizabeth c.5 dealt sharply with the persistent problem of rogues, vagabonds and sturdy beggars, and provided in one part for conviction by 'inquest of office' or by two credible witnesses on oath. The statute of 'artificers' (5 Elizabeth c.4) dealt with servants who refused to serve their master or 'unduly' departed from service. It did not in fact use the words 'witness' or 'evidence' *per se*, but referred to them obliquely by stating that, on receiving complaint from the master, the justices of the peace or head officer of a town should hear and examine the matter by 'suche proofes and good matter as to their discretions shall be thought sufficient', and commit the accused to ward if guilty. The statute in every other way followed the ordinance of 1349 very closely, though it obviously had similarities also with the act 1 Edward VI c.3. Indeed, the dropping of the word 'witnesses' may have stemmed from the great unpopularity of this Edwardian statute which had laid it down that any person leaving his master after being engaged for work should, if it was proved before two justices of the peace by two honest witnesses, become the master's slave. The other statute in which the evidence of witnesses was permitted to supersede trial by jury was 43 Elizabeth c.7, an act concerned with the despoliation of crops and breaking of hedges and fences. Those who committed such offences, together with their procurers and receivers, were to be convicted by their own confession or the testimony of one sufficient witness on oath before a J.P. or head officer of a town. The use of a single witness was quite new, while the act's stipulation he should be sworn before giving his testimony was demanding something which had only been required once before,[16] although a statute of four years earlier dealing with logwood users had made examination on oath mandatory in regard to the witnesses, whose testimony was an alternative to indictment.

The four Elizabethan statutes which demanded witnesses, not as a method of conviction but either as one type of formal accusation or as a necessary adjunct of any presentment, dealt with the licensing of badgers and drovers of cattle (5 Elizabeth c.12), seditious tales or prophecies against the queen (23 Elizabeth c.2), illicit use of logwood for dyeing cloth (39 Elizabeth c.11) and the deceitful stretching of cloth (39 Elizabeth c.20). The first and the last of these statutes used the depositions of witnesses as an alternative to indictments, the other two utilized witnesses only for the purpose of supplying evidence to the juries. There was one difference, however, in how the two latter acts did this. Whereas the statute about the use of logwood decreed that witnesses should be examined and bound over to testify at the next quarter sessions or gaol delivery (whither their examinations were to be dispatched) and thus followed the Marian committal act more closely than any other statute had done, the act against seditious tales and prophecies followed in the tradition of statutes on treason by stipulating that two witnesses must testify at the time of the indictment, as well as face to face with the accused at the arraignment.

The statutes involving the use of witnesses which were promulgated in Elizabeth's reign were thus not concerned in any way with felony but only with indictable trespass, that is to say misdemeanour. Because of the act 2/3 Philip and Mary c.10 there was no need to make provision in dealing with a new felony for witnesses and evidence at the indictment and arraignment. Because of the rooted opposition among common lawyers, there was no way in drafting acts to do with new felonies the government could arrange for summary procedure and conviction by means of witness. Even in regard to trespasses there was no great expansion in the use of witnesses, since most of the statutes were only intended to modify others in which witnesses already appeared. No fewer than five of the Elizabethan statutes were in fields where 'witness' statutes had appeared before: they dealt with deceitful practices in the making of cloth, servants who refused to work, vagabonds, and the buying and selling of commodities. In fact the only new fields were seditious words, which was really very close to treason, where rules on witnesses had been numerous, and despoliation of crops. Only the latter was an entirely new field, and the novelty and distinctiveness of the provisions were underlined by the fact that they only called for a single witness. Despoliation of crops had, of course, been a common offence in the sixteenth century but hitherto it had been dealt with by the normal procedure of indictment and jury trial.

In a small number of the statutes noticed above there is reference to witnesses giving their testimony on oath. Clearly, any consideration of witnesses and evidence would be incomplete without some study of the circumstances in which sworn testimony was preferred and what implications this had for judicial process as a whole. In regard to procedure at examinations, the first statute to stipulate men should answer on oath was 2 Henry V st.1 c.4, which was concerned with the breach of the ordinance and statute of labourers, the examination serving as the form of trial. Whether the oath was thought necessary because by the 1351 statute men had been sworn to obey the new work rates is possibility, but no more. The act 4 Edward IV c.2 demanded that loss of merchandise at sea when it was being exported must be proven in the exchequer by examination of the merchant or by two credible witnesses sworn, but this may have been out of deference to exchequer practice. It seems in regard to crime as a whole that in the earlier Tudor period suspects and witnesses were put on oath at their examination only infrequently, perhaps on the special orders of some high authority such as the council. Thus at the time of the northern rebellions in 1536–7 Robert Sotheby of Horncastle and William Levenyng of Acklom, two rebels in whom the government took a fair amount of interest, were both sworn before being examined, whereas the mass of their fellow dissidents were not.[17] Demanding an oath of an intended examinee, though rare, does not seem to have been limited to cases where the crime was thought to be treason.[18] Other evidence hints that oaths were only required from witnesses, not from the suspected culprit. This appears to be also the view of William Lambarde, writing in the 1580s, who, when he discusses examination on oath, does so almost entirely in reference to the bringers of suspected felons, saying that the intention of the common law was to have the misdeed proven 'by others', not to wring the facts from the suspect. He noted how the Marian 'bail' and 'committal' acts failed to state whether the examination should be on oath or not and how practice in his day varied according to the personal inclination of the justice of the peace in charge. For Lambarde the value of the oath was that, should the witness die soon after he had been examined, the examination might still be given in evidence at the trial. In the 1588 adition of *Eirenarcha* Lambarde implied that some justices of assize were in favour, which suggests that the government was also, or at least veering in that direction.[19] At the end of the century came the act 39 Elizabeth c.11 which ordered that logwood users and witnesses to their practices should be examined by justices of the peace or the head officers of towns by oath 'or otherwise', the examinations and depositions to be certified to the next quarter sessions or gaol delivery. The statute was recognizing that a difference of opinion still existed over whether witnesses should be sworn or not, even if the former was thought preferable.

There were five Tudor statutes which demanded sworn evidence as part of the formal process of accusation. The livery and retaining act of 1504 (19 Henry VII c.14) demanded chief constables and bailiffs of each hundred and constables of towns should supply whatever information they had about such crimes to the jurors on oath. The act 23 Elizabeth c.2 against seditious words laid it down that two witnesses on oath were essential at the indictment and arraignment. Very likely this statute drew some inspiration from an Elizabethan act (1 Elizabeth c,5) of earlier date concerned with treason, which required the offences to be proved by the testament, deposition and oath of two lawful and sufficient witnesses at the time of the indictment, as well as from a similar statute of 1571 (13 Elizabeth c.1). In a different but essentially parallel fashion, the act of 'six articles' required bishops or their officers in their sessions to take accusations by the depositions and oaths of two able and lawful persons.

No statute apart from these stated that witnesses must be sworn before they testified at indictment or arraignment, but the evidence of individual cases shows that they were usually sworn nonetheless. Why, then, did these five statutes have to make specific provision? The answer seems to be that three were connected with treason and sedition by 'words' the laws on which, because of political pressure, could not leave out the stipulation for sworn evidence. Another, the act of the 'six articles', which incidentally was also concerned with the expression of opinions, drew on the procedural practice of the ecclesiastical law, while the 1504 act on retaining had to arrange for the submission of evidence to the council as well as common law jurors, and the conciliar method was usually to swear witnesses. The five statutes were therefore designed to deal not with the usual run of offences and common law processes but with exceptional crimes or procedures.

The third manner in which witnesses on oath were utilized was as a method of summary conviction, superseding, that is to say, the functions of both the grand

and petty juries. There were only two statutes which provided this. One was 14 Elizabeth c.5, which allowed the testimony of 'credible' witnesses on oath to serve as one way of convicting men of being rogues, vagabonds and sturdy beggars. The previous act to deal with this problem, 1 Edward VI c.3, had only required the use of two 'honest' witnesses who were unsworn. The second act in the category was 43 Elizabeth c.7, which stipulated that abductors and despoilers of crops in fields and breakers of hedges and their accessaries might be convicted on the sworn testimony of a single witness. Of this we may say it was a startling innovation for such a frequent offence, one not too far removed from common theft, to be summarily proven by the word of a single witness. The oath was no doubt intended to make the process seem a little more reputable. Significantly the testimony was to be taken by a justice of the peace, mayor, bailiff or head of a town who had the power to administer an oath, the first time such a qualification had been mentioned in the statute book.

Taking together all the Tudor statutes which demanded testimony on oath, we notice that as many as four dealt with offences which might cost the accused his life. Three crimes were felony, while one was treason, but this was not for the first commission of the offence by any one person, but for the second. The best explanation of this is that three of the acts, namely 31 Henry VIII c.14, 1 Elizabeth c.5 and 23 Elizabeth c.2, dealt largely with the expressing of opinions, evidence about which was often unreliable and therefore in need of some special afforcement, both to impress the grand jury and to bring home to the witness the very serious consequences his testimony might have. The fourth statute concerned with felony which demanded evidence on oath was 14 Elizabeth c.5. It had a powerful justification in that the testimony of the witnesses was to work a summary conviction.

The use of witnesses not for the purpose of prosecution, but on behalf of the accused whether at indictment or arraignment, was one topic which received no clarification through statute, except in regard to the particular offences dealt with by the acts 34/5 Henry VIII c.1, 1 Edward VI c.1 and 31 Elizabeth c.4. The first two of these were concerned with offences of an ecclesiastical nature, namely 'contrary' books on religion and non-conforming preachers. They allowed the accused to clear himself at trial by the ecclesiastical arrangement of producing as many or more (and of as great honesty and credence) in the way of witnesses to speak on his behalf as had deposed against him. Such laws were exceptional in their provision, because they reflected a temporary marriage of secular and ecclesiastical judicial process and contradicted the crown's normal attitude, which was that there should be no permitting suspects' witnesses to appear and testify on their behalf. The third of the three acts, 31 Elizabeth c.4, followed in no established tradition; it was unique. It dealt with the very secular offence of embezzling royal armour, habiliments of war, and victuals, which it made into felony. Anyone accused of such an offence was to be admitted 'to make any lawfull proofe that he can by lawfull Witnesse or otherwise for his discharge and defence'. We may surmize that those who would have custody of such military materials would be members of the upper classes, probably nobility, and that this very special provision was included for their benefit.

Among the judges and legal advisers of the crown it seems to have been agreed that for all offences save those in the statutes above, witnesses should not be allowed to testify at arraignment contrary to the king's interest, that is to say on behalf of the accused. It is, of course, quite possible that he who was called to testify for the crown might at the bar give evidence which tended to the accused's acquittal. What was certainly not allowed was for the prisoner to produce his own witnesses. Marowe said that if one such wished to say something about a felony the J.P.'s might not question him 'pur ceo que le Roie est partie'. The rule was clearly demonstrated at the trial of Sir Nicholas Throckmorton in 1554, when his would-be testifier John Fitzwilliams, whom he had arranged to be present, was told by one of the judges to leave the court 'peradventure you would not be so ready in a good cause'. The implication was that any defence witness was a liar. When John Udall was on trial for seditious words in 1590 he offered at one point to produce several witnesses to give evidence on his behalf, but again the judges forbade it because they would be speaking against the crown.[20] During his trial, Throckmorton made the intriguing remark that Queen Mary had told her judges that 'notwithstanding the old error amongst you which did not admit any witness to speak or other matter to be heard in the favour of the adversary, her majesty being party, her highness's pleasure was that whatsoever could be brought in favour of the subject to be heard'. The only answer he received was apparently from Bromley, the chief justice of the king's bench, who claimed the remark was not made to him but to Morgan, the chief justice of common pleas. What the context of the original remark was, what exactly the queen had in mind is not clear. At any rate Throckmorton drew no benefit from his comments. There is a report of a trial of about four years later which suggests the queen raised the matter of defence witnesses a second time. In 1558 William Dalyson J.Q.B., and Attorney General Griffin defended to Mary their conduct in refusing to allow one Dionysius Thimbleby accused of highway robbery, the opportunity to call witnesses to prove an alibi. They said it was against the 'accustomed prerogatyve of the Crowne of this Realme' to suffer any witness to be sworn and examined against the queen in trial of felony or treason 'the same beinge first dulie proved for your majesty accordinge to your highness's lawes as of trewthe this was by dyverse wytnesses beinge honeste and credyble'.[21] The writers admitted that witnesses were heard at times on the prisoner's behalf but claimed this was at the justices' discretion. Clearly it was not allowed when there were crown witnesses testifying to the opposite effect. The duke of Norfolk, when on trial in 1572 is reported as having ssaid he had 'divers times prayed that if anything. .(he said). .were denied to be true' he might 'be driven to the proof of it'. To this Lord Burghley answered that he had not heard it 'reported to her majesty that you made any such request or desired to have any particular witnesses examined or proofs heard on your part'.[22] We do not know what the duke retorted, but as the report stands it suggests that the prisoner might well have a witness examined on his behalf and the examination be offered in court. Since supporting evidence and references to other similar occurrences is lacking, we cannot be sure if this case portended any major change in the use of witnesses.[23]

If the history of witnesses for the accused at arraignment is descernible only vaguely, that of those who spoke on his behalf at indictment is even more obscure. Obviously those persons with information who had been bound over to appear at the next sessions might give testimony which exonerated rather than incriminated the accused, yet since they had probably been examined by justices of the peace who would have made a summary of the evidence this was exceptional rather than common. That the accused might himself be present when bills of indictment were offered to the grand jury is quite likely, and it is therefore possible that he had the opportunity to offer his own evidence in reply. It is even possible that by the end of the sixteenth century he might, if the justices were willing, have been allowed to call his own witnesses to testify, but the evidence for this is fragmentary.[24] Two treason statutes, 5/6 Edward VI c.11 and 1 Elizabeth c.5, which demanded two witnesses should appear face to face with the accused at indictment as well as arraignment, must have promoted the giving of testimony by both sides on both of these occasions, but whether this became common practice in regard to other offences seems very doubtful.

However, at the preliminary examination of suspects before justices of the peace it was readily possible for persons to testify in their defence. On this point we have a clear and conclusive statement. Sir Thomas More, in his *Debellacion of Salem and Byzance*, when referring to the examination of murderers and thieves, mentions how their friends were wont 'to come forth for declaracion of them that are suspected and in trouble and depose for them'.[25] More wrote this in about the year 1533, and would have had in mind his experiences during the previous twenty years or so. Unfortunately we have no similar information from later in the century, but since in theory a justice of the peace had to take evidence from anyone claiming to be a witness, and since the duplicity of miscreants never abated, it is more than likely that the deceitful practice continued.

Examinations also figured in the history of evidence in a more important way. By the later sixteenth century it had become possible for the crown to offer at indictment or arraignment a witness's examination in place of the witnesss himself. Except where the crime was treason, it was not essential to bring witnesses in their own persons face to face with the accused. This development was logical enough for, as Lambarde noted, it obviated the danger of a witness dying before the next sessions arrived. A precaution sometimes taken by the crown, not so much to prove its own honesty as to impress the jurors, was to get a justice or court officer to affirm on oath that the testimony offered in writing was as originally set down and in no way altered. If the deposition was lost, then the justice could testify to his own knowledge of the deed as discovered at the taking of the deposition. A reporter of John Udall's trial noted in one place 'then there was much said to prove that the testimony of a man absent was sufficient if it were proved to be his upon the oaths of others'.[26] Who in these cases, when the witness was absent from the arraignment, actually put forward the testimony is not certain. Sir Thomas Smith wrote that when the absence of witnesses from the gaol delivery sessions was established, the justice of the peace who had committed the accused should hand over the examinations he had taken, but he did not suggest the justice should actually put the evidence to the court.[27] Although proof is lacking before the last years of Elizabeth, it seems very likely that this was done by counsel for the crown or some officer of the court.[28]

The qualitative sufficiency of witnesses' testimony in criminal causes was only subject to debate in the sixteenth century in regard to treason. In that area the issue was the use made by the crown of hearsay statements, that is to say of testimony from persons not called. This helped to create a demand for witnesses to be brought face to face with the accused at both indictment and trial. Descriptions of notable treason trials which show the accused challenging this governmental practice date from the reign of Mary. Sir Nicholas Throckmorton challenged a deposition by the duke of Suffolk which offered information the duke had received from his brother. Only a few days later, the judges at the trial of William Thomas ruled that one witness of his own knowledge and another by hearsay from him, although at third or fourth hand, were two sufficient witnesses where the crime was high treason.[29] Coke, writing in 1628, called this decision a 'strange conceit' and argued that accusation by hearsay was condemned by the judges in Lord Lumley's case in 1572.[30] From then to the end of Elizabeth's reign there is little evidence of the crown using hearsay statements against suspect traitors. Descriptive material relating to trials for lesser offences is very small, but an account of John Udall's trial for seditious words in 1590 shows him objecting to the crown offering a confession which stated the deposer had heard a third party say the accused was guilty of a particular offence.[31] Udall's expostulation seems to have had no effect, despite the fact that the statute regulating the offence for which he was being tried, 23 Elizabeth c.1, stipulated quite clearly that proof was to be by the testimony on oath of two witnesses who must meet the accused face to face. On occasions where the trial had considerable political significance the crown may have been none too scrupulous in choosing the evidence which it offered, but we must be careful not to conclude that it made use of hearsay testimony either frequently or in the face of other evidence which proved the contrary.

That evidence, its seeking, its production in court, and the witnessess who gave it, was a crucial area in Tudor judicial process there can be little doubt. A system had developed which demanded that accusations should be supported by the evidence of witnesses, not left at the simple statement of the accuser and the private enquiries of the jurors. More and more the witnesses appeared at the sessions and there was even one piece of statutory inducement (inducements had been hitherto reserved for informers) to procure more effective testimony against suspected criminals. The act 21 Henry VIII c.11 ordered that restitution should be made to the owner of stolen goods whose testimony was responsible for the conviction of the culprits 'in like manner as though such . . . felons were atteynted at the suit of the party in appeal'. This was an adoption of the procedure used in the old appeal of larceny to replace the usual practice whereby, if a thief was convicted on an indictment, the stolen goods forfeited to the crown. There was never any provision for the payment of expenses of witnesses in criminal cases, although such a step was mooted for a time in government circles in 1566, when alterations to the operation of the penal laws was under consideration. [32]

Any study of those statutes which were concerned with witnesses and the giving of evidence tends to create the impression that these things became increasingly important in judicial procedure because the government wanted it that way. It is just as possible that developments in the field of testimony reflected an equal desire on the part of the nation as a whole, or rather that part of it conscious of the functioning of the criminal law, to make judicial procedure more sophisticated and more likely to get at the truth. No member of this section of the population has left any real criticism of the legal developments scrutinized above. Apparently there was little fear that novel devices were infringing ancient liberties. Nor in fact should there have been, for as we have seen the Tudor laws of evidence, like those relating to summary jurisdiction, developed slowly, and in the main quite logically, from the practices of the later middle ages.

Thus mainly from the statutes but partly from other sources we are able to discover a fair amount about the history of witnesses and evidence in the fifteenth and sixteenth centuries and the growing concern about them, even if some of our knowledge has to be based on deductions from omissions in legislation and commentaries, and from procedure in special circumstances and in regard to new offences. Investigation reveals that the history of witnesses converges rather remarkably at some points with the history of summary justice as well as, more expectedly, with the certification of evidence and the making of indictments, both of whose developments can be reconstructed at second hand, so to speak, from the same sources. We can also see that in the sixteenth century the law ecclesiastical had considerable influence on the doing of justice in common law courts, at least where witnesses were concerned. It is lucky that the statutes can be made to tell us what they do for traditional sources of other kinds, Year Books, legal commentaries, and law reports, have very little to say on the subject, their attitude generally being one of disinterest, reminding us how Edward Coke, as Plucknett noted, was moved to say that 'evidence of witnesses to the jury is no part of a criminal trial, for trial is by jury, not by witnesses'.[33]

NOTES

1. J.Fortesque, *De Laudibus Legum Angliae*, ed. S.B. Chrimes (Cambridge, 1942), pp. 63, 75–7.
2. G.D.Squibb, *The High Court of Chivalry* (Oxford, 1959), pp. 14–15; J.G. Bellamy, *The Law of Treason in England in the Later Middle Ages* (Cambridge, 1970), p. 74.
3. Miss Putnam in her *Enforcement of the Statutes of Labourers* did not comment on this aspect of the judicial machinery established for enforcement.
4. *Calendar of Inquisitions Miscellaneous, 1399–1422*, no. 325. This is the same practice as described in the sixteenth century by Sir Thomas Smith in his *De Republica Anglorum*, ed. L.Alston (Cambridge, 1906), p. 99.
5. It is possible that one earlier Tudor act also intended the use of witnesses for giving evidence. The statute 11 Henry VII c.17 stipulated that justices of the peace could hear and determine accusations against those who had taken hawks' and swans' eggs either on inquisition (i.e. inquest) or information with proofs. These proofs may well have been the depositions of witnesses, but we cannot be sure.
6. Bayne did not seem to notice any such influence: of *Select Cases in the Council of Henry VII* ed. C.G. Bayne and W.H. Dunham Jr. (Selden Society, 75, 1958) pp. xxiv, lxxi, cxxii.
7. Thus, as we have seen above, under 19 Henry VII c.12 officers failing to enforce the act 11 Henry VII c.2 against vagabonds might, on examination, be punished as if convicted by due process.
8. This was an unsavoury practice which Thomas More in his *Debellacion of Salem and Byzance* could only defend by pointing to similar illicit behaviour on the part of secular justices: T. More, *The English Works of Sir Thomas More* (London, 1557), pp. 958–9.
9. See, for example, the Ilchester gaol breach of 1533 (P.R.O. SP 2/0/(14)) and the Witheryke murder case of 1538 (P.R.O. SP 1/131/199–217)
10. More, *Works*, p. 990.
11. The factor which finally decided the government on a piece of criminal legislation seems very frequently to have been a case which demonstrated loopholes in the existing law. Trying to prove this to be the basic cause is often a very laborious and inconclusive exercise. Langbein's thesis is that the act 2/3 Philip and Mary c.10 grew out of the 'bail' act, 1/2 Philip and Mary c.13: 'in the interval between Parliaments there dawned on someone the realization that the scheme just accepted by the Commons could have broader applicability than bail' (Langbein, *Prosecuting Crime* (p. 62).
12. These were 31 Henry VIII c.1 and 5/6 Edward VI c.4.
13. Langbein notices the close connection with the 'bail' act, 1/2 Philip and Mary c.13, but does not mention 1 Mary st.2 c.3, 31 Henry VIII c.14 and 1 Edward VI c.1 in this context, nor in fact the 'certification' statutes 13 Henry IV c.7, 28 Henry VIII c.10 and 31 Henry VIII c.14 which are dealt with below.
14. *State Trials*, ed. W. Cobbett and T.B. Howell (London, 1809), i. 873–81; English Reports, 1 Dyer 99b–100a.
15. The opportunities for justices of the peace to hear and determine felonies were slowly diminishing. See Cockburn, *A History of English Assizes*, pp. 86–91 and Langbein, *Prosecuting Crime*, pp. 105–6.
16. i.e. in 23 Elizabeth c.2

17. P.R.O. SP 1/110/136–45; P.R.O. SP 1/117/128–31.
18. See P.R.O. SP 1/ 246/10.
19. Langbein, *Prosecuting Crime*, p. 85; W. Lambarde, *Eirenarcha* (London, 1581), pp. 208–9 and *ibid*. (London, 1588), p. 216.

   Richard Crompton in his 1584 edition of Sir Anthony Fitzherbert's *L'Office et Aucthoritie de Justices de Peace* states 'Home ne serra examine sur son serement de chose que sounde a son reproche et *nullus tenetur seipsum perder* come le ql il fist tiel felony ou le qe il fuist periure ou tiel seble etc. car le ley intend qe home ne voile luy mesme descrediter ou accuser in tiel case (p. 152). By the early seventeenth there was a clear rule that witnesses should always be sworn before being examined, but not the accused: M. Dalton, *The County Justice* (London, 1618), p. 264.
20. B.H. Putnam, *Early Treatises on the Practice of the Justices of the Peace in the Fifteenth and Sixteenth Centuries* (Oxford, 1924), p. 409; *State Trials*, i, 885, 1304.
21. P.R.O. SP 11/13/47.
22. D. Jardine, *Criminal Trials* (London, 1832–5), i. 170.
23. There is a report of trial for murder in 1595 which states that 'as none of his (witnesses) being near' the suspect was found guilty: P.R.O. SP 12/254/55.
24. There is a possible reference in the Staffordshire quarter sessions rolls of 1597: *William Salt Archaeological Society*, *1932*, p. 302.
25. More, *Works*, pp. 987–8.
26. *State Trials*, i, 1282.
27. Smith, *De Republica*, p. 99.
28. Langbein's case that the justice of the peace who committed the suspect was the government's chief prosecuting agent is, I think, overstated. I am doubtful about justices of the peace being ready 'to assume where necessary the forensic role of prosecutor at trial' (Langbein, *Prosecuting Crime*, pp. 35–9). They may have played a key role in investigating crime outside the courtroom, but then they always had.
29. *State Trials*, i, 883; English Reports, 1 Dyer 99b–100a.
30. E. Coke, *The Third Part of Institutes of the Laws of England* (London, 1797), p. 25.
31. *State Trials*, i, 1283.
32. P.R.O. SP 12/13/43.
33. Plucknett, *Concise History of the Common Law*, p. 435.

4

THE LATE MEDIEVAL WORLD OF RIOT

The word 'riot' made its first appearance in a statute in 1361. The act, which was 34 Edward III c.1, gave authority to keepers of the peace to pursue, arrest, chastise and imprison 'offenders, rioters, and all other barrators'. What those responsible for the act had in mind was probably the unruly behaviour of the soldiery returning from the French war, men who refused or were unable to return to their erstwhile occupations and so turned instead to the pillaging and robbing they had practised overseas. The misdeeds of these 'rioters', so the statute affirmed was causing trouble and damage to the people of the realm and to merchants, presumably both English and foreign. Before this time the word 'riot' had not appeared in any official record and the connection with returning soldiers suggests it may have been imported from France. The meaning in 1361 was clearly imprecise perhaps being nothing more specific than 'boisterious wrongdoing' by a group of miscreants.[1] It was to take many years before the word ceased to be used in a very general sense; as late as 1437 the records of the king's council included within the term 'greet ryotes' robbery, arson, and manslaughter.[2] There is also some suggestion that 'riot' as a term placed as much emphasis on the violent nature of the deeds wrought as on the banding together, and thus traditional words like asssembling, confederating, or congregating illicitly, were deemed less appropriate by the drafters of the 1361 act.[3]

The words 'riot' and rioters' did not, in the years immediately following the statute, appear in official instruments again, those responsible for designing legislation and royal commands failing to incorporate them into their legal vocabulary. Yet to the lawyers who advised the king it must have become increasingly obvious that there was a need to create a new category of offence. In fact the act of 1361 may have been directed against a new category of miscreant, the person who was part of a large band which kept together with the avowed intent of breaking the law when a profitable opportunity presented itself. Those whom the statute had principally in mind were returning soldiers of the lower ranks who had little intention of going back to a humdrum labouring existence on the manor, preferring instead to wander, pillage, and rob. Such gangs were doubly dangerous because it was quite likely they would be joined by peasant fugitives who had offended against the labour laws.

There is little evidence to suggest the act of 1361 was a very useful tool for maintaining public order in the 1360s or 1370s; certainly few commissions were issued specifically under it. What to later generations was called riot, namely banding together for an illegal purpose and then some member of the band perpetrating the deed intended, did not exist as an offence and may not even have been a legal notion much before the end of Edward III's reign. Those who created such disturbances were usually dealt with under the statute of Northampton (2 Edward III c.3) which, although directed against those going with armed followers to judicial sessions, stipulated also that no man should go or ride armed by day or night or bring force in affray of the peace.[4] This was probably the most serviceable law the government had to deal with group disturbance at that time and it was used against offenders committing everything from open insurrection and assemblies or conventicles where the participants bound themselves together by oath to travelling with weapons or in armour in populated areas.[5] Progress towards the formulation of a distinct offence called riot was stimulated at the beginning of Richard II's reign by peasant restiveness, for example their refusal to pay or perform customary dues and services and their assembling and confederating together to resist their masters' demands. Similar truculence was to be found at this time in towns and was officially described as 'creating debates and contentions, and resisting attempts of officials to perform their offices'.[6] Whereas riding armed to cause disturbance, which was largely the preserve of the wealthier classes, had been dealt with under the statute of Northampton, peasant confederations resulted at the outset of Richard II's reign in a new law. This was the act 1 Richard II c.6, a piece of legislation prompted apparently by the complaints of all the elements or parliament, lords, commons, and clergy.[7] The statute attributed the peasant restiveness to their failure to gain discharge from traditional services despite evidence which they thought was in their favour to be found in Domesday Book. Their protests had taken the form of banding together in what were called great routs,[8] and promising each other to resist the demands of their lords by force, all of which was called in the statute an example likely to cause others to make similar riots. In this, the second appearance of the word 'riot' in the statutes, the meaning seems to have changed from 'boisterous wrongdoing' to 'group intransigence directed against social superiors'. It is noteworthy that the statute also referred to such miscreants as 'rebels', rebellion being at this time the traditional word to describe resistance by peasants against their lords; it was a trespass and never held by itself to be any form of treason.

In the next parliament, which met at Gloucester in October 1378, the word 'riot' was used again, but in a different sense. The relevant statute, 2 Richard II st.1 c.6, noting how men gathered in routs in Cheshire and the Welsh marches so as to take possession of lands and ravish women, and were lying in wait to injure, murder, or take persons for ransom, first conirmed the act which had been used to combat these crimes in the past (the statute of Northampton, 2 Edward III c.3)[9] and then stipulated new procedural methods for dealing with such 'assemblies, routs, and rioters' in the future. Clearly the routs were thought to be made up of rioters of a higher social station than those who were the object of the act of 1377. Entering lands and holding them by force as well as ravishing women were crimes traditionally associated with the squirarchy and above, and ambush was a preferred method of eliminating the opposition with the least danger to oneself. The act was short-lived, however. It was revoked by the same parliament which passed it, the reason being that the section allowing the arrest without indictment of those known to have been involved in the riots was considered too grievous; in other words, shortened procedure did not as yet have wide approval.

The parliament which met in November 1381 passed a law annulling all manumissions made by compulsion in what was called 'the time of the last rumour and riot' (i.e. the Peasants' Revolt).[10] The continuing connection of the word 'riot' with peasant restiveness was thus afirmed; it had not been severed by the fate of the act of 1378. Furthermore, to recommence that 'riot' was made by the 1381 statute into treason, or at least an offence carrying the normal penalties for that crime. In the parliament of 1394, which sat at a time of considerable unrest in Cheshire, Lancashire, and Yorkshire, the act of 1381 was rehearsed by way of a preamble to a new statute (17 Richard II c.8) which laid down the duties of sheriffs and other officers of the crown in such circumstances, and the help to be afforded them by subjects in general. It was, however, not an exact recital of the 1381 riot statute but one with a slight, yet significant, addition. This was that the king forbade anyone from making or beginning again not only the 'riot' or 'rumour' of 1381 but any other similar one. In other words, all such extensive riots now became treason. The connection of riot with treason, soon no doubt regretted by lawyers, must have come about through the use in the 1381 act of a word which had had very little legal use hitherto. It must have made its way into the statute rolls through the emotional demands of the parliamentary lords and commons, who used everyday language rather than words the lawyers would have chosen. There was, it is true, some need for legislation on the subject, since the treason laws in operation had little to say about peasant uprisings, which only by feats of construction could be said to amount to aiming at the death of the king or levying war against him (the major categories of treason). There was no treason of 'combination', as was to be found in Europe, and not until Edward VI's reign was it good law to interpret congregations hostile to authority as felony. That there were in subsequent decades charges and indictments under the 1381 act and its 1393 extension is certain, but there is no evidence any accused suffered the penalties for treason.[11] The statutes in this respect seem to have been hortative, mere threats, although their origin shows that a statement like Bayne's, that the use in accusations of the phrase 'in the manner of a new insurrection' was just for added impressiveness, needs qualification.[12] Another point of note was the manner in which the king in 1394 connected the 'riot and rumours' of that time with the nobility, warning them against making such disturbances in the future. By this the close tie between 'riot' and lower class uprising was weakened and in consequence the general scope of the offence was extended.

The statute on riots which legal writers of a later date heralded as being of the utmost importance, 13 Henry IV c.7, like the others before it, did not define riot or relate it to the social context. It was concerned almost exclusively with the methods by which justices of the peace should handle such disturbances in the local milieu and the legal procedure involved in getting the miscreants convicted: how they might record what they saw done (or make inquest if they arrived on the scene too late) and certify the events to the king's council.[13] As has been shown elsewhere, these novel judicial methods demonstrate how serious a problem riots were now becoming. The statute, perhaps because of its new summary way of dealing with riotous behaviour, was not immediately put into general operation. There had to be a complaint by the parliamentary commons and a confirmatory act with alternative procedures in case of default by the justices of the peace and sheriffs (2 Henry V st.1 c.4), before accusations were made under it. After this act there was no significant legislation on riot as such for thirty-eight years.

What, it may be asked, did riot as the subject of legislation and judicial enquiry in the early fifteenth century amount to? How far, if at all, had it changed from the 'boisterous wrongdoing' of 1361 and 'popular insurrection' of 1381 and 1394? The evidence suggests the word 'riot' by 1430 meant just as often what it had meant to those who were responsible for the statute 2 Richard II st. 1 c.6, which was to band together as in the manner of war, to lie in wait to beat, maim, and kill people, and to take possession of land on one's own authority and hold it by force. Such misdeeds were committed regularly during the feuding of the upper classes and the indications are that it was to this phenomenon that the word 'riot' was frequently applied, perhaps even more often than to popular uprisings. This is shown by several sources. The statute 4 Henry IV c.8, concerned in essence with forcible entries (with the taking of goods and chattels) and ousters by the great men of the realm for themselves or for their clients, referred to these misdeed as 'such riots and forcible entries'. Cases in the Patent Rolls refer to debates, strifes, dissensions, arising between X and Y over title and possession of the manors of A and B, and the king ordering the disputed properties to remain in the hands of Z until he decides what further action shall be taken.[14] Commonly in these cases the reason for such an order was to avoid 'riots' between the parties. A surviving justices' charge to jurors, which has been dated *circa* 1403–4, where it instructs them to investigate riots seems to be referring to the statutes of 1361 (34 Edward III c.1), 1378 (2 Richard II st.1 c.6), and to the peace commission of 1380, all of which give the impression of having been designed more to deal with upper classs trouble-makers than with lower class insurgents.[15]

This evidence we must set against references in the Patent Rolls where the word riot is found in close relationship with terms like 'insurrection', 'rebellion', 'confederations' and 'congregations', which signify large scale disobedience to authority. There are several examples of this but they seem usually connected with faction fights in towns.[16] Records of proceedings in chancery for the period under review show considerably more cases of 'riot' meaning insurrection or uprising than mere affray or entry with force.[17] Admittedly there were occasions when the word 'riot' was used, even as late as the early fifteenth century, in a way which confused the two different traditions. One plaintiff in chancery claimed a forcible entry into his property was a grievous example of insurrection and fell within the act of 1381.[18] In the Patent Rolls for the last years of Richard II's reign there are examples of riotous feuds between knights and esquires where the crown referred to the offences as insurrections in the same sentence.[19] Nonetheless such cases where the traditions were confused were not common. Clearly, then, although the word 'riot' was by the reign of Henry VI used commonly in reference to violent behaviour in the course of feuds, amongst the gentry it still retained a connection with popular rebellion.

To discover how the lawyers would have defined 'riot', had they been asked, at the beginning of the fifteenth century is no easy task therefore. Those who wrote legal treatises or commentaries, which dealt with the criminal law, in early Tudor times all gave fairly similar meanings to the word. Marowe in his lecture of 1503 on the conservation of the peace gave what became the classical definition of riot, namely that it was where more than two people were assembled intending to do something against the law and actually executed a deed to that purpose.[20] Pollard, writing in Henry VIII's time, said very much the same, merely turning Marowe's 'more than two people' into three or more.[21] Fitzherbert called riot an unlawful assembly for an evil intent with something done contrary to the law after the assembly was made, but he did not mention the matter of number.[22] If the lawyers who wrote in the earlier sixteenth century were agreed on what they meant by 'riot' the two definitions which survive from the fifteenth century were both different from theirs and different from each other. A justices' charge to jurors of *circa* 1444–5 declared riot *per se* was a group of persons going in forcible array against the king's peace and 'puttynge the kynges people in fere'. In a record of council the chief justice of the king's bench was reported as saying in November 1488 that a riot was where 'a man anie thinge attempteth with a multitude gathered beyond the wonted number followinge him whether with weapons or without' unless, he added, the gathering was for 'some comon good'. Neither of these definitions mentioned the number of persons necessary to make a riot.[23] Both made the point in a rudimentary way that the gathering must intend some misdeed, although neither suggested an actual offence must be committed before a riot had occurred. The charge of *circa* 1444–5 stipulated that the participants in a riot must go 'in forcible array' whereas in contrast and perhaps even in correction the chief justice said that whether they had weapons or not was immaterial. Thus it seems that a definition of riot which satisfied the lawyers was only worked out in the last decade of the fifteenth century, but there is no indication of by whom or which cases in law led to the definitive pronouncement on the matter.

The reason for the delay in defining exactly what riot meant was partly that the drafters of statutes relating to public order had once more shown a *penchant*, common in the later middle ages, of using an everyday word of an imprecise and general nature (perhaps suggested to them by the original petition), and partly that statutes on crime defined their legal terminology only very rarely. They were generally intended not for declaring the scope of an offence but for establishing procedure to be used in dealing with it judicially. Thus the act of 1361 gave authority to keepers of the peace to arrest recalcitrant ex-soldiers, that of 1377 gave lords whose villeins rose against them the right to have special commissions hear and determine the cases; the statute of 1378 allowed commissioners in each county to have the power to arrest rioters without waiting for their indictment 'or other process'; the act of 1381 made recommencing the riot that was the great revolt an offence carrying the penalties of treason; the act of 1411 provided *inter alia* for justices of the peace to convict men of riot simply on their 'record', which was their viewing of the incident, or if they did not see it to certify what they learned had happened, the certificate having the force of a presentment. In the years after these acts had been entered on the statute rolls the word 'riot', originally as we have seen a general term for group misbehaviour, achieved through its very appearance there and the common lawyers' growing acquaintance with it an identity it did not have originally, even if its role merely as an element in criminal law procedure remained always the dominant one.

Viewed in a legal light riot should have been of considerable value to the king as a category of indictment because it enabled him to prosecute the person present at a popular uprising or a forcible entry who did not actually commit an offence himself other than assembling. For the law on riot, probably by the mid-fifteenth century, made offenders of all those present in his company when the miscreant committed the deed; they did not have to do the same themselves. Thus the crown was in theory able in this instance to reach accessaries before the fact when the fact was only a trespass. This alone, if indicting jurors responded to the promptings of justices in the fifteenth century, and the evidence suggests they usually did, should have produced a spate of indictments for riot. Yet there was none; at least, what records we have do not show one, although admittedly there are very few peace rolls extant for the period after the accession of Henry V. Most of the surviving examples of what may be called the riotous type of offence in indictments are not of riot under that title but cases of lying in wait to kill or main, the charges presumably being brought under the peace commission of May 1380.[24] This type of ambush appeared in the same article as riot in a justices' charge to jurors of *circa* 1403 and lawyers may have become inclined to associate one with the other, particularly as with both offences simply for the mass of the participants to have intended a misdeed was a crime in itself.

The great shortage of cases of riot in common law records prior to the reign of Henry V, when other records like the rolls of parliament suggest they were a fairly frequent phenomenon, may have been caused by several factors. For example the riot laws may only have been drawn assiduously to the attention of the justices of the peace at about the time the peace rolls cease (*circa* 1400). Then there is the probability that the government may have considered that to use the statute of 1381, with its punishment as for treason, against those involved in local popular uprisings and group disturbance a measure too severe. There are in the peace rolls a number of indictments for around 1400 where men were accused of insurrection, being arrayed in the manner of war, and suchlike, and it was called felony, there being no mention of treason. In almost every case, however, the miscreants were also charged with something that was a traditional felony, like robbery or larceny, the indictment treating the numerous insurgents as accessaries to felony and using the insurrection as an aggravation.[25] Indictments claiming a group of persons had made armed insurrection which rated the offence as only trespass (i.e. as riot) did occur, but they were uncommon. The reluctance to use the statute in its proper form is very apparent. Indictments under the statute 1 Richard II c.6, which might have been used against the villeins of several manors who withdrew their services and made leagues in the later years of Henry IV, are rare and again the cause may be the lack of surviving peace rolls. It is also possible this type of crime was handled as an offence against the labour laws rather than as riot. If we look for a riot statute which was intended to be used against those involved in forcible entry into land or other property, which fifteenth century correspondence suggests was the situation in which riots most commonly occurred, we do not find one. There was no need for one since there was no shortage of statutes designed specifically to deal with forcible entry *per se*; 5 Richard II c.7, 15 Richard II c.2, 4 Henry IV cc.7 and 8, and 8 Henry VI c.9 demonstrate a variety of efforts to combat an offence which was a great danger to public order. Yet, as with riot, very few indictments of forcible entry appear in the records of the justices of peace.[26] One other possible reason for the lack of riot indictments may have been that those doing the indicting preferred to lay other charges, perhaps because they seemed to them more substantial and specific, like assault, lying in wait to kill or maim, larceny (where animals were driven off and crops taken), travelling armed (against the statute 2 Edward III c.3), and even forcible entry (which after 1429 could bring a fortunate victim treble damages). Finally there is the likelihood that bills of indictment for riot were being refused by grand juries and that, knowing this, those who wished to complain resorted to personal actions rather than the procedures of the criminal law.

It is no exaggeration to say that the statutes concerned with riot had no coherence as a group. One overlapped on to treason, another was itself overlaid by the laws on forcible entry, while what might have been a great deal of business was not handled under a riot statute but by indictments drawn under the peace commission of 1380 or even under the Northampton statute of 1329.[27] The terrain which riot laws should have occupied was already taken and riot, the common offence of the upper classes of the fifteenth and sixteenth centuries, was really the child of the procedural devices set out in the important act 13 Henry IV c.7. Through this it appeared in the records far more frequently than it had previously because the Henrician statute provided for cases to go before courts which were not of the common law. What the statute said was that when there was reported a riot, rout, or unlawful assembly two justices of the peace, the sheriff and the county posse, should go and arrest the miscreants.[28] The first three could then make a record of what mischief they had seen done, which was to work an instant conviction on the wrong-doers, who were then to be imprisoned until they made a fine with the king. If the trio failed to arrive at the riot before the rioters had dispersed they were to make an inquiry into what had happened, presumably by means of an inquest, and procedure would then follow the normal course. The statute also provided that if the truth could not be discovered in this manner then the trio should certify what had happened to the king and the council, the certificate having the force of a jury's presentment. To this the accused were to be put to answer. If they pleaded guilty they were to be punished by king and council; if they traversed the certificate then they were to be tried on the charges it contained in the king's bench. Failure of the accused to appear when summoned was to bring conviction. In the matter of the use of record the statute was not novel being, as it clearly stated, modelled on the earlier act 15 Richard II c.2. This, where complaint was made of a forcible entry, instructed justices of the peace to go to the scene of the offence and where they found anyone holding the land with force they were to arrest them and put them in gaol as convicted by the magistrates' record. They would later pay a fine for release.

The adoption of what we may call a form of summary justice suggests that by 1411 it had already met with some success.[29] The act of 1391 was apparently prompted by a petition which asked merely that the statutes against forcible entries and riot be enforced. Whether the radical step of summary conviction by justices of the peace, was proposed by the parliamentary commons, the lords, or the king and his advisers, is not known. Searching for the immediate causes of the 1411 riot act is likewise inconclusive, although there were several disturbances at that time which must have made the government nervous. In March 1411 the bondmen and tenants of Waltham abbey withdrew their services and created an insurrection. There were similar withdrawals and leaguing together at Chertsey and Torre abbeys.[30] There were three significant private feuds as well. A petition by the commons in the parliament of 1410 listed and complained strongly about the riots and felonies committed in Staffordshire by Hugh de Erdeswyk and his associates. In Lincoln and Lincolnshire in the spring of 1411 Sir Walter Tailboys, with a large band of men, caused much riotous disturbance in his efforts to kill Sir Thomas Chaworth, even to stopping the wool traffic between Lincoln, Hull, and Boston. In autumn of the same year, at the time when the parliament which enacted the riot statute was about to meet, there was an eruption, which took the form of a siege, at the castle of Cotyf in the Welsh marches, the antagonists being Sir Gilbert Denys and William Gamage on the one side and Joan the widow of Sir Richard Vernon on the other. These were not the only disruptive occurrences of that time; there were others possibly quite as serious but about which we know little. For example, in October 1411 a commission was issued in accordance with a petition of the commons in the last parliament for enquiry into all riots, 'rides of evildoers', maintenance, and livery giving, in the counties of Yorkshire, Nottinghamshire and Derbyshire; the inquisitions so taken were to be sent to the council, which suggests a connection with the riot act.[31]

The disturbances in Lincolnshire, Staffordshire, Wales, Yorkshire, Nottinghamshire and Derbyshire, or rather the government's response, heralded new solutions or attempted solutions. The Staffordshire riots led to an act which stated the miscreants involved should appear in parliament to answer, or stand convicted and forfeit all their property. The Lincolnshire rioters were to be arrested by two justices of the peace and forced to give sureties for their good behaviour. If they refused to do so the matter was to be certified to the king in chancery. Those besieging Cotyf castle, in contrast, were to be commanded to appear before the council on a certain day to answer. Then the king would, on the council's advice, do justice in the matter of any right or title which 'he two sides possessed. What these methods of dealing with riotous disturbance had in common was a failure to use the normal procedures of the common law. There was to be no reliance on indictment by jury and trial by jury. The device of summoning men to answer for riot and other crimes in parliament, although it was persisted with off and on for another half century, had no great future. Use of the king's council and the services of the chancellor in cases of riot, some complaints admittedly starting from petitions in parliament, was on the other hand to become popular.

As the ultimate method of dealing with riots, the statute of 1411 postulated the king's council or court of king's bench. In the next reign procedure was slightly amended by two statutes which allotted a significant role to the chancellor. The act 2 Henry V st.1 c.8 provided that when the two justices of the peace and the sheriff, who were required to visit the scene of any riot, defaulted in their duty the party grieved could obtain a commission for an inquiry into the disturbance apparently by informing the chancellor.[32] If the latter perchance heard of the riot without any complaint from the party who had suffered he was to instruct the justices of the peace and sheriff to perform their duties. Another act in the same parliament, 2 Henry V st.1 c.9, also connected the chancellor with riots, although in this instance there were other crimes involved also. It said that when those who had committed homicides, robberies, assemblies, rebellions and riots (a group of offences which the act elsewhere labelled collectively as riots) fled to the woods to avoid execution of the law, a bill was to be made for the king and delivered to the chancellor. He, on ascertaining its veracity (apparently by letters from two justices of the peace), was to order the sheriff to effect an arrest. If this failed, proclamation was to be made instructing the miscreant's appearance in the king's bench by a stated day or he would be held convicted.

The role of the chancellor in dealing with riots at this time ought not to surprise us if we remember how in the fourteenth century he was responsible for summoning the council *in cancellaria* when a knotty point of law arose there. Petitions were addressed to the chancellor primarily because he was the chief executive officer, for it was the council, or at least a number of councillors, who decided the case; in such judicial matters the chancellor was one amongst several who served as judges. There is no evidence in the fourteenth century that he operated a court in which he was the sole justice. It was probably the speed with which a person who suffered from riot could get his oppressors called before the chancellor or council, and the relative certainty of punishment if they defaulted, which made this mode of action popular. The instruments of summoning were privy seal letters, writs of *quibusdam de certis causis* and *sub poena*, which were often the subject of complaints in parliament to the effect that they were untrue, that remedies were available at common law and that the person summoned was not told the offence of which he was accused. Despite strident objection commencing in the 1340s the council persisted in using the writs and letters because it recognized it could not function properly as a judicial body if it relinquished them.[33] It also strengthened the method of getting the plaintiff and accused into court by demanding sureties for appearance. We can see, therefore, why the chancellor and the council were chosen to receive bills of complaint, which explains their mention in the 1411 act. A problem not so easily answered is why amongst these bills were the ones which concerned riot prominent even before the statute was conceived?

One answer might be that the council and the chancellor had a traditional duty to compose the feuds of the upper classes and that an outcome of many feuds was riot. Against this must be set the fact that in the last years of the fourteenth century complaints came before the chancellor which were based on contravention of the act 5 Richard II st.1 c.6 (the statute which forbade the recommencement of the great revolt of 1381 on pain of treason) or its rehearsal in 17 Richard II c.8, even if there were others based on the violation of the forcible entry act of 1391, where the misdeed could certainly be said to be feuding involving riot.[34] It was the latter type which was in time to become the staple criminal fare of the council, and we may take it that the act of 1411 was a corollary to the one of 1391 in the type of crime covered as well as procedure for, as we shall see, virtually all forcible entries involved riot. Emphasis on these two statutes, and later that of 1411 in particular, did not mean that all offences complained of to the chancellor and council in this period came logically under them. One of 1395–6 claimed that a bill fixed on the door of the church of St. Martin's, Leicester, was a riot and the perpetrators soon likely to make an insurrection. Another of *circa* 1404 claimed the election of Thomas Burton as abbot of Melsa was a wilfully made insurrection.[35] However, these seem to have been in the minority, or perhaps complainants become more adept at turning the mischief done to them into something more resembling riot. Another reason why riot from early on became staple conciliar judicial business was that the council was usually ready to receive complaints of misbehaviour where the party grieved claimed that because of his antagonist's social status and local influence he could get no satisfaction at common law. This was because (although it was not often stated) of the manner in which juries, both petty and of indictment, could be intimidated by powerful men. Such men of course, because of their landed interests and those of their clients, were likely to be involved in a good number of riot cases during their careers. The crown could also argue that riot and the feuding of which it was part, where they involved the magnates could easily take on political overtones if there was a substantial party of opposition in the realm from which one side could seek support. Quick and decisive action, which meant conciliar intervention, was therefore essential.

One effect of the riot act of 1411 was the appearance of the word 'riot' among the crimes to be enquired into by commissions of oyer and terminer for virtually the first time. There had been one earlier example, as we have seen: this was in regard to the counties of Yorkshire, Nottinghamshire, and Derbyshire, and occurred in October 1411, just before the parliament which promulgated the act met. In 1414 came several; they were issued to enquire into riots and offences of a similar type in Norwich, Nuneham (Oxfordshire), and the counties of Lincolnshire, Nottinghamshire, and Derbyshire.[36] From Henry VI's reign riot occurred regularly as an offence to be investigated and dealt with by oyer and terminer commissions.[37] Royal action against riot named as such which we can clearly identify as directed against gentry or nobility at feud only appeared regularly in records at the end of the second decade of the fifteenth century. From 1418 we find conciliar ordinances which committed land in dispute to the keeping of a third party until further order, the reason usually given being the evidence of riots and other evils between the adversaries.[38] From around 1440 'riot' appeared regularly in another type of legal instrument, the special pardon. It did not appear alone but usually figured in a list which might include such general categories and specific offences as felonies, murders, trespasses, insurrections, congregations, contempts, and extortions. By this time offenders seeking a pardon, if they had been involved in a gentleman's feud or an urban factional disturbance, made sure the word 'riot' was included, where earlier they had not bothered.[39] We may therefore assume that after a slow early development the crime was by this time well established both in lawyers' minds and public consciousness, and furthermore that statutes on riot were at last being operated with some consistency. In addition it seems the term was understood and used in a way that was precise and technical, even if there still occurred in the 1430s (especially in conciliar records) instances of its use in a very general way.[40]

In considering the field of late medieval riot we should be foolish to concern ourselves with only the development of the legal notion of riot itself. We have already seen how riot did not find a distinctive place in the lawyers' vocabulary without difficulty and how the concept of riot sprang from more than one tradition in criminal law. This early confusion arose because riot was a necessary concomitant of two other forms of misbehaviour, namely insurrection and forcible entry (entry into land using force). The former, although relatively spectacular, was very much rarer than the latter and thus did not have the same effect on the later development of the law of riot. Forcible entry, on the other hand, was probably the most common crime committed by the upper classes and had an essential, even a dominant role in riot as it stood in law and riot as it stood in the wider social context, in what might be called 'the world of riot' or 'the gentlemen's wars'. The first occasion on which forcible entry was officially equated with riot was in the statute 4 Henry IV c.8 (the making of forcible entries by great men with the taking of goods and chattels was called 'tielx riotes et forcibles entrees') but it is clear that the latter was very likely to occur when the former did, and indeed had done so in the past when for forcible entry there was disseisin and for riot something like riding or going armed or making an assault or larceny in a group; the situations were the same even if the vocabulary was different.

The term 'forcible entry' appeared in the statute book for the first time in 1381. The act 5 Richard II c.7 forbade anyone from entering land except where entry was allowed by law and then not with a strong hand, as it was put, but only in a peaceable manner.[41] Until this time references in legal records to moves to occupy land without the authority of a court had always gone under the term 'disseisin', although by the 1370s we do read of 'forcible disseisin', the adjective being used where it had never been found necessary before. The slowly declining popularity of the action of novel disseisin was only one reason for the emergence of the term 'forcible entry'. Very likely it came into common use because of the new legal process associated with it. This was that those who occupied lands illegally might, from 1381, be indicted for their offence where hitherto they were only subject to personal actions, as for example of novel disseisin or trespass. Theoretically the king was taking a direct interest in charges being brought against illegal entrants and was asking people of the locality to bring such charges. Title to the land, it should be noted, was in these proceedings quite immaterial; only whether the entry was forcible was being tried.

Entries into land using force and the often accompanying event of ouster of the occupier had a long history. They were prompted by a number of factors, some emotional and irrational but many legal and technical. Some entries were permissible because the party out of possession had the better title, being in fact the rightful owner, although of course this had not been decided by judicial verdict at the time of entry; it was to be a result of the dispossessed party pleading in court. In the thirteenth century it had been shown to be important for the preservation of his title that the owner should make an entry and establish seisin, since the encroacher-occupier who was left undisturbed in possession of the land for a considerable period could develop actual rights to it, and the courts might forbid the owner from occupying land and even award it to the usurper if he did. As the law stood, it did not pay a party claiming land to be other than aggressive. Should the claimant, indeed the rightful owner, be over-cautious and start a suit in law to recover the land this might be held as admitting that his antagonist was seised, and therefore the owner might lose the right to enter. In the fourteenth century, on the face of it, there was less necessity to enter so as to preserve a right of entry.[42] The loss of right of entry merely through sueing one's opponent in court disappeared in Edward II's reign. The immediate exercise of entry right was still necessary when an adversary enfeoffed a third party in the land in dispute; if it was not exercised then it was 'tolled' i.e. permanently lost. This rule endured to the 1390s but was then abandoned. Longer lived still was the dictum that descent cast tolled right of entry, descent cast being when the opponent in occupation died and his claim to the land passed to his heir. If the owner had not exercised his right of entry in the adversary's lifetime then it would cease to exist unless he could show a record of a recovery against the new adversary's ancestor, or some other document extinguishing their right at an earlier time. In a case of 1351 it was stated the owner should have protested and constantly raised contention up to the time of the occupier's death. Fourteen years later these protests and contentions were required to take the form of attempting to enter, while in a case in Henry IV's reign it was held that such an intrusion had to be made in the last year of the occupier's life. This rule continued right through the fifteenth century, eventually being amended by the act 32 Henry VIII cc.7, 23 and 33, which stipulated there must have been an attempt to enter within five years of the death for a right of entry to subsist. One other feature of the law encouraged entry, and indeed effective entry, rather than a mere show of entering. This was where the occupier had been in possession for a long time. Should the claimant make only a token entry, that is to say enter and withdraw, and then sue out a writ of novel disseisin, he would likely be defeated by the length of his opponent's seisin. If however he entered effectively the opponent, now dispossessed, would have to sue and without the benefit of continued long seisin.[43]

Despite the encouragement of entry by the judicial attitude to descent cast and benefits under the assize of novel disseisin for those who made effective entry, there was a fourteenth century tendency to ensure wherever possible that situations involving violence were limited. There was a new sensitivity to the use of force by all classes, as the emphasis in the 1381 act that all future entries must be peaceable clearly shows. Judges, so it has been argued, in their interpretations of the law did what they could to preserve the longevity of rights of entry so that, secure in the knowledge that time and passivity did not work against them in law, men who claimed land but were out of possession would not feel they must make entry immediately.[44] Social tensions may also have been eased through the act of 1381 making forcible entry a criminal offence, which allowed charges to be laid and determined without verdicts on titles to land; only whether the entry was by force was considered. Rather oddly, there are few indictments for forcible entry to be found in the surviving peace rolls of the late fourteenth and early fifteenth centuries, although there are more in one of the only two extant rolls of the later fifteenth century and in the coram rege rolls of Edward IV's reign; in the reign of Henry VIII they became not uncommon.[45] After the promulgation of a second statute on forcible entry in 1391 (15 Richard II c.2) it is possible many such cases were handled summarily by justices of the peace. The statute required one or several justices of the peace, on complaint made, to visit the place where the entry had occurred and if they found anyone holding property by force to imprison them as being convict by the justices' own record, procedure that was even more draconian than that modelled on it in 1411 to deal with riot. As has been pointed out elsewhere, there is no suggestion any files or notes of these summary convictions have survived. We must, I think, accept the evidence of what literary material remains, that forcible entries were common place throughout the later middle ages and early Tudor period. If they were not, then there would have been lacking a basic reason for the frequent promulgation of statutes against not only riot but illicit retaining, livery giving, and maintenance in the crucial period 1380–1430. There were other remedies against forcible entry as well as the laying of criminal charges. Those grieved could bring personal actions of forcible entry, novel disseisin, trespass, and entry in the nature of an assize. These must have been quite popular among those not in possession of their land, because if prosecuted successfully they could bring damages, double damages if under the act 4 Henry IV c.8,[46] or treble damages if under 8 Henry VI c.9, but it is not possible to assess the frequency of such suits with exactitude at the present time.[47]

We must turn now from riot and forcible entry as they stood in legal theory to their role in everyday living. We may ask how it was, with the welter of preventative and remedial legislation, these crimes continued to be perpetrated so frequently. Did men adapt their conduct to evade the legal sanctions and if so how? Could the laws be safely ignored given a supporting patron or a long purse? To answer such questions as these we must look at contemporary correspondence as well as the records of the courts and the commentaries of the lawyers.

Actual entry into land held by an adversary was always a potential danger to public order. The rules as to how a party entitled to disseize might carry it out were several, and they altered periodically to keep pace with social realities. In the thirteenth century a would-be entrant with good title could ask the sheriff to assist him and this the latter was by law permitted to do, but he must only do it if he felt the cause was sound and he was legally liable if he did so on behalf of a party whose claim was later found deficient.[48] We may take it, therefore, that sheriffs generally only gave aid in this matter to those whose friendship was valuable. Most claimants determined to disseize felt the sheriff's aid would not be forthcoming, and therefore took a following of their own with them to effect the task. The number of supporters taken with him by any person bent on making an entry depended on whether he was entering merely to exercise a claim to entry (so he could say in court at a later date he had seisin) or whether he intended actually to oust the occupier and his household from the land. By the end of the thirteenth century the requirements for the proper effecting of the former had become such that the danger of confrontation with one's adversary and therefore affray had been diminished, even if it was never removed. In Edward I's reign it was held a man had taken seisin if he came to the land in an open manner, in daylight, entered it, declared he was taking control, and commanded the occupier face to face to leave.[49] By the late fourteenth century it was only required of the entrant, if he feared he might be killed, that he go as close to the land as was safe before announcing the claim;[50] in the fifteenth century he was allowed to adopt this procedure where the threat was not to life but only to limb. Thus in a notorious incident in the Paston correspondence when Friar Hawteyn came to enter Oxnead manor against Edmund Paston in *circa* 1445 and was ordered by the latter to withdraw or suffer bloody penalty, he told those who had come with him to observe how he was kept out; then with his hands he scooped up some earth asking them to bear record how he was taking possession of his inheritance.[51]

When the purpose of the entry was, as in Hawteyn's case, merely to assert a claim, the entrant needed only followers sufficient in number to bear witness and to protect him from assault. When the aim was to occupy and hold the land in dispute then entrants preferred to take with them as many men as they could muster: household servants, retainers, the servants of friends, tenants, other followers of their own lord, and even men hired just for the occasion at a set rate per day with bouche of court. Wrote Henry Makney to William Stonor 'Y purpose to entere the manere of Makney with Godes grace . . . I pray youe sende me a gode lade or ii that y be note bete owte ayene'.[52] Robert Pilkington's account of his great cause in the late fifteenth century tells of his foes raising help from several acquaintances by telling them in prosaic terms to help them now if they wanted their help in the future. Bands of as many as five hundred adherents were by no means unknown in fifteenth century forcible entries and it seems likely that the gentry and nobility of that time were tempted into spending large sums to recruit extensive assistance. As Serjeant Billing pointed out to one notorious perpetrator of riot and forcible entry in Norfolk, 'Yt is the gyse of yowre contre-men to spend alle the good they haue on men and levery, gownys, and hors and harnes'.[53] Not until 1495 was it an offence for one trying to enter to take on such an enterprise what was considered an excessive number of men, the acceptable size of such a band being limited to the number who would customarily attend on the claimant. This explains very clearly why members of the upper classes were always zealous to have a full household and the largest of retinues their pockets could afford.[54] These recruiting practices were not, of course, confined only to the would-be entrant. The party in occupation, if he suspected an effort was to be made to oust him, would also seek the services of able-bodied men and collect weapons.

In contrast to the matter of number there were, right through the later middle ages, established rules as to the equipment and behaviour of such bands. After the middle of the thirteenth century their members were not supposed to carry arms; if they did they were committing an offence, even if later on it was found the claimant's title to the land was superior and thus the entry was justifiable. From the later thirteenth century, assault on the adversary's person was not permissible and by 1411 even threats on the part of the intruders by word of mouth were illegal.[55] In the later fourteenth century at least if such attacks should occur retaliation by the aggrieved party was considered lawful. This dictum may have developed from the act of 1347 (21 Edward III c.34) which permitted the party entered on to use force to defend his goods if he had been in quiet possession for three years or more. The force he could utilize for this purpose was only the company he had in his house, which by a later legal interpretation, since it was probably where the goods were located, could also be defended.[56] Looking further back, it seems fair to assume the statute affirming the legality of force to defend goods may have derived from thirteenth and early fourteenth century prohibitions against lawful disseisors seizing the personal property of the party ousted.[57] Whatever the origins of the notion, its practical effects are obvious: if they had the right to defend their goods and houses men were very likely to consider they could use force in defence of their lands in addition.

The manner in which force was used in the feuds over property in the fourteenth and fifteenth centuries is interesting. One reason for the large numbers of men used to support forcible entries may well have been a desire to overawe the opposition rather than successfully assault and defeat it in battle. In an age when there were no weapons, like modern firearms, which would compensate for lack of numbers, every sword and armoured torso was important to have. The short pieces we have describing entries (they concern the fifteenth and sixteenth centuries) show force was used in a very circumscribed way. The intruders would seize crops, and livestock, break doors and windows, no doubt to gain entry, and throw out the occupants bodily. Actual fights between occupants and intruders seem to have been the exception rather than the rule. Certainly by the fifteenth century deaths were few. No one on either side seems to have been killed in Robert Pilkington's quarrel with the Ainsworths, which lasted from 1478 or before to after the accession of Henry VIII. In the Paston letters, which are full of entries into land, there is only clear mention of two homicides in that pursuit, and the rarity of the event is proven by the great concern it aroused and the extended legal proceedings which resulted. In the Plumpton correspondence similarly only one person seems to have been killed in a forcible entry or riot.[58] This lack of casualties is in line with other facets of these 'gentlemen's wars' of the later middle ages. For example, there are many reports of ambushes laid with the intention of killing adversaries, but although servants may have suffered cracked heads and flesh wounds very few principals died or were even badly wounded. When a death did result it was usually through a chance missile, not in hand to hand combat, which again suggests little determination to close with the foe and finish him off.[59]

Although historians have talked a great deal about the abuses of livery giving and receiving, of illicit retaining, of the maintenance of parties engaged in law suits by powerful men, as being at the heart of the disruption of public order in fourteenth and fifteenth century England, a very good case can be made for forcible entry and riot being the prime causes, with the other evils springing from them. Because that was where their wealth was centred, the upper classes thought first and foremost about their property in land and ways of extending and defending it, as the Plumpton, Stonor, and Paston correspondence clearly shows. Because of the complex rules of inheritance and devising created largely by the fact that land, unlike goods and chattels, could not be willed but must be settled on someone in the holder's lifetime, and also because of the looseness of the law of marriage at a time when few men or widows failed to remarry on the death of their spouse, few titles to land were legally impregnable. If you did possess land which had this blessing then it was foolish to sell it, as Margaret Paston once tried to make her son John acknowledge.[60] This insecurity in land holding tempted men who had some claim to one manor or another to try their luck and make an entry, whether a token one or one ousting the current occupier, as a hopefully beneficial precursor to a trial of title in the courts. One way of making an entry was to distrain the tenants in the land in dispute. The taking of their chattels because they failed to perform customs and pay dues and rent to the claimant might be adduced as evidence to prove seisin in court at a later time. So might the holding of a manor court in which the tenants recognized the holder as their lord, or the collecting of rents. Both these figure prominently in contemporary letters, the holding of a manor court having the additional advantage of providing the opportunity for tenants loyal to the claimant to get decrees against their own and their patrons' enemies.[61] If we accept the evidence of the Plumpton and Paston correspondence, it helped his case when title to land was the issue, if the claimant came in person to the disputed manor to take a distress. For example, Sir Robert Plumpton in 1501 was advised to do this and to stay a while and be seen among tenants and friends, which suggests that having the respect of the lower class inhabitants was important for legal purposes.[62] In these circumstances, as when making an entry for purpose of ouster, a retinue in train was helpful and persuasive, especially if in livery. There can be little doubt that men intending to enter retained or hired whoever was available, and took their chance on being indicted under such statutes as 1 Richard II c.7, 13 Richard II st.3, 20 Richard II c.2, 1 Henry IV c.7, 2 Henry IV c.21, 7 Henry IV c.14, and 8 Henry VI c.4.

When the cause progressed as far as trial in court, and actual title was likely to be decided, there came the business of labouring the jurors and obtaining support among the politically great. In May 1500, when an action of novel disseisin against him was imminent, Sir Robert Plumpton was told that the best line of action was 'to make many friends and of the best'. A year later, when others were about to sue him Sir Robert was advised by his solicitor to 'make your frynds to take your part as frynds hold doe'. Of course, it was not always easy to rally such support. Friends for legal business, as John Smyth in his history of the Berkeleys pointed out, could not be got without great expenses and greater promises.[63] In much the same way, claimants to land might seek support in their suit from those lords with whom they had already entered into a client relationship by becoming their retainers. Indeed, the relationship had probably been entered into by both parties with a view to mutual aid in quarrels over land, the lord wanting men to ride with him when he wished to make an ouster, the retainer looking for 'good lordship', which meant his master using influence to obtain a satisfactory outcome to his own entry when it came before the courts. Robert Pilkington's narrative of his quarrel with John Ainsworth and his allies shows the writer, through supplication, getting his 'special good lords' the earl of Derby and his son Lord Strange to write to judges and other judicial officials asking for a remedy for their client and for him to be 'well dealt with'.[64] This may have been, as the writers claimed, a request for only 'lawful favour', but given the social importance of the supplicants it was only a very short step from tampering with justice. A justification for such intervention, although not offered by contemporaries, was that it might prevent judges from favouring the other party, and stop sharp practice such as the manipulation of procedure by court officials so that your opponent had an unfair advantage.

There can be little doubt that late medieval men thought assiduous labouring of the jury could prevent defeat when one's case was weak. It might be the litigant's lord who took on the task, but more frequently it was the parties themselves. To 'labour' meant to explain your claim to the land in dispute to individual jurors and perhaps even show them your 'evidences'. Much money and energy were spent in discovering the names of the jurors and men of substance and authority, such as bailiffs, hundredmen, and manor lords, in the hundreds and wapentakes from which the two sets of twelve jurors were to be drawn. The men of local importance would be rewarded for attempting to influence the jurors, who were their fellow villagers or tenants; the jurors, the antagonists would try to persuade to see the case their way, or not appear at the trial. Few jurors ever wished to make the journey to court, for it was at their own expense, and thus if one party provided lodging for them in the location where the trial was held, they were likely to feel beholden and sympathetic to their benefactor's cause. Whenever possible the plaintiff and the defendant tried to load the jury with their relatives ('sib or allied'), their friends, their tenants ('retained by fee or livery'), their former household servants, servants of gentlemen who supported them, and even those of the sheriff, if he was thought sympathetic.[65]

In the quarrels of the squirarchy and the nobility, the seeking of good lordship meant gathering the support of the most influential of the magnates; these were not necessarily those with the most ancient title or even possessed of the greatest wealth, but rather those closest to the king. Other members of the upper classes were of assistance only against adversaries of relatively mean circumstances, and where the land at issue was not of great value. The Paston correspondence shows that family on several occasions seeking the favour, even the intervention, of the ultimate good lord, the king, in matters of entry and title to land. In June 1469 John Paston II lobbied Lord Rivers and his son Lord Scales, both high in the royal favour, to speak with the king concerning his dispute over land with the duke of Norfolk. In 1479, when quarrelling with the duke of Suffolk over the manors of Hellesdon and Drayton, John Paston III planned to persuade Lord Hastings to win over the bishop of Ely and they together to get the king to take Paston's service and his quarrel. He also had a scheme whereby two gentlemen who lay nightly with the king in his chamber would interest Edward in his problem.[66] Although historians have not commented on it in regard to this period, it was common knowledge among contemporaries that suits over land progressed best in law for a party if his or his patron's political star was ascending. Margaret Paston told her elder son, when he was beginning a suit against the duke of Suffolk, that the moment was opportune as the latter was not in the best favour with the king, and also 'ye have the voyse in this contre that ye may do as meche wyth the kyng as ony knygth that ys longyng to the Corte'. She added for good measure that John ought to marry into the queen's blood and then all would go well with his suit. To show in much more detail than this how influence affected court verdicts is difficult. Magnates may have sought to influence jurors rather than judges and used the sheriffs as their tools; they were certainly well placed to affect the outcome. Well known is the occasion in 1450 when the sheriff of Norfolk was instructed by the king to swear in a jury (i.e. select it) which would acquit Lord Moleyns.[67] Perhaps there was no need for actual threats or douceurs. Jurors in cases to do with title to land may have had such noses for changes in the political climate that they automatically decided in favour of the party who was likely to be a powerful figure in the future, and therefore the more able to do them mischief if they crossed him.

The wide social ramifications of feuds over land ensured the crown would not sit by and allow forcible entries and their attendent riots to be settled solely by means of the common law, efficient as the assize of novel disseisin had been for the first two hundred years, and as useful as indictments for forcible entry and actions of trespass, of forcible entry, of entry in the nature of an assize, were by the earlier years of the fifteenth century. By that time remedies such as these were not preventing forcible entries from occurring, and they may have been on the increase. There seems amongst those engaged in quarrels over property to have been a tendency to make forcible entries and oust occupiers with some recklessness. Sometimes those entering were keen to take rents, suggesting that ready cash and produce were particularly valuable, perhaps because it was an age of inflated households, large retinues, and much conspicuous expenditure in the form of livery giving and 'open house'.[68] Often the miscreants seem to have believed that although they had entered by force, taken chattels, committed assault, or broken the peace in some other manner, it might all be forgiven if in a trial their title was found to be the superior, and indeed there was a lot of truth in this. If they lost subsequently in court, then the fine and the damages would be the greater for such misbehaviour, but the risk seems to have been considered well worth taking, particularly since men who lost the verdict and where their opponents were given seisin by the sheriff were known to enter again when the latter had departed, and thus recommence the quarrel.[69]

One prominent feature of the history of riot and forcible entry in the fifteenth century was the role of the king's council. As that century progressed, the methods used to investigate those offences and summon the accused before council became more efficient, and there were efforts to make the sanctions for failing to appear somewhat heavier. By 1443 the council assumed that riots would be reported by complaints of individuals; that writs would go out to two local justices of the peace instructing them to go to the place of the riot, arrest any rioters present, and put them in gaol until they paid a fine.[70] If no rioters were discovered, the justices of the peace were to make enquiry by means of an inquest and certify their findings 'after the fourme of the statut'. Two lords of council or a lord and a judge were then to be sent to hear and determine the cases, except apparently where the rioters were 'notable persones'. These miscreants were to be summoned before the king and council at a certain day by writ of privy seal. The statute referred to must have been 13 Henry IV c.7, possibly as amended by 2 Henry V c.8, but the procedure stipulated in the instance of 1443 was slightly different from the original. The act of 1411 made no mention of how the justices of the peace would come to hear of the riot, whereas the procedure outlined in 1443 assumed they would be told to go to the place of the riot by writ, complaint apparently going directly to the council.[71] The use of a commission of oyer and terminer was not stipulated in the 1411 act, although those offenders presented were to be 'put to answer' and if found guilty to be punished at the discretion of king and council, a statement which seems to indicate trial before the council, even if it did allow for other judicial process. The summoning before council by privy seal of 'notable persones' involved in the riot had no parallel in the statute at all. The procedure decided on by the council in 1443 may have been peculiar to a single case, but it gives the impression of being an exercising of all the legal devices allowable, being a full display of how riot should now be handled in the light of experience or, as in this case, when it seemed important men were involved and the riot could be politically dangerous.

The statute 8 Henry VI c.9, which extended the processes stipulated in cases of forcible entry in 15 Richard II c.2 to those who made peaceable entries but held by force afterwards, or who entered by force but then removed themselves, envisaged, like its precursor, remedy being in response to a complaint by an individual to a justice of the peace. But it seems likely that it was royal policy soon after this to encourage those who suffered from forcible entry to bring their grievances directly to council, parliament, or the chancellor, or persuade them to bring an action of trespass or novel disseisin;[72] the inducement which the act of 1430 offered in the last case was treble damages to the successful litigant. These alternatives to seeking indictments for riot or forcible entry were very necessary because of the frequency with which one's enemies were able, through gaining the partisanship of the grand jury or the justices of the peace, to ensure no charge was brought against those known to have committed the offence against you. The king was not, of course, entirely powerless, but the mid-fifteenth century was a time when local magnates sometimes felt, and with reason, they could control the normal process of accusation at the sessions of the peace in their region.

Complaint to council, parliament, or the chancellor circumvented this and other obstacles, such as being unable to offer the grand jury the names of many of the rioters or entrants, an ignorance which also precluded any private suit against them. The complaint would usually lead to a writ of privy seal summoning the offender to answer, the writ having the attraction of not necessarily passing through the hands of the local sheriff of his officers; it could also penetrate any franchise. Complaints against writs summoning persons to answer in courts which were not of the common law had occurred from the first part of Edward III's reign onward, but the crown persisted in their use and resisted parliamentary pressure for their abolition.[73] In the reign of Henry IV it conceded the *sub poena*, one species, but perhaps the most important, of these writs, should only be used where the chancellor or council deemed it necessary, and in 1436, in the act 15 Henry VI c.4, the crown conceded no *sub poena* writ should be issued until surety was found to satisfy any party grieved for damages and expenses. A later request in parliament for their suppression, and another for their enrolment and the inclusion in each writ of the reason for its dispatch were refused, although the commons' suggestion in the former case that anyone receiving such a writ should declare the action ought properly to come under the common law and he need not appear before the council was duly noted by the lawyers and made use of in the future.[74] In 1453 the king and his advisers, apparently taking profit from complaints caused by a wave of riots and other trespasses, laid down a procedure to make the writs more effective. There was established a system of proclamations summoning persons before the council or the chancellor, which, if ignored by the party they were directed at, could lead progressively to forfeiture of fees or offices held under the king, then of any title and lands.[75] This act seems to have owed something to earlier legislation, for example the statute of 1414 (2 Henry V st.1 c.9) which provided for writs of proclamation directing a person whom the sheriff had failed to take to be summoned to appear for various felonies or riot in the king's bench on a certain day or stand convicted. A connection can also be seen with the act of 1429 (8 Henry VI c.27), which ordered letters of privy seal for the making of a proclamation that no one should riotously pillage those travelling the River Severn on pain of being held a traitor, and with what may be called a private bill passed by parliament in the session of 1439 against a particular offender who would not appear to answer to a letter of privy seal but now must appear within eleven months or stand convicted of treason.[76] The novelty in the act of 1453 was that the penalties enforced the appearance of the rioters before the council or the chancellor, rather than the king's bench or parliament. The act was supposed to operate for a period of seven years, but the procedure seems to have continued in use in Edward IV's reign.[77] It was, however, available only for 'great cause of riot' and related cases (forcible entry and unlawful assembly) if we judge by the statement of one plaintiff or his counsel in 1488.[78]

This plaintiff said the rule was made in the 'last parliament holden at Westminster' and may therefore have been referring to the statute 3 Henry VII c.1 (later given the name 'Pro Camera Stellata') or perhaps to the debate on the parliamentary bill on which it was based.[79] Here we reach an area of great and continuing historical debate, namely the intention of that act and the relationship of riot and similar upper class misbehaviour with council. Viewed with the earlier history of riot in mind, it seems the statute of 1487 was intended to offer a new speedy procedure against those committing riots and the other related trespasses, embracery, maintenance, and the illicit giving of livery and empanelling of jurors. Accusation was to be made not by indictment but by bill or information to the chancellor. Those accused were to be summoned not through the sheriff but by letters of privy seal, and they were to be tried before a new tribunal consisting of the chancellor, treasurer, keeper of the privy seal (or two of them), a bishop and a temporal lord of the council, and two judges. Those who were the victims of riot, as we have seen, had already in the fifteenth century enjoyed the benefit of information, bills, and privy seal writs, although they had not been available hither to for the other crimes.[80] One advantage those grieved by riots drew from the 1487 act was that they no longer needed to have their bill supported by the letters of two justices of the peace in testimony, as had been required by the act 2 Henry V st.1 c.9, or rely on the sheriff to arrest the miscreants. Nor could the case end in trial in the king's bench, where pardons abounded. Probably the act of 1487 was designed to avoid, when dealing with a type of trespass so dangerous to public order, having to rely on the justices of the peace and the sheriff. This was because at that point in time the king and his legal advisers had concluded that a major cause of such disorder was interference with the criminal processs of the common law by those who operated a large part of the system, abetted by their lords and clients. For the first time an alternative system, reaching from original complaint to verdict without utilizing the traditional forms and officers of the common law, had been constructed, even if it only concerned a small number of trespasses.

Why was it necessary, it may be asked, to constitute a new tribunal for the purposes of trial? Would not the council have served? The answer must be that smaller numbers of justices promised greater efficiency, as well as the exclusion of councillors whose clients and interests were involved. We may also fairly surmise that the new body was intended to be, by its very nature, exempt from the several statutes of the fourteenth and fifteenth centuries designed to limit the judicial activity and authority of the council. Henry VII's reign, as Bayne pointed out, was very fertile in the creation of judicial machinery and in legal experiment in general.[81] Another innovation which can be found in the 1487 statute and in the workings of the court which it instituted concerned accusation. The majority of the extant proceedings under the act, eight cases out of ten, came as a result of accusations by royal office-holders, and not private parties. The statute of 2 Henry V st.1 c.9 had talked of complaints being made about riots and felonies to the chancellor and then bills being made for the king, but these may have been bills of indictment; there is little evidence of direct prosecution by the crown before 1487, and the Henrician examples confirm there was an attempt to construct a whole alternative system of criminal procedure. Although the 1487 act did not refer to forcible entry specifically, all the types of crimes that were mentioned frequently had their origin in a quarrel over illegal entry into land. There must have been a feeling in the 1487 parliament that neither of the basic forcible entry or riot acts (15 Richard II c.2 and 13 Henry IV c.7) was fulfilling its purpose and they needed assistance.

The act of 1487 was probably as important as a token of governmental policy on public order as for its practical effect. This policy, however, must have changed somewhere between the years 1487 and 1495, when there were promulgated two further acts concerned largely with riot. 11 Henry VII c.3 dealt with basically the same offences as 3 Henry VII c.1, the 'Star Chamber' act, had done, and its essence was that it allowed an information in regard to any of these crimes to stand in place of an indictment. 11 Henry VII c.7 was concerned only with riots and unlawful assemblies, and was directed against participants who went into hiding and leaders whom no one dared to accuse.[82] Accusation was to be made by other means as well as indictment, by bill in one case and by information in the other, but the second act, reminding us of the act of 1453, made failure to appear in court to answer to bring automatic conviction. Obviously the statutes overlapped, for there was little need for riot and unlawful assembly to be in the first at all when they were thoroughly dealt with in the second. We may assume, therefore, considerable debate and consequent amendment of the bills on their course through parliament, with perhaps the striking of a bargain between king and *generosi*. Maybe the king had to sacrifice the tribunal of 1487 in 1495 in order to get bill or information on riot allowed in addition to indictment at the lower level of criminal justice, i.e. the peace sessions.[83] The role of what we may call non-common law criminal process was also reinforced by another provision. The second act stipulated that where the rioters or assemblers numbered more than forty, or if they were less than forty but the offence was considered by the justices of the peace to be heinous, the leaders of the riot or assembly were to be tried before council. With this exception, trial under these two acts was apparently to be under the common law. The king, it seems, had decided that, as long as the method of accusation was not at the mercy of the local magnates, the justices of the peace should be allowed to help with the great problem of riot.

Since riot cases in the fifteenth century came with increasing frequency under conciliar jurisdiction of one sort or another, we must consider what was their ultimate outcome. Was in fact title to freehold land decided there? Despite fourteenth century statutes stipulating no man should be put out of his freehold unless put to answer and judged according to the course of the law,[84] which presumably precluded trial before council, it seems quite clear that in the next century judgments were given there as to which party had the better title to the property in dispute. An early clear reference to this practice appears in October 1412 when, in regard to an attempted forcible entry at Cotyf castle in Wales, it was declared that the king on his council's advice would do justice to the parties in regard to any right or title they had in the property.[85] The council seems to have continued to decide title in the next reign. There are several references to debates as to title, as it was put, taking place before it, and apparently they were likely to take so long to decide that it was thought worthwhile at times to put the land in dispute into the keeping of a third party in the meantime, so that riots between the factions should be avoided.[86] It was not always that the arguments or procedure were lengthy; sometimes the cause was other business which was occupying the council. One of council's big attractions must have been its flexibility in comparison with the courts of common law.[87] The original complaint there may have sought only a temporary cessation in a feud or restoration of property seized by an antagonist. When actually before the council, a party might then request that the title to the disputed land be tried.[88] The council would therefore order both parties to produce their evidences and give them time to search these out. When the documents had been examined and testimony heard the council would issue a decree awarding the property to one party or the other, but often in a way which was curiously indefinite.[89] For example, the decree might be stated as only being valid if the defeated party could not produce further evidence justifying his claim. In other words the council saw its decrees as being amendable, an attitude which gave comfort and hope for the future to the side which did not have the advantage. All this contrasted markedly with procedure under the common law, where judgments were reversed but rarely and only with the greatest difficulty, by means of a writ of error.[90] Although the evidence from the fifteenth century is not extensive it seems fair to say that it was conciliar policy to persuade the parties to come to a long term or final agreement between themselves, an attitude well appreciated by landholders who knew how common law judgments awarded everything to the winning side and nothing at all to the loser.

Quite often, perhaps in one quarter of the pre-Tudor cases where complaints of riot sprang from forcible entry into land, a question of title arose, and the council ordered the quarrel to be settled by arbitration. Many cases which had been started in common law courts, chancery, and even parliament, also went to arbitrators. These were a group of persons, not justices in their office, who were vested with authority by the parties to examine the conflict and decide a fair settlement on the facts. Such settlements, sometimes called treaties, were outside the common law and thus are to be found but rarely in contemporary legal records. This may account for the lack of interest historians hitherto have shown in them. On the other hand, chroniclers were well aware of arbitration and its value to litigants and society, and letter writers of the fifteenth century referred to it quite often as a natural part of the feuding phenomenon. How did arbitration come about? It was a common recourse of a party which saw large litigation expenses ahead and no great likelihood of a favourable verdict in court. When in 1415 the abbot and convent of Crowland were engaged in their dispute over forcible entry by the inhabitants of Multon and Weston into the island of 'le Purceynt', and the men of Spalding over fishing and the taking of turves and sedge from the waters and lands of Crowland, they found their suit at Westminster progressing none too well because of the support offered to the people of Spalding by the duke of Lancaster and the machinations of the lords of the two villages. The prior, says the chronicler, saw the suit 'lay at the mercy of a cast of the die'.[91] These factors, together with the dream experienced by the convent's legal counsel, convinced the prior he must seek arbitration. In contrast, in 1470 Sir John Paston II, whose men had killed two of the duke of Norfolk's followers at the siege of Caistor, was harried by appeals of homicide by the widows so as to force him into a treaty.[92] Willingness to aribitrate might also result from the advice of the very judges who were hearing the dispute in a court of common law or chancery.[93] The reasons for the judges' recommendations are not absolutely clear but may have been that they saw a case before them where the arguments for each side were evenly balanced, and they knew that the common law made one side an absolute winner and the other an absolute loser; by arbitration, on the other hand, there could be some form of compromise and perhaps a lasting peace between the contestants. Concern for public order and the danger to it of long-lasting feud seem also to have played a part in the pressuring of the parties to accept arbitrators. Fifteenth century magnates took it as part of the obligations of lordship that they or their officers should quell quarrels between their retainers, but gently and reasonably. The earl of Northumberland, perhaps in June 1490, asked Sir Robert Plumpton, probably because he was steward of the manor of Spofforth, to make a treaty between one of his servants and a tenant of that lordship, while on another occasion he requested him to replace a violated award with another. The Plumpton correspondence shows the earl himself trying to quiet several other dissensions among his feed men, although not as an elected arbitrator but through his social position.[94] These feudal settlements of quarrels were known in the parlance of the time as 'directions', but they seem to have followed much the same form as arbitrations in regard to procedure and awards. There is also indication that treaties brought much relief to those living in the locality of the parties involved in dispute. Sir Richard Bingham, J.K.B., wrote to Sir William Plumpton in January 1462 that a proposed settlement would be not only 'for the ease of you both' but also 'the rest of the contry'.[95] We may take it, therefore, that there existed considerable social pressure on those at feud to settle their disputes in a relatively rapid and direct way if possible, which meant primarily by arbitration.

The process of arbitration could be started in several ways. Justices or a great magnate, as we have seen, might suggest it to the king's council or those to whom it had delegated authority, or the parties themselves might ask their friends, or retainers to arrange it.[96] We may assume that if arbitration was suggested by justices or the council the parties felt obliged to agree to it and that they also accepted the arbitrators whom those authorites named.[97] If the two sides sought arbitration of their own volition, perhaps at a love-day, then the number of arbitrators must be decided between them and who exactly they should be. Two or three per side was the usual number, and occasionally it was agreed an umpire should be chosen in case the arbitrators became deadlocked in their debates or failed to complete their task in a specified time.[98] Sometimes it was left to the arbitrators to choose the umpire. The actual appointing of the arbitrators probably had to be done at a fixed time and place, perhaps a church or a court sessions. If the two parties were important men in their region the arbitrators might be great magnates, lay or ecclesiastical, and men of rank equivalent to their own. In the quarrel between Sir Robert Plumpton and Bubwith and Burgh, two clerks who had acted as plaintiffs on Sir Richard Empson's behalf they included the bishop of Winchester, Lovel the lord treasurer, the earl of Surrey, the judge Robert Brudenell, and John Ernley the attorney general.[99] The dispute in 1444–8 between the mayor and commonalty of Exeter on the one side, and the dean and chapter of Exeter cathedral on the other was committed to the arbitration of the two chief justices and the archbishop of Canterbury, although the latter was replaced by the chancellor. Because he could not find time to deal with the matter the chancellor subsequently entrusted the task to Chief Justice Richard Newton and two important local men, Sir Philip Courtenay and Sir William Bonville.[100] Delegation was not always because of other business. The settlement of the quarrel between Sir William Plumpton and the earl of Westmorland in 1435 was eventually left to one squire and one lawyer representing each side because six earlier arbitrators and one umpire had failed to compose it.[101] In 1498 in the long dispute between Robert Pilkington and John Ainsworth, the parties agreed to accept the award of the earl of Shrewsbury and the lawyer Thomas Keble, then king's serjeant. This episode is very instructive, as it shows that not every arbitrator played an active role. The earl told Pilkington to put his side of the dispute to Keble as he was learned in the law and whatever he said he, Shrewsbury, 'would be agreeable to the same'.[102] Among the upper classes and lawyers virtually anyone might serve as an arbitrator, even the king or the queen. In February 1483 Edward IV took on the task of sole arbitrator in the dispute between Sir Robert Plumpton and the heirs general of his late father, Sir William. He died before he could make the award and it was left to Richard III to finish, which he did, but with the advice of the lords of council and the judges of the two benches.[103]

At the time the arbitrators were chosen and agreed on it was customary for the two parties to enter into a bond to follow the award when made, the size of the bond being related to the wealth of the parties (it was of course the same for each) and perhaps the land at issue.[104] Other things which might be agreed on by the parties at this point were that both sides should send their men home from the disputed property, and, as in the Plumpton versus Rocliffe, Pierpont and Constable arbitration of 1510, for neither party to vex the other or its servants or tenants by entry, distress, writ, privy seal or indictment, which meant a moratorium in the use of force, or action or accusation under the common law.[105] Any actions then in progress were usually to be abandoned: we notice that in the case of the mayor and commonalty versus the bishop, dean, and chapter of Exeter the archbishop of Canterbury asked the bishop to stop from proceeding in his current action of trespass before the justices of nisi prius.[106]

'Treaty' sessions, where the actual business of making an award took place, were commonly held, or at least started, at the time of the assizes.[107] This must have been because the judges and lawyers, who often served as arbitrators, heard and read the evidence when they were professionally engaged in that region in the common law courts. This was the heart of the arbitration process, the hearing of the evidence, when the arbitrator or arbitrators as one observer put it, 'did indifferently his true, tendre, and diligent labor and parte for the gode, appesyng and welfare of bothe parties'.[108] Before the arbitrators were called counsel for both parties (presumably on separate occasions) who were expected to plead their principal's case and show his titles i.e charters, fines, recoveries, to the land which was the cause of the conflict.[109] Thus, in their quarrel with the men of Multon and Weston in 1415, the abbot and convent of Crowland produced charters of 716 and 948 with their confirmations by later kings, a judgment by justices in eyre of 9 Edward I, a release of the lord of the manor of Multon, and accounts of various manor bailiffs from the isle of 'le Purceynt', which was the centre of the dispute. The monk recounting this episode gives the further information that when the men of Multon and Weston had shown their evidences they were asked by the arbitrators if they could say anything against those of the abbot and convent, an interesting point suggestive of answer in conciliar process. A similar case arbitrated between Crowland abbey and the men of Spalding and Pinchbeck in July 1415 shows the latter being asked whether they agreed with the land boundaries as stated by the former. The settlement of this particular dispute demonstrates another interesting stage in procedure. The arbitrators, after an adjournment to a new meeting place, asked both parties and their counsel to each set down in writing on a roll all the evidences, allegations, and replications they had already offered. The contents of these rolls, which might be improved with new material in the interim, the two sides and their counsel were to 'shew and set forth' on a set day. [110] It seems that when the arbitrators from the two sides had examined all the evidence they made proposals and counter proposals for treaty which were then reported back to the actual disputants for their approval or refusal. If the parties found the proposals acceptable then there soon followed the formal announcement of the award.

Awards as made by the arbitrators of any dispute were likely to be lengthy and take many forms. Frequently they mentioned early on that the parties were to show the old enmity was dead. Thus in the arbitration of June 1415 between the prior of Worcester on the one side and Thomas Burdet, esquire, of Arow, Warwickshire, and his son Nicholas on the other, the first item was that the two sides should be friends. [111] We do not meet in the fifteenth century, as we do in the sixteenth, awards which stipulated the parties should drink together or hear a sermon together, although on the other hand the Tudor period does not show, as the Lancastrian does, any example of one party having to do penance: Nicholas Burdet, mentioned above, had to offer a five pound taper of wax in Worcester cathedral and ask pardon there for his trespass against God and the church. Since the aim of any arbitration was usually to settle not one but all the disputes existing between two parties, the stipulations in the awards were wide-ranging. Thus the final agreement made in 1448 between the bishop, dean, and chapter, aand the mayor, bailiffs, and commonalty of Exeter stated firstly that the bishop's action of trespass should continue, but that the judgment should not be to the disturbance of the mayor and the city (meaning presumably that the bishop promised not to execute any judgement given in his favour), secondly that the bishop should have his fee in the city, thirdly that the mayor and bailiffs should have the power to make arrests, fourthly that the tenants of the bishop who lived within the city walls were to keep night watch, and fifthly that the mayor and bailiffs would never seek from parliament power to make arrests to the hurt of the authority of the justices of the peace of the shire of Devon. [112] The quarrel between Crowland abbey and the men of Spalding and Pinchbeck was caused, according to the chronicler, by the entry of the latter by force and in large numbers into a marsh, and their illicit fishing in a pool owned by the monks. Subsequently they had taken turf, sedge, and bulrushes from the former. The arbitration award was therefore concerned with determining what rights the entrants actually had in the marshes and waters. The abbey was found to own the marsh (called 'Goggisland') as it claimed, as well as a stream called 'le Lode' within it. The men of Spalding and Pinchbeck were held to have no right to the land or water but, as with most arbitration awards, the overall losers did not depart empty handed. They were given passage for their boats on 'le Lode' and the privilege of pasturing their cattle on a section of 'Goggisland' with the taking of estovers there, even if they were explicitly denied the right to take fowl, fish, or dig earth. The award concluded with a warning as to the future conduct of the Spalding and Pinchbeck men. Those of them who were principals in the arbitration and entered into bonds to accept it were not to excite others to implead or molest the abbot and convent in regard to their possession of 'Goggisland'. The arbitrators also felt there was danger of future riot, and warned the commons of Spalding and Pinchbeck to use the pasture and take estovers as the common law demanded, and without making assemblies or leagues.[113]

If these two arbitrations were similar to the majority of such awards, there were also specimens where stronger measures than compromise were introduced to ensure violence did not erupt again. Thus in the prior of Worcester—Burdet award, Thomas Burdet was bound to the chief arbitrator Richard, earl of Warwick, in the sum of 300 marks, that neither he nor his son should do future damage or corporal injury to his erstwhile enemies, the prior, the monks, or their servants. An award of May 1449 by Queen Margaret in regard to a quarrel between Lord Ferrers of Groby and his followers on the one side, and the citizens of Leicester on the other, decreed that the followers who had beaten and wounded one William Neuby should pay him one hundred marks in three instalments in satisfaction, and that Ferrers should give no livery to men in Leicester nor maintain them against 'the rule of our towne of Leycestre'.[114] This particular case was clearly of a character different from the Crowland and Exeter arbitrations in that it dealt with violent deeds where the possession of land was not apparently the underlying issue even if the offences occurring in the dispute were only trespasses, as in the more usual type of arbitrations. In the 1450s, however, there were two instances where the quarrels arbitrated had resulted in homicide. In one of 1458 the arbitrator was the duke of York and the dispute was between Henry Pierpont on the one side and Thomas Hastings and Henry Ferrers on the other, Pierpont claiming the latter pair had killed his brother Robert. The duke's award was that Hastings, Ferrers, and William, lord Hastings should pay Pierpont £40 in instalments and he in return would cease any appeals of homicide and actions of trespass which he had commenced, and would not seek to gain the indictment of anyone for the death.[115] A feud where arbitration was similarly intended to avoid prosecution for a criminal offence was that between Sir John Gresley and Roger Vernon, two of the Derbyshire gentry.

After they had been summoned before the council in July 1455 their quarrel was given to the duke of Buckingham to arbitrate. His award, as one historian has pointed out, reminds us of the tariff system for injuries as found in the Anglo-Saxon codes: those considered responsible for homicide were to pay £13–6–8, for a head wound 13/4, for a broken leg bone 40/–, and for any lesser wound 6/ 8.[116] Again, what we have before us is a system of justice which was an alternative to the common law; it was deemed necessary because that law could not be trusted to give fair results.

The question naturally arises whether arbitration awards were more permanent and immutable than the judgments of the courts of common law. A Tudor nobleman holding office claimed the settling of civil causes by arbitration was the best way, because the normal course of the law was prone to create enduring hatred[117]; furthermore, this would help to settle 'the meaner causes depending on them'.[118] That these ancillary quarrels existed also in late medieval society is borne out by the evidence already pointed to of arbitrators (and the common law itself) insisting, when they undertook to make a settlement, that the parties should cease personal actions under the common law against each other and make no effort to get their foes indicted. Since arbitration tended to bring to a halt 'meaner causes', subsidiary reasons for friction between two parties were removed and the chances of a lasting peace increased. On the other hand there is undoubtedly some evidence of awards being ignored and quarrels recommencing.[119] Yet it is not strong, and we may conclude that arbitration was, as society thought, the best way of settling feuds and actions at law.[120] One additional reason for this was the low cost of arbitration in contrast with the large sums which might be spent in courts, on lawyers' fees, and furthermore on travel for whereas many common law and conciliar cases ended up at Westminster, arbitrations were held and awards given in the localities of the disputants.[121] The implementation of the award was the task of the parties themselves, no doubt under the supervision of the arbitrators; it was not the job of the sheriff to put one of the disputants into possession. If there were quarrels over the meaning of any section of the award it was probably the arbitrators who clarified or interpreted.[122] If one party refused subsequently to abide by the award, then he forfeited the bond he had entered into guaranteeing he would. If he or his sureties refused to pay, then there had at last to be recourse to the common law in the form of an action for debt.

Riot, then, in the later middle ages was largely an offence committed by the gentry, although the word had little connection with them when it first appeared in the statutes in the mid-fourteenth century. The crucial statute in the history of riot was 13 Henry IV c.7 by reason of the procedure which it established for dealing with that offence rather than any indication which it gave concerning its scope. The procedure connected riot firmly and long-lastingly with the king's council and it was procedure quite distinct from that which was normal under the common law. Rather it was similar in nature to some of the varieties of summary or truncated procedure we have noticed in chapter two above, and had close connections with that utilized in the handling of forcible entry, a parallel and related crime. Both forcible entry and riot, the predominating offences in the late medieval 'gentlemen's wars', seem to have been by-products of the laws pertaining to the claiming of land, the first being incidentally and the second very directly a danger to the maintenance of public order. The king and his legal advisers saw rightly in the fifteenth century that in addition to introducing judicial machinery for the quicker and more efficient handling of forcible entries and riots, some assistance had also to be given to that part of the legal system which dealt with land cases, the basic cause of the disturbances. To this end there seems to have been a tendency among the king's councillors and justices of encouraging arbitration between contesting parties, and the policy appears to have had considerable success.

NOTES

1. Only the form *riotour* (committer of riot) appears in the statute.
2. *Proceedings and Ordinances of the Privy Council*, ed. N.H. Nicolas (Rec. Comm., 1834–7), v, 83.
3. Although they appeared in preambles to commissions which seem to have been drafted under the act: *William Salt Archaeological Society*, xiv (1893), 112.
4. However, the commission of the peace of 21 December 1338 for Somerset commanding the enforcement of the statute of Northampton ordered in addition the taking and imprisoning of those making illicit congregations and conventicles or leading armed groups to perpetrate misdeeds: B.H. Putnam, *Proceedings before the Justices of the Peace in the Fourteenth and Fifteenth Centuries* (London, 1938), p. 151. There do not seem to have been any other examples of this supplementary rule, which appears in some ways to have anticipated the authority given to justices of the peace in regard to riot in the fifteenth century.
5. Special commissions under the statute of Northampton are to be found in *Calendar of Patent Rolls, 1367–70*, pp. 272, 428, *ibid., 1370–4*, p. 238, ibid., *1377–81*, pp. 294, 251, 565. Commissions of the peace in this period were generally based on the statutes of Winchester (1285), Northampton (1328), and Westminster (1332).
6. For example *Cal. Pat. Rolls, 1364–7*, p. 391, *ibid., 1377–81*, pp. 204–5, 251, 299, 304.
7. The statute was no dead letter: see *Cal. Pat. Rolls, 1377–81*, pp. 299, 578.
8. A rout, according to Marowe, was the band or assembly which committed a riot. The word was much more ancient than riot, having appeared in the thirteenth century.
9. And still used later; see *Cal. Pat. Rolls, 1377–81*, p. 565 and *Calendar of Inquisitions, Miscellaneous, 1392–9*, nos. 61, 149.
10. 5 Richard II st.1 c.6.
11. See *William Salt Arch. Soc.*, New Ser., iii (1901), p. 125; *Select Pleas in Chancery*, ed. W.P. Baildon (Selden Soc., 70, 1896), pp. 7, 75, 77, 83, 90, 106, and Putnam, *Proceedings*, p. 246.
12. *Select Cases in the Council of Henry VII*, p. cxxxvii.
13. On the rise of summary jurisdiction see chapter two. The procedure adopted in 13 Henry IV c.7 was largely based on that in 15 Richard II c.2, an act against forcible entries.
14. See *Cal. Pat. Rolls, 1416–22*, pp. 135, 181, 295, 317.
15. Putnam, *Proceedings*, p. 12.

16. Cal. Pat. Rolls, 1413–16, pp. 176 221; ibid., 1422–9, pp. 225, 278.
17. See Select Pleas in Chancery, pp. 7, 75, 83, 106; 'Monastic Chancery Proceedings', ed. J.S. Purvis, Yorkshire Achaeological Society Record Series, lxxxviii (1934), 44.
18. Select Pleas in Chancery, p. 83.
19. Cal. Pat. Rolls, 1396–9 pp. 309, 365, 503.
20. Putnam, Early Treaties p. 339
21. British Museum, Harleian MS. 388 f. 205. J.H. Baker argues this reporter was Sir Richard rather than John Pollard: Reports of Sir John Spelman, i, xxv.
22. A. Fitzherbert, The Newe Boke of Justices of the Peas (London, 1538), f. 64.
23. The Boke of Justyces of Peas (1506), n.p.; B.M. Additional MS.4521 f. 105.
24. Cases that can be called ambush with assault number six out of 184 in the Staffordshire peace rolls of 1409–14 and two out of 48 in the Leicestershire peace rolls of 1410–14: Putnam, Proceedings, pp. 91–103, 295–303.
    Congregating with an unlawful intent when, in contrast with riot, none of those congregated committed a misdeed to further that intent subsequently, was by the sixteenth century the crime of unlawful assembly. Setting an ambush with intent to maim or kill clearly amounted to unlawful assembly as long as there were sufficient persons lying in wait. As with riot, we find no actual definition of unlawful assembly until the Tudor period.
25. Putnam, Proceedings, pp. 305, 314, 316, 403, 446.
26. Forcible entry into land as an offence appears only twice in the peace roll indictments in Putnam's Proceedings, and both cases are from Edward IV's reign. There is also one indictment for forcible entry into a church from the North Riding of Yorkshire, dated July 1392.
27. Plucknett's analytical index of Putnam's indictments shows the former but does not distinguish the latter: Putnam, Proceedings, pp. 475–6, 482. The use of the Northampton statute shows itself clearly in the patent rolls.
28. Discussion of this statute by historical writers has been very slight.
29. See chapter two.
30. Cal. Pat. Rolls, 1408–13, pp. 285–6, 310.
31. Rotuli Parliamentorum (Rec. Comm., 1767–77), iii, 630–2; Cal. Pat. Rolls, 1408–13, pp. 317, 374; Calendar of Close Rolls, 1408–13, p. 407.
32. See for example Cal.Inquis., Misc., 1399–1422, no.589 which shows the justices visited the scene of the riot at some point within the subsequent month and found no riot, assembly or rout, the miscreants having withdrawn before their arrival; the enquiry took place a month after the writ was issued. This underlines the weakness of the system introduced by the act of 1411: if the J.P.s and sheriff did not get to the riot while it was in progress they could not convict summarily by record, and enquiry devolved on juries, which could be corrupted.
33. Rot. Parl., iii, 21, 267, 446, 471, ibid., iv, 84, 156, 201, 344.
34. See Select Pleas in Chancery, pp. 75, 77, 83. The act of 1391 confirmed, incidentally, all statutes dealing with insurrections, 'grantz chivaches', riots, routs, and assemblies, in disturbance of the peace.
35. Ibid., p. 106; Yorks. Arch. Soc. Rec. Ser., lxxxviii, 87.
36. Cal. Pat. Rolls, 1413–16, pp. 176, 221, 222.
37. Ibid., pp. 275, 278; Ibid., 1429–36 pp. 218, 468; Ibid., 1436–41, pp. 505, 572,; ibid., 1441–6, pp. 246, 337; ibid., 1446–52, pp. 41, 137, 187, 320, 377, 431. There were also from Henry V's reign a good number of commissions just to enquire into riots: for example ibid., 1429–36, pp. 218, 468. ibid.,1436–41, pp. 87, 145, 147, 371, 505.
38. For example ibid, 1416–22, pp. 135, 181, 237.
39. See ibid., 1436–41, pp. 162, 438–9, 507, 553, 561.
40. For example Nicolas, v, 18, 83, ibid., vi, 211.
41. The actual words 'forcible entry' appeared for the first time in a statute in 1391 (15 Richard II c.2).

42. To say, as does M.S. Arnold (*American Journal of Legal History*, xviii (1974) 366) that by the reign of Edward III 'self help had triumphed completely' is, I think, going too far.

43. See D.W. Sutherland, *The Assize of Novel Disseisin* (Oxford, 1973), pp. 153–69.

44. *Ibid.*, pp. 157–8.

45. Norfolk Record Office, Norfolk Quarter Sessions Files, 24 Henry VIII, show eleven indictments of forcible entry out of a total of 254.

46. Under this statute damages might be awarded following an inquest for the king as well as suit by a party.

47. Sutherland provides figures for such personal actions from the 1430s: Sutherland, pp. 178–80.

48. *Henrici de Bracton de Legibus et Consuetudinibus Angliae*, ed. G.E. Woodbine with revisions and a translation by S.E. Thorne (Cambridge, Mass., 1977), iii, 24–5.

49. *Year Books, 33–35 Edward I*, ed. A.J. Horwood (Rolls Series, 1874), pp. 53–5.

50. *Year Books, Liber Assisarum*, 38 Edward III no.23; *ibid.*, 39 Edward III no.11; *Year Books*, Pasch., 49 Edward III no.7.

51. *Paston Letters and Papers of the Fifteenth Century*, ed. N. Davis (Oxford, 1976), ii, 522.

52. *Plumpton Correspondence*, ed. T. Stapleton (Camden Soc., 4, 1839), pp. liv–v; *The Stonor Letters and Papers, 1290–1483*, ed. C.L. Kingsford (Camden Soc., 3rd Ser., 30, 1919), no. 190. See *Paston Letters*, ed. Davis, i, 346, for an illustration of both parties seeking to recruit the same men.

53. Historical Manuscripts Commission, *Report on Manuscripts in Various Collections*, ii, 31–2; *Plumpton Correspondence*, p. lvii; *Paston Letters*, ed. Davis, i, 154.

54. *Year Books* Hil. 19 Henry VII no.2. A good example of the recognized need to have a garrison perpetually about one in times of feud is to be found in *Paston Letters*, ed. Davis, i, 330–1.

55. Sutherland, pp. 120–1.

56. *Les Reportes del Cases in Camera Stellata, 1593 to 1609, from the original MS. of John Hawarde*, ed. W.P. Baildon (London, 1894), pp. 140–1.

57. *Year Books*, 3 Edward II no. 26; *Year Books of Edward II. The Eyre of London, 14 Edward II, A.D. 1321*, ed. H. Cam (Selden Soc., 85, 1968), p. 327.

58. *Paston Letters*, ed. Davis, i, 363, 550, 560, 561; *Plumpton Correspondence*, p. 164.

59. The Plumpton cartulary shows the archbishop of York complaining that in May 1440 Sir William Plumpton and a band of the tenants of the forest of Knaresborough (a'great and notable fellowship') had ambushed his officers and servants near Boroughbridge, killed two of them and maimed three. The victims, so it was claimed, had had a thousand arrows shot at them: *Plumpton Correspondence*, pp. lviii–lxii. This was bloody combat, by fifteenth century riot standards.

60. *Paston Letters*, ed. Davis, i, 362.

61. *Ibid.*, i, 529, 532, 618. *Plumpton Correspondence*, p. 111. It is interesting how agricultural practice and yields almost never figure in the fifteenth century correspondence of the land-owning classes.

62. *Plumpton Correspondence*, p. 156. See also *Paston Letters*, ed. Davis p. 133, where John Paston I sends his wife Margaret to Hellesdon, Drayton and Sparham manors to show herself to the tenants so as to forestall any attempted distraint of rents there by the duke of Suffolk.

63. *Plumpton Correspondence*, pp. 150, 153; J. Smyth, *Lives of the Berkeleys*, ed. J. Maclean (Gloucester, 1883), p. 166.

64. *Paston Letters*, ed. Davis, i, 401; *Report on Various Collections*, ii, 35, 40, 44, 52.

65. Pilkington's account of the packing, labouring, and pressuring of the jury in the special assise taken out against him by John Ainsworth and his allies at Michaelmas 1496 is very instructive. The Derbyshire sheriff had 'great reward' at this time to make a panel of Ainsworth's 'kynnysmen, lyancez and olde servandes, (and) sybmen'; on a later occasion a jury in the same quarrel was said by Pilkington to be his enemies' 'boundmen' and 'dyvers ways syb or alyed, olde hawshad servandes, free tenandes reteynyd be fee or lyverey' and

'gayne dwellers' of them. Ainsworth's relatives the Savages appeared in person to labour the jury 'and said to eyvre man on that whest that the Byschop of London', who was a Savage, 'wold not for V hundrethe marks that mater passyd agaynys Aynysworth that day'. Pilkington also made 'grete labur' to the second panel in 'all the dewellyng placys of thayme that were on the whest' in both the Scarsdale and Chapel en le Frith wapentakes: *Report on Various Collections*, ii, 39–42. See also Sir Robert Plumpton's complaint about an assize jury panel of 1502–3: *Plumpton Correspondence*, pp. cix–cx.

67. *Paston Letters*, ed. Davis, i, 543, 617.
67. *Ibid.*, i, 381, ii, 71.
68. *Report on Various Collections*, ii, 31, 34; *Paston Letters*, ed. Davis, i, 530. A shortage of ready cash amongst the upper classes is suggested by John Paston I's frequent financial embarrassment.
69. *Stonor Letters*, no.313; *Report on Various Collections*, ii, 52–4.
70. Nicolas, vi, 268–70; *Foedera*, ed. T. Rymer (The Hague, 1741), v. 120.
71. The justices of the peace and sheriff were to take from any rioters they found 'any defensable wepen': Nicolas, vi, 270.
72. For example, the act 4 Henry IV c.8 provided the opportunity for those who were the victims of forcible entry to swear to the chancellor that they had suffered such an offence and on this the latter would grant a special assize. If the plaintiff then gained the verdict in court he would get double damages and the defendant would be imprisoned.
73. See footnote 33.
74. *Rot. Parl.*, ii, 471, iv, 84, 156.
75. I.S. Leadam said the act gave council power to initiate proceedings but a petition, bill, or suggestion, must have been needed to trigger the mechanism: see *Select Cases in the Star Chamber, A.D. 1477–1509*, ed. I.S. Leadam (Selden Soc., 16, 1903), p. lx.
76. *Rot. Parl.*, v. 14, 15.
77. *Year Books*, Mich., 14 Edward IV no.1. However if we judge by his antagonist's petition to council the many misdeeds of Roger Kynaston seem only to have led to writs of proclamation for arrest without danger of the heavy penalties mentioned in 1453: F. Palgrave, *Essay upon the Original Authority of the King's Council* (London, 1834), pp. 141–2. The reason may have been that the antagonist, Lord Strange, hoped to acquire the lands himself; or it may have been that the writs were subsequent to an arbitration award, one which provoked Kynaston's violent behaviour.
78. Or where the supplicant lived in grievous poverty.
79. *Select Cases in the Star Chamber, A.D. 1477–1509*, pp. 20–1.
80. The giving or taking of livery illicitly seems to have been an exception: see 8 Edward IV c.2.
81. *Select Cases in the Council of Henry VII*, p. lxi. See also chapters two and three for innovations in regard to summary procedure and witnesses.
82. 11 Henry VII c.3 envisaged information being brought to justices of assize as well as justices of the peace. Under 11 Henry VII c.7 the bills were to go to justices of the peace alone.
83. Both of the statutes of 1495 provided for costs and damages to be paid by the informer should his suggestion be found untrue at the trial.
84. 25 Edward III st.5 c.4, 28 Edward III c.3.
85. *Cal. Close Rolls, 1408–13*, p. 403. Judgment on title may have been a new departure, perhaps stemming from the authorization or confirmation of conciliar jurisdiction over riot in certain circumstances by the act 13 Henry IV c.7.
86. *Cal. Pat. Rolls, 1416–22*, pp. 181, 237, 238, 253, 414.
87. A decision by council was never a cheap way of settling a quarrel, as the Paston letters show: *Paston Letters*, ed. Davis, i, 495.
88. *Report on Various Collections*, ii, 32–3.
89. *Select Cases in the Council of Henry VII*, p. clxvii; c.f. p. clxii where the abbot of Shrewsbury won absolutely against the bailiffs of that town.

90. As for example Robert Pilkington discovered: 'we were in purpas to have discontenued owre wrytt of errouor because we were commaundet at the tranete terme afore to bryng in presedence from the comyn place of othere maters in like case adjugyt': *Report on Various Collections*, ii, 54.

91. *Ingulph's Chronicle of the Abbey of Croyland*, ed. H.T. Riley (London, 1854), p. 368. Conversely those who felt sure of victory in the courts did not want arbitration. In Henry VIII's reign Sir Edward Willoughby made great play of the fact he had allowed a treaty when at an advantage in law: 'Willoughby Letters of the first half of the Sixteenth Century'. ed. M.A. Welch, *Thoroton Society Record Series*, xxiv (1967), 90. For an interesting demonstration from the late fourteenth century of litigation and manoeuvring by the interested parties which might precede arbitration see J.B. Post, 'Courts, councils and arbitrators in the Ladbroke manor dispute, 1382–1400'; *Medieval Legal Records edited in memory of C.A.F. Meekings*, ed. R.F. Hunnisett and J.B. Post (London 1978), pp. 290–7.

92. *Paston Letters*, ed. Davis, i. 560.

93. *Report on Various Collections*, ii, 41.

94. *Plumpton Correspondence*, pp. 32, 33, 45–6, 72–3, 76.

95. *Ibid.*, p. 4.

96. In Robert Pilkington's great cause, commissioners sent out to enquire whether indictments had been prompted by malice arranged a meeting of the friends of each party in order to treat: *Report on Various Collections*, ii, 35.

97. Judges of the bench who had been hearing the case under the common law sometimes offered themselves as arbitrators.

98. Historical Manuscripts Commission, *Fifth Report*, p. 303; *Plumpton Correspondence*, p. li.

99. *Plumpton Correspondence*, pp. 11, cvii–viii, cxiv.

100. *Letters and Papers of John Shillingford, Mayor of Exeter, 1447–50*, ed. S.A. Moore (Camden Soc., New Ser., 2, 1872), pp. 70–1.

101. *Plumpton Correspondence*, pp. li–lii.

102. *Report on Various Collections*, ii, 41.

103. *Plumpton Correspondence*, pp. lxxxix–xc. Earlier kings had done the same, for example Edward III in 1363: *Cal. Pat. Rolls, 1361–4*, p. 380.

104. In the case of Sir Robert Plumpton versus Robert Bubwith and Richard Burgh (the agents of Sir Richard Empson) the bonds set at the meeting of 10 January 1515 were for 1000 marks: *Plumpton Correspondence*, p. cxix.

105. *Ibid.*, p. 210.

106. *Letters and Papers of John Shillingford,*, p. 41.

107. *Plumpton Correspondence*, p. 210.

108. *Letters and Papers of John Shillingford*, p. 50.

109. *Plumpton Correspondence*, p. cxx,

110. *Chronicle of Croyland*, pp. 371–3, 376–83.

111. H.M.C. *Fifth Report*, p. 303.

112. *Letters and Papers of John Shillingford*, pp. 136–40.

113. *Chronicle of Croyland*, pp. 383–6.

114. H.M.C. *Fifth Report*, p. 303; Historical Manuscripts Commission, *Eighth Report*, p. 415.

115. W. Dugdale, *The Baronage of England* (London 1675–6), 1, 580; see also J.T. Rosenthal, 'Feuds and private peace-making: a fifteenth century example', *Nottingham Mediaeval Studies*, xiv (1970), 88–90.

116. *William Salt Arch. Soc.*, New Ser., i (1899), 57–8; R.L. Storey, *The End of the House of Lancaster* (London, 1966), p. 155.

117. This was the earl of Sussex, then president of the council of the north, and the date was March 1569, the time of the northern rebellion: Public Record Office, SP 15/ 14/ 33.

118. For ancillary actions see *Report on Various Collections*, ii, 38.

119. For example *Plumpton Correspondence*, pp. 45–6.

120. After an award (1515) much in their favour in their dispute with the two agents of Sir Richard Empson, Sir Robert and William Plumpton quickly enfeoffed others in the manor in question to their own use. Whether this was because they thought the award would not be accepted for long by the other party or because of the usual feudal and political reasons is not clear: *Plumpton Correspondence*, p. cxxiii.
121. For example *Plumpton Correspondence*, p. 4.
122. *Ibid.*, p. xcv.

5

INFORMATION AND THE PENAL LAWS

To inform in the late medieval legal sense was to tell a justice or court about a crime without putting the accusation into proper juridicial form, as for example must be done in a presentment or an appeal and even, although perhaps in an amateurish way, in a bill of indictment. It was really no more than a suggestion for the proper investigation of an offence by the justices with the understanding that there was a social evil to be corrected. In this way, being oriented towards the benefit of society rather than the person, it was somewhat different from the petition. It need not originate in written form and sometimes it took the guise of a mere word in the justice's ear. When charges of this sort first appeared they were usually called *querelae* or plaints.[1]

Perhaps the most important attribute of information in this period was that the informer, once the charge was laid, was able to withdraw into obscurity without any legal responsibilities. He was not, like other accusers, expected to give sureties that he would prosecute, or, if the case failed, be at personal risk in the matter of damages and cost or of conspiracy. It was not his case. He provided the justices or court with material for the laying of charges, although that material, we may admit, was often nothing more than local gossip and rumour. Because such information allowed justices to prompt juries of presentment and indictment as to local offences, they were usually sympathetic to the informer. On the other hand, because the informer was not legally accountable, being a shadowy figure whose name might never be known and who might accuse out of malice, there was a hostility towards him at large.

Except in regard to the crime of treason, the history of information can only be traced back with any accuracy to the second half of the thirteenth century. On returning from sojourns abroad in 1275 and 1289 Edward I invited by proclamation the submission of *querelae*, which in essence were complaints about local administration and the doing of justice. It has been suggested the idea derived from the complaints invited in the period 1258–60 (which were to be founded on the *capitula* of general eyre of 1254) and those embodied in the first statute of Westminster.[2] In 1289–93 it was ordered that *querelae* were to be submitted in writing, but there was no stipulation they should be written down by the complainant. Those supplicating were to tell their grievance to clerks provided by the crown whose task it was to cast the complaints into proper written form. Prior to 1280 these *querelae* seem to have been offered to the justices in oral form and it is perhaps here we should look, therefore, for the origins of the information. Both in their beginnings and their early development infomations cannot have been very different from bills in eyre. The king's intention was to persuade his subjects to speak freely about maladministration occurring whilst he was away, more freely than they would if the normal methods of accusation by appeal, presentment and indictment were utilized. The difference between *querelae* and the usual methods of accusation was clearly explained by one of those suspected of maladministration, the associate justice Salomon de Roffa. The normal practice, he said, was for a bill offered in this manner to the justices to be delivered to twelve jurors.[3] These, if it seemed true, would present its contents in their verdict: if it seemed false they would deny it. For Salomon the *querela*, plaint or information was an untried bill, of indictment nothing more, but which was sufficient to arraign a person on without further checking.

There was one important limitation on the scope of the plaint and its written counterpart the bill. It could not be used for the arraignment of a person where the offence was a felony; it would only serve for a misdemeanour.[4] This is not to say the king may not have tried to extend the practice to more serious crimes.[5] However Maitland's opinion, which was supported by Plucknett, that the crown could put men on trial for treason and felony in Edward I's reign merely on information needs considerable qualification in regard to the second type of crime, and even perhaps our reservations.[6] Often those arraigned on bills before commissions of trailbaston in that period were reckoned to have been guilty of calculated violence for purposes of intimidation or of conspiring to defeat the doing of justice.[7] Indeed the very word 'informer' first appeared in legislation in the *Articuli super Cartas* in association with conspirators, and evil procurers of assizes, inquests and juries.[8]

In the reigns of Edward II and Edward III despite the demise of trailbaston and the general eyre there were very likely other occasions when men were deliberately or inadvertently put to answer on information or suggestion alone. The names of almost all of those so treated are lost to us, as are the details of the cases, but legal commentary and the remedial legislation enacted proves the actual occurrence. In a case which occurred at Trinity term 7 Edward III the judges argued that the king would not put anyone to answer unless it was on indictment or in response to a private suit.[9] Chief Justice William Herle, however, took the line that if the offence was trespass the king might not require these forms of accusation, implying thereby that a mere information was sufficient. Nonetheless the opinion of the majority may well have had a long-lasting effect and indeed may have been responsible for virtually all penal acts being framed in a manner which appeared to encourage personal actions rather than the clandestine reporting of rumours. A little later the act 25 Edward III st.5 c.4, noting that Magna Carta had said no one should be imprisoned or put out of his freehold save by the law of the land, stipulated that no one should be taken (supply 'and put to answer') merely on petition or suggestion made to the king or council, unless it was by indictment or presentment or process made writ original.[10] Twelve years after this the problem still remained and there had to be enacted another statute (37 Edward III c.18) which ordered that suggestions (i.e. informations) to the king should go before the chancellor, treasurer and Grand Council, surety taken that these would be pursued, and if the suit failed a penalty paid.[11] In a case in Ireland in 1390 concerning the farm of the deanery of Dublin the justiciar and chancellor of Ireland put a clerk to answer, as his attorneys argued later in the English king's bench, on an information without anything in the way of record or original writ or a bill, and gave judgment thereon. When the case was heard in Dublin the clerk, John Carlisle, argued quite rightly that in Magna Carta and several other 'statutes' (he could have included 42 Edward III c.3) it was stated no man could be made to answer in court to any suit on mere information, without that is, original writ, present- ment or due process of law.[12] Why it should be so is not clear, but this is the last reference to the issue of arraignment on mere information until the reign of Elizabeth. Perhaps the growth of conciliar justice made fifteenth century men less sensitive on this score. Another reason may have been the enactment in the fourteenth century of a number of statutes which stipulated information as the proper method of accusation for a distinctive and limited number of offences. The crown seems to have conceded the illegality of information in general so as to acquire its approved use in a narrower area, probably the original one. While most types of crime were excluded, the crown now made increasing use for various sorts of corruption on the part of officials of the new method of prosecution which eliminated the necessity of using juries of presentment or indictment. It recognized that the jurors' knowledge of ministers' delinquencies and of economic sharp practice was strictly limited, and that their inclination to enquire privately with any diligence diminished year by year.

By the sixteenth century information had become closely associated with the so-called penal laws. These were statutes which set a pecuniary penalty to be paid by the committer of the statutory offence and which usually permitted the miscreant to be put on trial on mere information as well as on indictment or by a personal action. The forfeiture which the offender incurred was divided: part went to the king and another part to the informer or mover of the action. The reason for this was the belief that the informer or party was acting as prosecutor on the king's behalf, and so deserving of a share. The first act of this type seems to have been 12 Edward II c.6, which was directed against the taking of the assizes of wine or victuals by those holding office in city or borough. It deemed that if they should do so the merchandise involved should be forfeit to the king, who would give a third to the party who sued the offender. There followed over thirty years later, the act 25 Edward III st.3 c.1; this, which stipulated the measuring of whole cloths by the king's aulneger, allowed the purchaser to measure also and to sue under the act if he found the cloth defective. If this deficiency was confirmed by jury trial the buyer was to receive half the cloth's value and the king the other half. By another section of this act successful suit by a party against forestallers of wine, victuals and merchandise would win them half of the things forestalled and thus forfeited (25 Edward III st.3 c.3). By another act of the same period, 27 Edward III st.2 c.10, a party who successfully complained about merchants' deceitful use of weights and measures was to have 'the quatreble of that which he shall be endamaged'. By the act 38 Edward III st.1 c.12 jurors receiving bribes from parties and being attainted of the same at the suit of the other party 'sueing for self or for the king' were to pay in fines ten times what had been taken, half going to the prosecuting party. The term 'sue for himself and the king' had occurred in court records before 1300 and had appeared several times in the records of trailbaston commissioners in 1305, but not with the suer receiving formally at least, a share of any forfeiture or special damages.[13]

In these fourteenth century statutes the crown was encouraging the party who had suffered from the corruption, negligence or malpractice of officials to sue the miscreants by offering part of the forfeiture or additional damages as a reward for a successfful conviction, but there was no mention of action by any informer or prosecutor who had not suffered personally from the misfeasance. This essential element of fifteenth and sixteenth century 'penal' laws had originated quite separately. The first mention of the admission of an uninvolved prosecutor is to be found in the *Articuli super Cartas* (28 Edward I c.11) of Edward I, where they deal with the offence of champerty, that is to say assisting a party in his suit so as to receive a share of the disputed property involved. The *Articuli* stated that any officer convicted of the crime was to forfeit the value of the part that he had purchased 'for such maintenance' and, more importantly, that 'for this Attein-dre whosoever will shall be received to sue for the king'. This procedure seems to have been ahead of its time, for nothing similar was promulgated for sixty years or so, and then uninvolved prosecutors were only admitted to sue if the injured party would not. Thus the act 34 Edward III c.8 stated that a party who considered the jury hearing the case to have taken bribes could sue, but so also might any other person, he acting on the kings behalf. Should this uninvolved suer be successful he should have half the fine, while the party injured should recover damages. We may fairly assume that under this act the secondary suer could only sue if the party would not. Certainly that was the principle clearly laid down in the next statute of relevance, 36 Edward III c.3. This act ordered that when royal purveyors accepted bribes not to take things or 'to grieve men out of hatred' they could be sued by any party who considered himself injured. If the party would not bring a suit then 'he that will sue for the king' was to have for his labour the third penny of what was recovered. The next year an act was passed which said nothing about any party but returned to the formula of the *Articuli super Cartas* and utilized any man who would sue for the king. This was the statute 37 Edward III c.6, which stipulated enquiry by commissioners into merchants who dealt illicitly in more than one type of merchandise. The uninvolved suer was to have 'the Fourth Peny of the forfeiture of him that so shall be attained at his suit'.

As yet, it will be noticed, there was no use in these categories of statutes of the words 'informer' or 'information', and indeed no mention (with a single exception) of the legal method by which the suers should proceed in their suits. The word 'inform' or its derivatives appeared in the statute book for the first time in the *Articuli super Cartas*, but then not until 1361. The act 34 Edward III c.1 stated that a justice of the peace, either on information received or without it, might award a precept to anyone to find surety for good bearing or surety of the peace. Furthermore the justices were to inform themselves about robbers who would not labour and arrest those indicted or suspected. Here, as in the *Articuli super Cartas*, the word was being used in a non-technical sense, the sense of receiving communications or discovering. There is no hint that the informer has any legal standing or his position is precisely defined. Indeed the word 'suggestion' which appeared, as we have seen, in the act 37 Edward III c.18 is much closer to the 'information' of the late fifteenth and sixteenth centuries. It is in the sense of 'discover' or 'search out' that the verb 'to be informed' appears frequently in judicial commissions of the late fourteenth and early fifteenth centuries. These usually instructed the commissioners to make an enquiry into some situation which was causing the king financial loss and had been recently reported. Thus an information of 1401 had told the king that the abbot of Cirencester was attempting to accroach on and usurp the king's rights in Cirencester, one of June 1397 had reported that the lands of Thomas Swanneland of North Mimms, merchant, were being wasted by farmers, and another, in 1420, had told the king that beds, sheets and curtains had been purloined from Windsor castle. On the other hand a commission was issued in February 1421 which instructed the commissioners to inform themselves by means of information and examination about all cases of smuggling, escapes of felons, forfeitures and escheats concealed from the king since 1399 in the counties of Somerset and Dorset.[14] In fact the commissioners enquired partly by the more usual method of inquest, but there do survive three informations about smuggling where the record clearly states information was laid before the commissioners by X, or Y and Z. In this case the informers were examined before the commissioners on oath on articles already prepared, the 'information' being their answers. This example from 1421 was by no means the first. A commission to William la Zouche of Harringworth and others in January 1375 resulted in a certificate by the commissioners to the effect that three men had been brought before them, sworn, and then examined 'for the information of the commissioners'.[15] We may conclude that the method by which the crown was first told informally of all these offences had come to be known as 'being informed' and the product of examining persons with knowledge of the offence was given the title, at about this point in time, of an 'information'. There is some slight suggestion that one of these commissions, that of January 1375, was to investigate the offence on behalf of the king's council and it is possible that either council or the exchequer was the court to which the findings of the other commissions were returned.

'Information' and 'informing' only assumed a permanent and clearly defined legal form under the common law in the later fifteenth century. As we shall notice in more detail later, there were between the accession of Henry IV and the death of Richard III a good number of penal laws making their appearance in the statute book, yet only five contained the word 'inform' or its derivatives in a special technical sense. The act 2 Henry VI c.6, which controlled the export of gold and silver, said that he who discovered any violation and informed the treasurer or the council should have a quarter of the forfeiture. The statute 18 Henry VI c.17, which was intended to regulate the measuring and gauging of wine, said rather similarly that 'Every person that espieth any of the forfeitures aforesaid and thereof doth inform the Treasurer of England or the Barons of the Exchequer shall have half of the same forfeitures for his labour'. The act 33 Henry VI c.1, which was directed against servants who embezzled their masters' goods after their deaths, permitted the executors to give information about the offence to the chancellor so that if on proclamation the suspect did not appear in the king's bench within fifteen days he should stand convicted of felony. The subject of the fourth of this group of statutes was fraudulent cloth manufacture.[16] Justices of the peace, mayors, bailiffs and stewards of wapentakes and leets were empowered upon information or complaint of offence to cause the accused party to come before them and be examined, the examination serving as one method of trial. Here, in contrast with certain commissions of enquiry issued in the late fourteenth century, the examination was to be of the accused, not the accuser, suggesting that one form of information had acquired a close link with summary procedure. The fifth statute of this group is 8 Edward IV c.2 and it is a vital one, not only in the history of information but, as we have already seen, of examination and summary procedure. The offence the statute was designed to combat was the illegal giving of livery or taking of retainers. It allowed any person, who wanted, to sue or complain in the king's bench, common pleas, or before justices of the peace, oyer and terminer or gaol delivery in their sessions, by means of giving information to the king. This way they were to be admitted to sue for the king and themselves, with the information standing in the place of a bill or an original writ. Presumably the verbal information was written down by a clerk in the court because the suspect, so it was stated, was to be put to answer to 'such bill or bills by such information'. Furthermore the informer was to take an oath that his complaint was rightful. The judges would then examine those accused and try the, either by means of the examination or some other way they thought suitable. This was the statute in which information was securely linked with sueing 'for the king and himself' for the first time and one essential element of the Tudor 'penal law' thus created, 'Information' as a method of bringing a charge was, at least in regard to illicit livery giving and retaining, given a legal definition: it was to stand in the place of a written bill (not of an actual indictment, as in the earlier fourteenth century) or, if the suit was to take the form of a private one, an original writ. It was also laid down that process, the securing of the accused person's presence in court to answer, should be as when the case was initiated by original writ. The medieval suspicion of the informer, the man who did not risk anything by his accusation and was often motivated by hatred or greed, shows itself in the provision for the oath on the informer's part to the effect that his charge was rightful. Additionally we should note that the act also set the pattern for many later penal laws in its giving to the justices the power to award costs at discretion to the informer who, being referred to as the party complainant, was to have half the forfeitures. Execution of the judgment in this regard was to be as in recovery of debt or in cases of trespass. One way in which the act differed from sixteenth century penal acts was in its separation of the information laying from the process of recovery. Tudor acts simply stated the penalty on the offender and then laid down the manner in which it might be sued for stipulating information merely as one method amongst several. In considering the more general significance of this important statute we should notice the manner in which the 'suggestion' of medieval times, which is best described as a private word to the justices leading occasionally to a bill of indictment, turned into the 'information' of the late fifteenth century, which was a method of bringing a personal action against a particular party with the crown's support. This suggests that the traditional criminal process in which charges were brought by juries of presentment was thought to be in regard to certain crimes in need off supplementation by a new device, namely information operating under a statute. The criminal law was, it seems, being reinforced by the use of personal actions.

In the later medieval period between the beginning of Edward I's reign and the death of Richard III there were no fewer than 69 penal statutes passed by parliament. Ten such statutes permitted suits by the party grieved alone, 59 allowed anyone to sue, although they sometimes permitted the injured party the first opportunity. The ten, which were 12 Edward II c.6, 25 Edward III st.3 c.1, 25 Edward III st.3 c.10, 27 Edward III st.2 c.10, 8 Henry VI c.9, 9 Henry VI c.7, 23 Henry VI c.6, 23 Henry VI c.9, 4 Edward IV c.1 and 17 Edward IV c.7, were obviously not an earlier, more primitive type of penal act, as their date of origin shows. Nor did they deal with one particular category of offence. The misdemeanours they covered were negligence or delinquency by officials (aulnegers, borough and city officers, and sheriffs), forestalling, using defective weights and measures, and selling non-standard tiles. These were very much the type of offence the 59 other statutes were concerned with. The only comment to be made is that the first four of the 'party' acts preceded (if we omit 28 Edward I c.11) the first of the 'any suer' ones and may thus have been the unperfected version of such laws, reflecting a belief that the wrong was only the concern of the party grieved, and not for the crown to investigate in the most efficient manner possible.

The main concern of the 59 penal laws under which any one could sue was trading practice. This included offences in the manufacture, shipment and sale of commodities and the delinquencies of officials concerned with economic life. Thus eight statutes dealt with methods being used to export materials and manufactures illegally, four were concerned with the same in regard to imports, while six were intended to punish those breaking laws covering processes of manufacture. The only other category of any size in this group comprised laws for dealing with negligent, delinquent or unqualified officials. Of these there were no fewer than fifteen, two dealing with customs officials, two with aulnegers, three with sheriffs, three with bailiffs and two with escheators. There were also two acts where the intent was the punishment of corrupt jurors, two which were aimed at the illegal giving or taking of livery and two concerned with breaking the rules of retailing. The remaining nineteen were one of a kind. They were meant to combat such distinctive and perhaps temporary threats to trade as the use of barrels of illegal size, the harassing of aliens, the high cost of bows, the use made by Italian merchants of the money they received for their imports, failure to send certificates of export to the exchequer, illicit plating with gold or silver and illegally receiving apprentices, but there were also acts which handled problems which were much less clearly of a commercial or economic type. The subject of one was permitting forbidden games within one's own house, (17 Edward IV c.2) a second (33 Henry VI c.7) limited the number of attornies in East Anglia, a third (22 Edward IV c.1) set rules about apparel while a fourth (22 Edward IV c.6) stipulated the penalties for those having games of swans who were not the sons of lords. However, this type of penal act was relatively rare, totalling no more than fourteen.

We must now consider in what manner and in which courts actions under these late medieval penal laws were to be brought. Virtually all these statutes laid it down that the injured party or, as we have seen was very much more common, any of the king's lieges, should bring a suit against the delinquent person. By the later fourteenth century, starting from 34 Edward III c.8, penal acts usually said that those who would sue under them would be sueing for the king, a provision which had appeared in only one earlier act, the archetypal 28 Edward I c.11. It is in this act that we find for the first time a stipulated degree of forfeiture or penalty and, juxtaposed, a provision that the person whose suit resulted in the conviction of the offender should have it. It was, however, not the first statute to divide the forfeiture/penalty into two so that the king got half and the successful suer half. This policy was begun in 25 Edward III st.3 c.1 but thereafter, as we shall see, some form of division of the forfeited money or goods was standard practice. It was a feature of nearly all penal acts (the most notable exception being 8 Edward IV c.2) not to mention the laying of information specifically, but simply to state the offence, the penalty, and then to provide the methods by which the suer might recover his share of the penalty. The laying of information usually made its appearance as one of these. The earliest penal laws talked only of 'suit' or 'sueing', without any further definition. They did not suggest by what particular private action the suit should be brought. A change occurred only in the reign of Henry VI. The act 8 Henry VI c.9 which was concerned with entry into land and forcibly holding it thereafter said, quite vaguely, that the party should sue by bill; but then, more significantly, the statute 23 Henry VI c.7 against delinquent sheriffs ordered that suit should be by action of debt. Thenceforward this was the most common method of sueing under the medieval penal laws it being a stipulation in 26 of them between 1445–85. Other methods which were utilized were sueing by writ of trespass (28 Henry VI c.5), by writ of debt (18 Henry VI c.11, 33 Henry VI c.6), and by bill of debt in the exchequer (4 Edward IV c.1). From 12 Edward IV c.7 onwards there were several acts which ordered suit not merely by the words 'action of debt' *tout court* but by 'action of debt by writ at the common law' (or 'action of debt according to the common law') and by 'bill or plaint according to the custom of the town' where the offence was committed. 'By bill or plaint' was simply an allowance of cherished urban legal custom in suits of debt. Action of debt was intended to gain not only the forfeiture, but damages and costs for the suer in addition. As well as those which invited men to sue there were a number of statutes which ordered the delinquent party to be informed on or 'espied'. These were 2 Henry VI c.5, 2 Henry VI c.6, 8 Henry VI c.17, 10 Henry VI c.8, 18 Henry VI c.17, 7 Edward IV c.3, and 17 Edward IV c.1, and there were two others 8 Edward IV c.1 and 8 Edward IV c.2, which combined the two different types by allowing men both to give information and sue. Although the last statute dealt with the illegal giving of livery, the other eight were essentially concerned with commerce and largely with illegal exporting. Those of this group of statutes which originated in the reign of Henry VI were designed to ensure the 'espials' and informers made their accusations to the treasurer or the exchequer, but no such rubric appeared in the Edwardian acts. From all this we can clearly see that the commonly held idea of penal statutes being usually involved with informing and the information being given in the exchequer is quite erroneous.[17] Such practice in medieval times at least was provided for in explicit terms only infrequently, occurring in a very limited number of offences under acts of the reigns of Henry VI and Edward IV.

The novelty of information into the exchequer and the equivocal position of the device within the common law at this time is revealed in a case of Michaelmas term 37 Henry VI in the exchequer chamber.[18] Information had been laid under the statute 8 Henry VI c.17 and the accused was apparently convicted but then obtained a pardon. The question which the judges argued was whether the pardon barred the party's suit as well as the king's and whether the informer was in fact a party. The distinctive nature of penal laws being operated by information was noted. One judge, Chief Justice Fortescue, argued that the informer had no action under the statute and if he wished to sue it must be by bill or original writ and not by 'suggestion' (information). Against this and to the effect that the informer must have had suit argued Yelverton and Markham, justices of the king's bench, the latter pointing out that anyone wishing to have advantage of the statute was wont to come to the exchequer and make his 'suggestion' 'et sur ceo il avera proses saunz ascun autre bille oue et ceo serra dit soun suist'. Clearly at the end of Henry VI's reign information was still a minor and relatively new method of operating the penal laws and its implications, especially in regard to suits, were not readily apparent even to the sharpest legal brains of the period.

The vast majority of the fourteenth and fifteenth century penal laws did not specify before which justices suit, or information, should be brought. Only twelve statutes gave proper direction in this respect. The fourteenth century acts 28 Edward I c.11 and 34 Edward III c.8 provided for suit respectively before the justices where 'the plea hangeth' and in the same court where the offence (the taking of bribes by jurors) had been committed. Three statutes specified the exchequer, although one of these said 'before the Barons of the Exchequer' and another the 'Treasurer and Barons'. Two specified the treasurer and another the treasurer and the council. One (12 Edward II c.6) gave jurisdiction to hear and determine to the chancellor, treasurer, and barons of the exchequer, justices of the benches, and justices of assize. The statute 33 Henry VI c.7 laid down that the suer should sue by action of debt before justices of the peace. The livery act 8 Edward IV c.2 provided comprehensively for information to be given in the king's bench, common pleas, or before justices of oyer and terminer, gaol delivery or justices of the peace. Those sueing under 4 Edward IV c.1 were even more amply provided for: they could inform in any court. Of the nine fifteenth century statutes which mentioned the court no fewer than six involved laying information or 'espying' and communicating the discovery informally to authority, a vastly higher percentage than in penal acts as a whole.

It was, of course, the essence of penal laws to set fines and forteitures, but there were variations in the manner in which the 69 medieval statutes did so. By the earliest act, 28 Edward I c.11, the penalty paid by the official convicted of champerty which went to the suer was the value of the part that the former had 'purchased for such maintenance', but the second, third and fourth penal acts (12 Edward II c.6, 25 Edward III st.3 cc.1, 3) set a pattern for the future by dividing the forfeited goods between the successful suer (in these cases the party) and the king. This did not mean that from 1352 penalties and their sharing were standardized. The statute 27 Edward III st.2 c.10 gave to the complaining party 'the quatreble of that he shall be indamaged' while the offender was fined and sent to gaol for a year. Under the act 34 Edward III c.8 the successful suer was to have half of the fine and the original injured party and the suer were to recover their damages. Somewhat similarly by the act 36 Edward III c.3 the party, if he sued successfully, was to have treble damages and the suer for the king, should the party fail to take action, was to have the third penny 'for his labour'. The normal late medieval practice in penal laws whereby parties were forgotten and a suer on the king's behalf was allotted half the stated penalty arrived with the statute 38 Edward III st.1 c.12. From 1406 this formula was in regular use, appearing in no fewer than 37 of the 60 statutes passed between this time and the end of Richard III's reign. Under another eight acts the suer was awarded a third part of the forfeiture.[19] For this provision in the three early acts (8 Henry V c.3, 3 Henry VI c.3, 8 Henry VI c.17) there is no reason apparent, but the other five were directed at towns. They gave the urban authorities, who in three cases were the mayor and in the fourth (4 Edward IV c.7) the governors of the relevant guild, a third, like the king and the suer. There were also three penal acts which gave to the suer only a quarter of the penalty, although the reason why parliament decided on this smaller fraction is not at all clear. There were two statutes which gave to informers, not suers, one third of the forfeiture, two others awarding them one quarter and four which gave them a half.

There were a small number of acts which awarded to the suer or informer something in addition to a percentage of the forfeiture. Damages, double damages or treble damages were specifically provided for the successful suer under six penal statutes, two of which were promulgated in Edward III's reign and four in Henry VI's.[20] In every instance the offence legislated against was some form of delinquency by an official such as a sheriff or escheator. Three other acts awarded against the convicted party costs or double costs. In six of these eight cases[21] the suer, who might on a successful action secure costs of damages, was supposed to be the party who suffered the original offence. In one case, under 23 Henry VI c.10, the suer might be anyone, in another (8 Edward IV c.2) he was an informer (who, if successful, might be awarded costs at the justice's discretion). There was of course no need for special provision for damages and costs in the penal laws in those instances where the suer was ordered to proceed by action of debt (i.e. from 23 Henry VI onwards), since the successful action would itself gain them.

In turning to the penal statutes of the Tudor era we are entering a field of study which has exercised the minds of historians considerably more than the medieval one. The result has been clear demonstration that the acts were inspired largely by the government and did not usually originate with other sections of the community: furthermore that they were not a device intended merely for the raising of money. This confirms what the medieval period seems to tell us. The most striking feature of the Tudor penal laws is their very great number. There were 26 acts which deserve the title 'penal' promulgated in Henry VII's reign, and no fewer than 103 under Henry VIII. Some of course had only a short life, being soon repealed or through their own stipulation becoming void after a limited number of years, yet there were as many as 11 from Edward VI's reign and 30 from Elizabeth's still in operation halfway through the reign of James I.[22]

The offences dealt with by the Tudor acts were quite similar to those covered by their medieval predecessors. A majority were concerned with misdeeds in the fields of commerce and manufacture ranging from the quality of manufactured goods and demarcation of work to be done by men of different trades to controls on the export and import of commodities. As many as 19 of the statutes of Henry VII contained provisions which fell in this category and 42 of Henry VIII's, although there had been only thirteen similar acts passed before 1485. The manufacture of cloth and its export figured in fourteen penal statutes of Henry VIII and two of his father's, in contrast with eight originating in the whole medieval period. Under Henry VIII were promulgated fifteen penal acts which may be said to have aimed at the regulation of rural life through, for example, controlling the cutting of trees and the killing of certain types of cattle, making rules about the destruction of pests, the sowing of some crops, and the breeding of horses, although in his father's reign there had been only one, as there had in the middle ages. The reign of Henry VIII also saw the enactment of six penal laws concerned with clerical jurisdiction and offences committed by the clergy, whereas there had been none similar before 1509. In another important category the increase in new laws was less pronounced. The later medieval era produced ten penal statutes which were aimed at the detection and conviction of negligent or delinquent officials: the reign of Henry VII added one more, and that of his son another fourteen. The manufacture of leather, like the import and sale of wine, was the subject of one specific medieval penal law, two under Henry VII and three in the next reign. There had been one medieval sumptuary law: the reign of Henry VII produced nothing further but the subsequent one gave birth to four. In the period before 1485 there were enacted three penal laws dealing with bows, crossbows and guns, their manufacture, cost and use: another act was passed under Henry VII and four under Henry VIII. The obstruction of streams and rivers by weirs, fishgarths, and the like occasioned one medieval act, one in Henry VII's time and five under Henry VIII. On the other hand there were three medieval penal statutes concerning corrupt jurors, one under Henry VII and two under Henry VIII, while in the field of illegal livery giving and retaining there were in those periods two, one and two acts respectively. One peculiarity concerned coins, their export, import and making. There had been medieval penal acts on this: Henry VII's reign produced four, but there were none enacted under Henry VIII. A substantial number of Tudor penal laws (six in Henry VII's reign, nineteen in Henry VIII's) dealt not with offences of a commercial-industrial nature or touching delinquent officials or any of the categories mentioned above. They had nothing in common with other penal acts as regards the nature of the offence. The crimes they were concerned with included such varied things as buying books for resale, refusing to help whip youths who had quit their jobs, demanding payments for the freeing of apprentices, contravening articles about the qualifications and behaviour of surgeons and barbers, keeping more than four alien servants, and breaking oaths of obedience to town bye-laws. That each of these misdemeanours might be construed as vaguely threatening the public weal and jeopardizing social control is the nearest we can get to discerning a common element.

By the reign of Henry VIII it had become usual for penal statutes to decree that actions should be brought by 'suers'. There were, it is true, still a few which referred instead to the 'party sueing' (which was virtually the same thing) or 'the finder' or 'the seizer' or 'the prover', but these became increasingly rare. Four of Henry VII's penal laws mentioned the finder bringing the action, and one the seizer. In the subsequent reign six statutes referred to finders and six to seizers: significantly, only two were after 1534, which seems to have been about the time when, as we shall see, a standard phraseology appeared.[23] The words 'finder' and 'seizer' were used in acts which usually concerned manufacturing or commercial arrangements of a technical nature where officials of a town or guild were expected to search, examine and regulate the quality and production of the wares or the method of sale.

It was usual for Tudor penal acts to divide the forfeiture equally between the suer and the king, but there were occasional exceptions:[24] there were, for example, two such statutes under Henry VII and seven under Henry VIII. Of these nine, three gave a share to the mayor of any town where the offence was committed[25]: in two cases this was a third of the total but in the other the mayor got half, the crown taking nothing. Two other acts in this group gave a share to owners of franchises within which the offence had been committed (33 Henry VIII cc.6 and 7) while a further two (19 Henry VII c.18 and 34/5 Henry VIII c.9) for no obvious reason gave the king respectively two-thirds and three-quarters of the penalty. One act originated a trend which found full flower later in the century. This was 27 Henry VIII c.25, under which half the penalty went to the poor box rather than to the king. This was unique in Henry VIII's reign but under Elizabeth penal statutes gave shares of the penalty to, for example, churchwardens (5 Elizabeth c.3, 35 Elizabeth c.2), the parish (5 Elizabeth c.5), the poor (5 Elizabeth c.3), and to charity (35 Elizabeth c.1). As well as implying a social conscience this suggests that penal acts were becoming increasingly unpopular and that to ensure their safe passage through parliament it was sometimes wise for the crown to give its share of the penalty to a worthy local cause.[26]   The methods of action by which the suer was to recover the penalty to which he considered himself by his discovery to be entitled became increasingly standardized as the Tudor period progressed.[27] Under Henry VII eleven statutes made action of debt by itself the method, although one other had 'action of debt, plaint, bill or information' and yet another 'action of debt, bill or information': also 12 Henry VII c.6 stipulated 'by writ, plaint, bill or information' and 3 Henry VII c.7 'by writ, bill or information'. Writ, of course, meant starting a common law action by original writ, a bill here was a complaint to quarter sessions justices or judges on a commission, and a plaint was probably a bill to the justices of an urban court. An information by this time was an accusation, normally written down, giving the name and status of the informer, the date, together with the name of the offender and details of the offence. Whether the suer invariably cited the statute against which the offence was committed is uncertain, though probable. Informations in the exchequer usually requested in addition that half of the penalty be granted to the informer. Most interestingly it was not until well into Elizabeth's reign that statutes concerned with the penal laws separated information from other forms of suit. By 1588 the formula had arisen 'to inform or sue on a penal act', which suggests that by that time informations were quite the commonest form of action. In the reign of Henry VIII there were only eight penal statutes enacted which stipulated action of debt by itself, whereas there were as many as 43 which required the suer by 'action of debt, bill, plaint or information' or if we accept the formula 'writ, bill, plaint or information' as amounting to something similar, then 67. There were also another six where the suit was to be by 'bill, plaint or information'. If we examine the matter chronologically it is obvious that what came to be the standard verbal arrangement, namely suit by 'action of debt, bill, plaint or information', was popularized and made pre-eminent by the Reformation Parliament. In Tudor times, at least, it was never superseded. It was also quite common from Henry VII's time for penal acts to contain a clause which gave a degree of advantage to the suer. This was done by stipulating that the defendant might not use dilatory proceedings, namely essoins, claiming the king's protection, or defending himself by wager of law. The last of these was made necessary because the act 5 Henry IV c.8 had allowed compurgation in actions of debt in cities.

The court in which the action was to be brought was rarely stated by early Tudor penal acts. Only six of the acts passed by Henry VII's parliaments gave clear indiction in this regard. Three of these stipulated that the suit should be in the exchequer while three others spoke of 'any court' (12 Henry VII c.6) or 'any king's court of record' (11 Henry VII cc.8 and 27). The penal acts of the first two decades of Henry VIII gave little indiction as to which courts suers under them might go to, but those originating in the Reformation Parliament usually stipulated 'any court', 'any king's court' or 'any court of record'. From about 1540 these variations largely disappeared and the rubric became standardized as 'in the king's courts of record', a form which persisted for the rest of the century. There were three penal acts of Henry VIII which called for use of the exchequer as the court, 4 Henry VIII c.6, 6 Henry VIII c.1, and 25 Henry VIII c.4, but the last of the three was really only embellishing the usual formula of 'any court' by the addition of the words 'including the Exchequer or court of pie powder' and thus although the exchequer was obviously in continuous use for penal law actions there was felt to be no need for specific reference to it from fairly early in Wolsey's ascendancy.

The effectiveness of the penal laws as a tool of state policy is an important question, but one difficult to answer satisfactorily. There can be little doubt that those laws and 'information' were meant to regulate economic life and to provide for the bringing to account of delinquent officials quite sincerely, just as they were intended as an antidote to other, non-economic crimes. They were never designed simply as a means of providing the crown with an additional source of revenue.[28] They were clearly an effort to utilize personal actions to deal with criminal offences, a way to provide the crown with criminal charges in an age when the normal methods of accusation, appeal, presentment and bill of indictment were not forthcoming, especially for what must have been regarded as lesser, newly instituted, offences. In the fifteenth and early sixteenth century the king was coming to rely on a corps of amateur prosecutors, some admittedly royal officials though of a non-judicial type, who took less legal risk than other accusers and who were frequently encouraged by the chance of financial reward in the shape of a percentage of the forfeiture incurred. The new methods of prosecution, like conciliar justice, were carefully kept away from really serious offences, the felonies, which called for punishment by the loss of life, limb, and the whole of the convicted person's possessions. How frequent was the use of information and prosecutions under the penal laws will probably never be known, except for those brought into the exchequer or king's bench. The virtual total loss of the records of the justices of assize, before whom many cases which had started in the exchequer had been sent by *nisi prius*, of the justices of oyer and terminer, and justices of the peace, between the mid-fifteenth and mid-sixteenth century, stops any proper assessment for that period: yet the same records for the later sixteenth are quite uninformative, containing surprisingly few examples of informations. Even when in the 1590's the rules of legal administration should have preserved a good proportion few seem to have survived, at least from the local courts. That the 'common information belongs to a class of sessions decument peculiarly subject to loss' seems irrefutable.[29] Happily, investigations into penal law cases before one of the great central courts have been more successful. Informations laid in the exchequer show an increase from 44 in 1486 (with a total of 1804 for the period 1485 to 1509) to an average of 150 for the Michaelmas terms of the 1550s. There was an average of 477 for that term in the years from 1597 and 1602, one of 515 for 1584–9, and an even higher one (of 538) for 1564–8. As to the different types of offences, it has been reckoned that some 63 per cent of the informations laid in Henry VII's exchequer concerned customs violations (usually smuggling), seven and a half per cent were related to misdeeds by customs officials, and about 21 per cent were 'domestic' offences, a label meant to include extortions by sheriffs, illegal livery-giving and retaining, usury, violations of trade and manufacturing regulations by artisans, and the exorbitant pricing of retail goods.[30] According to another investigator for the century and a half subsequent to 1519, actions in the exchequer were composed of 26 per cent customs and foreign trade offences,

43 per cent marketing offences (engrossing, forestalling, regrating), six per cent manufacturing offences (cloth and leather), four per cent agrarian offences (cutting wood, enclosing, overlarge sheep flocks), and four per cent misdemeanours against the labour laws (failure to be apprenticed, breach of service). [31] How representative the exchequer cases were of the types of penal law offences coming before other justices is unknown, although we may surmize that a higher prooportion of 'domestic' offences may have been handled by the local courts. How many actions overall were founded on information rather than action of debt, bill, plaint or writ is also uncertain, but it has been reckoned that of apprenticeship cases in the exchequer and queen's bench brought under the statute 5 Elizabeth c.4 the total amounted to 80 per cent. [32]

As has already been shown, the penal laws and the use of information were well developed by the end of the medieval era and beginning to create, as most legal instruments do in the course of time, their own abuses. Within a few years of Henry VII's accession complaint was made by the parliamentary commons against collusion in the bringing of 'actions popular', as they were called. [33] Apparently offenders against penal acts were causing actions to be commenced against themselves with the intended plaintiff's approval. If on the other hand the plaintiff would not fall in with the defendant's plan the latter would delay the case and in the interval arrange for a similar action to be brought against him by some friend to which he would plead guilty or concede, as the resultant act stated, thereby barring the action of the original plaintiff. The statute which was promulgated to stop this duplicity allowed the plaintiff meeting such a bar to aver covin, and if it was found, to have the action regardless, and judgment.

The operation of the penal laws became a political issue on at least one other occasion in Henry VII's reign. The statute 11 Henry VII c.3, as we have seen, gave justices of assize and justices of the peace power to hear and determine cases, where the accusation took the form of a mere information, under the statutes on riots, retaining, livery-giving, embracery, maintenance, excessive wages, unlawful games, inordinate apparel and other 'enormities'. It has been argued (for example by W.S. Holdsworth) that this act gave justices of the peace the right to hear and determine all, not merely some, statutory misdemeanours, but this is transparently untrue since no mention is made for example of economic offences or the delinquencies of officials. [34] That the justices made use of this authority is quite definite, since an act was repealed in the first parliament of Henry VIII (1 Henry VIII c.6) on complaint that men were 'craftily' feigning informations, that is to say concocting them maliciously, deceitfully, and probably quite untruthfully. The repeal must have been a defeat for the crown, which needed accusations in virtually any form if the feuding of the gentry and their abuse of authority were to be controlled. Very likely the hostile climate towards penal laws and informing was a result of the notorious activities of Empson and Dudley in 1503–6, though it is not clear whether they enforced this particular act diligently or not. One opinion has been that the two ministers were set to work 'on the medieval penal statutes augmented by the tillage acts' but there is no reason why the penal acts of Henry VII were not utilized.[35] Empson and Dudley acquired their great unpopularity because they enforced penal laws already on the statute books but hitherto not put into operation. Their encouragement of the bringing of actions, informations (using, according to Hall, 'a company of accusers (commonly called promoters)') or presentments where the act provided for it, created much perjury.[36] The result was therefore a statute (1 Henry VIII c.4) which stipulated that such accusations should be made within three years of the committing of the offence, if brought on the king's behalf, or one year if by anyone else. The situation was, however, altered to the crown's advantage by the act 7 Henry VIII c.3 which allowed four years after the offence in which actions solely on the king's behalf might be brought, although where the suit was for the king and the suer (*qui tam . . . quam*) or for the suer alone it must be brought within twelve months. After this there were no more complaints about men being troubled long after the offence was committed, or at least none which were capable of producing reformatory action on the part of the government, until 1588, when 7 Henry VIII c.3 was repealed and the time limit made two years if at the king's suit and one if the action was a *qui tam*.

In the later part of Henry VIII's reign there were two issues connected with penal laws and information which caused concern and criticism. Henry Brinklow in *Roderyck Mors* complained bitterly that promoters, that is to say professional informers, were not being punished if their suit failed since the king wished to encourage them: furthermore the king never paid costs or damages because his lawyers argued the crown 'must pay no charges'.[37] Brinklow begged parliament to alter this and pass a law stipulating the king should pay damages when a promoter lost his suit. An attempt to remedy this unfairness had been made by the act 11 Henry VII c.3, which provided that unsuccessful informers on the king's behalf concerning illicit retaining and liveries, embracery, maintenance, and excessive wages were to be compelled, if the justices so decided, to give costs and damages to the accused. Unfortunately, as we have seen, this act was repealed at the outset of Henry VIII's reign. Of the new penal acts promulgated under Henry VIII only two made provision for damages and both were exceptional in their general form. One, which gave costs as well, was directed against those who cited men before a spiritual court outside their diocese, while the other was aimed against suits by officials of stannary courts against persons seeking to enforce the statute 23 Henry VIII c.8.

The other issue was enforcement, or rather utilization, of the laws provided. Despite the inducement of the penalty shared between crown and suer, actions were not being brought under penal acts frequently enough, and when they were brought it was usually out of malice. Presentments, or lack of them, under other statutes against crime must also have been causing concern. It was apparently this climate which gave birth to an unofficial scheme, generally regarded as dating from *circa* 1534, for the erection of a court of six 'conservators of the common weal'. Of these at least three were to be utter-barristers. The court, a quorum of which was to be three conservators, one being learned in the law, was to sit at Whitehall and hear and determine cases under all statutes 'penal and popular' enacted since the accession of Henry VII[38]; this probably meant all acts wherein a punishment was stipulated for the offender and included those where the forfeiture went to the king alone, as well as those where it was shared with the suer.[39] Following searches on the conservators' orders information was to be laid by a staff of serjeants and trial was to be as usual under the common law in actions of debt or trespass. If the prosecution was successful the serjeants were to take the penalties, if not they were to pay double damages to the party, or what the court thought reasonable. If the offender appeared and confessed his fault the conservators could mitigate the set penalty and fine him at their discretion and decide what share of the latter should go to the prosecuting serjeant. If the accused traversed the charge, trial could be arranged before the justices of assize as an alternative to the conservators. If he failed to appear within three months of being instructed he was to be held as automatically convicted. There can be no denying the hint of Star Chamber procedure which appears in several parts of this novel plan.[40] Plucknett pointed also to a degree of similarity to the tribunal established to enforce the so-called 'Star Chamber' act of 1487.[41] One proviso at the end of the draft strengthens this conciliar illusion. By it the conservators were given authority to summon (by *sub poena*) not only offenders under the penal laws but perpetrators of any act hurtful to the commonwealth not falling under any statute.[42] This ambitious arrangement was not intended to supersede the authority of justices already concerned with the operation of the penal laws but rather to supplement it. The scheme categorically stated that justices of assize, justices of the peace, and justices of sewers were to retain their powers in this field. How close the government came to implementing this scheme is not known, but its rather fanciful and occasionally non-legal vocabulary and the very width of its suggestions argue against governmental origin or governmental sponsorship.

In addition to simply providing an additional number of prosecutions under the penal laws the aim of the drafters of the proposed law may have been to supplant those informers motivated solely by greed or malice. That was what three unsuccessful parliamentary bills of the years 1543–7 were designed to accomplish. There followed in 1552 the establishment by the privy council of a committee to meet before and after each of the law terms, for the purpose of encouraging informations from those who had the good of the state at heart.[43] The committee, which had ten members including the lord privy seal, the lord chamberlain and the solicitor general, was to decide which penal laws needed to be enforced and to supervise the same, enquiring first into the 'greatest' offenders. What was actually accomplished we do not know. In 1558 a plan for commissioning a small number of men to inform was actually put into operation, but the letters patent were revoked again only a few months later. Eight years after this, at a time when there was much hostility towards informers, a scheme was offered to Cecil for operating the penal laws in an entirely novel manner.[44] It suggested that the penal laws relating to usury, tillage, apparel, engrossing of corn, illicit retainers, unlawful games, horses, and non-residents and pluralities, where they were enquirable before the justices of the peace, ought for greater efficiency to be entrusted to a number of justices commissioned for each shire. These were to receive from five substantial men in each hundred presentments of offences against the statutes which they in turn had received from two of the most substantial men in each parish, and which the five considered to be true. The five could also present offences which they knew of personally. At the quarter sessions, so as to avoid delay, these presentments were to be put to both the usual juries of indictment and a jury specially assembled for the purpose. If either would not find the indictment true, despite strong evidence, the jurors and offenders were to be bound to appear at the next assizes or the evidence certified thither. Trial, if the accused did not confess at the quarter sessions, was to be before the justices of assize: or by *nisi prius* or on information (with the indictment serving as evidence) in any court of record at Westminster. The scheme also contained the provision that under the penal laws it mentioned there should be no opportunity for a common informer to prosecute by information. Reliance was to be entirely on presentments, the reverse of the policy which had prevailed in the second half of Henry VII's reign. As to the penal laws not involved in the plan, informers were to be restricted in other ways. Only the party grieved or the attorney-general or his officers should be allowed to bring an action unless special permission, in the form of a commission, had been granted by the lord chancellor, lord keeper and lord treasurer: such commissions were only to be held during good behaviour. Informations might only be laid under the penal laws concerned with the royal revenue, subsidies or customs. Every informer was to put in a bond for his honest behaviour. Justices were to give costs for wrongful vexation or unnecessary delay if the informer lost his case. No one was to compound for a penalty except with the court's approval. All these suggestions were very relevant and sensible, indeed they went to the very heart of the unsatisfactory world of penal laws and informing, yet there was no parliamentary act resulting to give sanction to these rules for informers or the plan for presentments to commissioners.

It is possible that the scheme or something like it may have come before parliament, but we cannot be sure. A bill concerned with informations was passed by the commons early in the 1566–7 session but was amended by the lords in a way the lower house found unacceptable, and so lapsed. We also know that in December 1566 the commons, who angrily criticized a commission intended to enforce penal acts, sent a committee to the house of lords, which successfully asked it to intervene for the revocation of all such commissions, and that Queen Elizabeth was annoyed by their action.[45] Not, in fact, until 1576 was there legislation putting into force some of the recommendations of the scheme of

1566. At that time the act 18 Elizabeth c.5 stipulated informers must pursue their action under a penal statute in person or by an attorney, not by a deputy: this made groups of informers unprofitable. The name of the prosecutor, the act sued under, were to be endorsed on every process and there was to be no compounding for the penalty with the defendant without leave of the court. If the prosecutor discontinued or neglected his suit, or lost at trial, he must pay costs to the defendant. Unfortunately nothing was said about limiting suit to the party grieved or limiting the number of penal statutes under which information could be laid: nor was there any arrangement for special justices or a system for eliciting presentments. This was probably because the crown was now wedded to a much cheaper policy of granting patents to one man or a group of men by which they received a monopoly of action-bringing under particular statutes or in particular parts of the country.[46] Despite the act 18 Elizabeth c.5 these men were usually given the power of compounding with those against whom they brought suit and, because of their local monopoly, this gave them ample opportunity for blackmail.

One of the great abuses of the penal law system under Elizabeth seems to have been the way in which those who were sueing chose the courts at Westminster for their action rather than the assizes or the quarter sessions. It was apparently quite common for informers to lay their information in the exchequer or the queen's bench against provincial offenders who, realizing that a jury in a Westminster court would be much less likely to favour their defence than one of their own locality, and bearing in mind the expense of a journey to the capital, would be very ready to compound.[47] To some extent actions under the penal laws had been directed to Westminster by judicial policy anyway, for in 1564 at a judges' meeting it was decided that the phrase in many penal statutes about suit having to be in any court of record meant in fact in one of the four courts at Westminster.[48] This rule was moderated in 1588, when an act stipulated that suits on penal statutes where the offence concerned bows, illegal games or using any art or mystery without apprenticeship were to be prosecuted at quarter sessions or assizes in the county where the offence was committed.[49] Eventually it was an extension of this rule of 1588 by the statute 21 James I c.24 so as to include virtually all other offences under penal statutes which reduced actions from a flood to a very meagre trickle.

In addition to being an integral part of the penal laws, information has an important history, so far not touched on, as an element in summary or non-standard criminal procedure. In the medieval period it did not show much prominence in the field, the word appearing in one form or other in a mere eight statutes and in only two in a way which supplanted, or truncated, normal process. One of these was the act 4 Edward IV c.1 whereby justices of the peace, mayors, constables and stewards of leets were empowered to hear and decide cases concerning the non-payment of cloth workers' wages and the defaults of those workers in their occupation on receiving information and complaints.

Apparently the complaint or information was to serve as an indictment and there was to follow trial by examination or by 'other due proof'. The other act, one concerned with illegal retaining and livery-giving, was 8 Edward IV c.2, which we have already met. It allowed for information to be laid in the king's bench, common pleas, the courts of justices of oyer and terminer, gaol delivery and justices of the peace, and to stand in place of a bill of indictment. The subsequent trial could be by means of exam as well as by jury. Under the Tudors, acts of this sort providing for informing as an alternative type of accusation in the courts of the common law became quite frequent. There were two under Henry VII, namely 11 Henry VII cc.3 and 17, the second dealing with the taking of swans' and hawks' eggs, the first with the more serious problems of riots, illicit retaining, embracery, maintenance and the payment of excessive wages. 11 Henry VII c.3 put information in the place of presentment; 11 Henry VII c.17 allowed justices of the peace to enquire either by inquest or by information 'and proofs'. Under both acts actual trial was to follow the normal common law pattern. The use of information as an alternative to presentment appeared in eight of the statutes of Henry VIII, four of them being passed in the same session of the Reformation Parliament (24 Henry VIII cc.1, 4, 7, 9). The offences dealt with were all different, killing of cattle, keeping of stallions, the limits of sheep ownership, the sowing of flax and hemp, the misbehaviour of leather curriers, vagabonds, beggars, illicit liveries, maintenance, forestalling and the defaults of justices of the peace in enforcing statutes. Of considerable interest is the fact that each of these eight acts, as well as the two of the previous reign, gave authority for the information to be received by justices of the peace. The usual formula was for the justices to enquire, hear and determine the offences by information and presentment. Only in 11 Henry VII c.3 and 33 Henry VIII c.5 were they to share responsibility with the justices of assize, although in the second section of 33 Henry VIII c.10 justices of the peace's slackness in handling offences listed in the first part of the act was set to be dealt with by the assize judges. Two of the acts made provision for trial of the offender by methods other than the usual. 22 Henry VIII c.12 stated that if he should deny the information it should be proved by sufficient witness; 24 Henry VIII c.4 allowed, if the charge was made by information, for conviction by examination. Such practices disappeared after the death of Henry VIII.

'Information' appeared also in acts of Henry VII and Henry VIII dealing with criminal offences by other than the usual common law methods, as it had in those of the medieval era. By 1 Henry VII c.7 information against hunters who wore disguises was to go either to the justices of the peace or the council: under 19 Henry VII c.14 against illegal retaining the informer was to be admitted before the chancellor and the keeper of the great seal in the Star Chamber, before the king's bench or the council. 31 Henry VIII c.14 allowed bishops to take informations by the oaths of two lawful persons as well as accusations by juries of indictment: 32 Henry VIII c.50 permitted persons trying to avoid being rated for the subsidy to be 'proved' by presentment, examination or information before two commissioners, the barons of the exchequer or two justices of the peace. Were it not for the early history of information showing a clear connection with the common law it would be tempting to speculate that other courts were having an influence. What seems to have developed, particularly in the reigns of Henry VII and Henry VIII, was a readiness by common law courts and other courts, conciliar, ecclesiastical and novel, to accept each other's procedural practices and an acceptance of certain crimes as presentable in a variety of these courts. The reigns of Edward VI, Mary and Elizabeth were noticeably lacking in new statutes which provided for accusation by information before other than courts of common law.

Under the later Tudors 'information' appeared in statutes almost entirely as an alternative form of accusation before the courts of common law, although there were sometimes several alternatives, not just presentment, mentioned. Thus the act 5/6 Edward VI c.14 stipulated that justices of the peace in their quarter sessions should hear and determine offences of forestalling, regrating and engrossing by inquisition, presentment, bill, information, or the examination of two witnesses. 5 Elizabeth c.9 said that justices of assize, justices of gaol delivery and justices of the peace, where perjury occurred in a suit before them should enquire by inquisition, presentment, bill, information 'or otherwise lawfully' hear and determine. 5 Elizabeth c.21 ordered justices of oyer and terminer, justices of assize, of gaol delivery and of the peace, to hear and determine cases where fish, deer, or hawks had been unlawfully taken, by indictment, bills of complaint, information or 'other action'. It is noteworthy that a good proportion of the statutes which provided for accusation by means of information as an alternative to presentment or even indictment also permitted in another of their sections any person to sue the offender on his own and the king's behalf by means of information, action of debt, plaint or original writ, and to keep a share of the forfeiture if successful. They were, that is to say, acts dealing with criminal justice and penal acts providing private actions at the same time. There was only one such act in Henry VII's reign but seven in his son's. By the time of Elizabeth they had become quite common, there being as many as four emanating from the parliamentary session of 1563 alone.

Much has been written by historians about information and the penal acts as methods of raising revenue and regulating the economy, and how the system through its abuses created problems for the crown. What has received much less attention was how information fitted into the criminal law as a method of prosecution. A problem of considerable size which faced later medieval English kings in regard to the doing of justice was the fact that they had no public prosecutor and were dependent on their subjects at large to bring charges against misdoers. Sometimes presentments, which provided the indictments, were hard to elicit: not infrequently juries seem to have been reluctant, through fear or favour, to point the finger at known miscreants. The other standard form of accusation, the appeal, was only allowed for felonies. Thus, faced in the later thirteenth century with the corruption and the abuse of authority of officials of various types and prompted, no doubt, to do something about it by complaint in parliament, the king allowed charges to be brought against misdoers without the usual vetting process by a grand jury. In the fourteenth century the crown succeeded in extending this system of crime reporting to commercial and industrial misdemeanours, but had to confirm it was not to be used in regard to other criminal trespasses except where authorized by parliament, nor in cases of felony. If he lost in this area the king and thus public order benefited from this time in another, through statutes which allowed information to be laid by delators not personally involved in the offence, as well as by the victim. Furthermore in many cases there was provided reward for him if successful in the form of a portion of the money or goods the accused forfeited on conviction. Sometimes there was damages and costs in addition, as befitted a process which was assuming some of the attributes of personal actions. The Tudor age saw the opening of virtually all levels of the courts to the informer, but it was plagued by much abuse of the system. The hostility which this aroused among most classes must have been a major cause of the schemes to establish a regulated system of information-laying with officials as informers, decisions taken as to which of the vast number of penal laws should be enforced, information used as material for presentments only, and informers being forbidden to compound and being liable to costs themselves when the case was lost. However the crown took up instead the idea of granting patents to selected and professional informers, believing that through such monopolists it would have greater control. Finally we must remember that as with witnesses, examination, riot, and forcible entry, the history of the informer and the bringing of information demonstrates on investigation some close links with the history of summary and truncated process, the non-traditional, alternative, form of criminal process which has been the dominant theme in this study so far.

NOTES

1. The traditional account of the history of information is to be found in W.S. Holdsworth's *History of English Law*, 236–41. For the role of the plaint see A. Harding, 'Plaints and Bills in the History of English Law, mainly in the period 1250–1350', *Legal History Studies, 1972*, ed. D. Jenkins (Cardiff, 1975), pp. 66–77.
2. F.M. Powicke, *The Thirteenth Century*, (Oxford, 1953), pp.352–5.
3. *State Trials of the Reign of Edward I, 1289–93*, ed. T.F. Tout and H. Johnstone (Camden Soc., 3rd ser., 1906), pp. 69–70. Often *querelae* seem to have been preceded by appeals of felony which were abandoned, the bringer opting for a complaint which simply alleged a breach of the peace: *Legal History Studies, 1972*, p. 72
4. See below.
5. See *Select Cases in King's Bench, II*, ed. G.O. Sayles (Selden Soc., 57, 1938), pp. 25–6 and *Memoranda de Parliamento*, ed. F.W. Maitland (Rolls Series, 1893), p. 280.

6. F. Pollock and F.W. Maitland, *The History of English Law before the time of* Edward I (Cambridge, 1895), ii, 662; Plucknett, *A Concise History of the Common Law*, p. 430.
7. *Legal History Studies, 1972*, pp. 76, 85.
8. 28 Edward I c.11.
9. *Year Books*, 7 Edward III Trin. pl. 12. See also *A Cambridgeshire Gaol Delivery Roll, 1332–1334*, ed. E.G. Kimball (Cambridge, 1978), pp. 60, 64, 69.
10. Fourteenth century parliaments were often worried by the fear of imprecise and general accusations of crimes, and pressed for all charges to contain solid facts: see 25 Edward III c.9.
11. The act 38 Edward III c.9 ordered the informer to be put in prison until damages were paid.
    The two acts 25 Edward III st.5 c.4 and 37 Edward III c.18 may well have been directed chiefly against the use of the council for dealing with criminal cases and titles to land, rather than against informations as such. Certainly the act 42 Edward III c.3, which said no man should be put to answer without presentment before justices, or matter of record, or by due process and writ original, was a remedy against the citing of men before council by writ.
12. *Select Cases in King's Bench, VII*, ed. G.O. Sayles (Selden Soc., 88, 1971), pp. 70, 74.
13. See for example *Select Cases in King's Bench, II*, p. 137 and A. Harding, 'Early Trailbaston proceedings from the Lincoln roll of 1305', *Medieval Legal Records edited in memory of C.A.F. Meekings*, p. 150.
14. *Calendar of Inquisitions Miscellaneous, 1399–1422*, nos. 27, 600, 608; *ibid., 1392–99*, no. 164.
15. *Ibid., Edward III*, iii, no. 969.
16. 4 Edward IV c.1.
17. Plucknett was careful not to confuse the two. He pointed out that the essence of a penal law was the prohibition of some act, and allowing men to sue the offender and recover the penalty as the act provided: see 'Some Proposed Legislation of Henry VIII'. *Transactions of the Royal Historical Society*, 4th Ser., xix (1936), 125.
18. *Select Cases in the Exchequer, 1377–1461*, ed. M. Hemmant (Selden Soc., 51, 1933) pp. 144–6.
19. 8 Henry V c.3, 3 Henry VI c.3, 8 Henry VI c.17, 1 Richard III c.8, 1 Richard III c.10, 4 Edward IV c.7.
20. 34 Edward III c.8, 36 Edward III c.3, 9 Henry VI c.7, 23 Henry VI cc.9, 10, 17.
21. 34 Edward III c.8, 36 Edward III c.3, 9 Henry VI c.7, 23 Henry VI cc.10, 13, 17, 17 Edward IV c.7, 8 Edward IV c.2.
22. M.W. Beresford, 'The Common Informer, the Penal Statutes and Economic Regulation', *Economic History Review*, 2nd Ser., x (1957–8), 222.
23. Also used were the words 'detector' (34/5 Henry VIII c.1), 'pursuer' (25 Henry VIII c.17 and 27 Henry VIII c.14), 'presenter' (25 Henry VIII c.9), 'searcher' (34/5 Henry VIII c.10).
24. Some of the acts gave the crown's part of the penalty not to the king *tout court* but to his use (e.g. 32 Henry VIII c.17) or his heirs and successors as well as himself (32 Henry VIII cc.14 and 16 and 35 Elizabeth cc.8 and 12). The formula of Edward IV's reign whereby the forfeiture went to the 'king's house' was not renewed.
25. 4 Henry VII c.23, 25 Henry VIII c.5, 34/5 Henry VIII c.10.
26. A scheme offered to Cecil in 1566 proposing the encouragement of presentment rather than informations and penal law suits suggested that the fines, after allowances had been provided for the presenters and witnesses, ought to be given half to the parish and half to the house of correction for the setting on work of rogues and vagrants: P.R.O. SP 15/13/43.
27. It ought perhaps to be pointed out here that statutes awarding damages against the person convicted were very few: there were none in Henry VII's reign and only three in that of his son (23 Henry VIII c.9, 27 Henry VIII c.23 and 35 Henry VIII c.10).
28. As G.R. Elton has pointed out: 'State Planning in Early Tudor England', *Economic History Review*, 2nd. Ser., xiii (1961), 439.
29. M. G. Davies, *The Enforcement of English Apprenticeship* (Cambridge, Massachusetts, 1956), p. 29.

30. The statistics for Henry VII's reign are drawn from Dr. D.J. Guth's Ph.D. dissertation *Exchequer Law Enforcement, 1485–1509* (University of Pittsburgh, 1967).

31. Beresford, *Econ. Hist. Rev.*, 226.

32. Davies, p. 31. One advantage of proceeding by information may have been that the king's attorney, once the accused had pleaded not guilty, stepped in as prosecutor. This is what Guth found usually happened in Henry VII's exchequer. The informer's moiety was not at risk. Guth found that 1359 out of 1804 cases came to a decision but that 40 per cent of the time the result was dismissal: *Exchequer Law Enforcement*, pp. 103, 137, 172.

33. *Rot. Parl.*, vi, 437. The remedial act was 4 Henry VII c.20.

34. *History of English Law*, ix, 241.

35. Beresford, *Econ. Hist. Rev.*, 222.

36. Hall held one great abuse was that defendants commonly never knew there was a suit under the penal laws brought against them until they heard they had lost it through non-appearance. Apparently at this time the suit did not have to be brought in the county where the offence was committed: it might be in a court 200 miles away: Hall, *Chronicle* (London, 1809), p. 502. Empson and Dudley also packed inquest juries with perjurers.

37. H. Brinklow, *The Complaynt of Roderyck Mors* (Early English Text Soc., 1874), p. 22.

38. The scheme's reference to an act of '4 Henry VIII' must be to 1 Henry VIII c.4, rather than 7 Henry VIII c.3 as Elton suggests in 'Parliamentary Drafts', *Bulletin of the Institute of Historical Research*, xxv, no. 72, 123.

39. F. Pulton's *Abstract of Penal Laws* (London, 1577) included both types. Guth found a number of cases where informers in the exchequer claimed a moiety of the forfeiture even though the statutes in question did not mention any: *Exchequer Law Enforcement* p. 87. Their claim must have been based on the terms of the letters patent these informers must have possessed.

40. For example defendants could also make an answer in writing: P.R.O. SP 1/88/30.

41. Plucknett, *Trans. Roy. Hist. Soc.*, 4th ser., xix (1936), 131.

42. They were also empowered to call on the escheators to enquire into all offences under the penal laws: P.R.O. SP 1/88/36.

43. P.R.O. SP 10/14/16. A quorum of six was required. The statutes to be enforced were to be proclaimed after parliament ceased to sit.

44. P.R.O. SP 15/13/43. A proclamation of that year (1566) stated that informers under the penal laws were being beaten up in and about Westminster Hall: *Tudor Royal Proclamations, II*, ed. P.L. Hughes and J.F. Larkin (New Haven, 1969), pp. 288–9.

45. J.E. Neale, *Elizabeth I and her Parliaments, 1559–81* (London, 1953), p. 170: C. Read, *Mr Secretary Cecil and Queen Elizabeth* (London, 1955), p. 370.

46. By the act 29 Elizabeth c.5 a defendant in a penal suit who lived far from London could answer by attorney but, of course, this might be a considerable expense.

47. For a list of these see Beresford, *Econ. Hist. Rev.*, 233.

48. English Reports, 2 Dyer 236.

49. This was the first time an act spoke only of information and not about other actions under the penal laws in addition.

6

BENEFIT OF CLERGY IN THE FIFTEENTH AND SIXTEENTH CENTURIES

By the early years of the fifteenth century the *privilegium fori*, whereby criminous clerks who had committed felony might be allowed the opportunity to escape from the rigours of temporal justice, had become clearly defined both as to the type of offence and the class of person falling within its orbit. A clerk (*clericus*) who so benefited could be a man in holy orders, that is to say of the ecclesiastical rank of subdeacon or above, one who was in lesser ecclesiastical orders, or thirdly a layman who claimed to be *clericus* and on examination had been found so. It is quite possible that in the reign of Henry II the term *clericus*, when used in a judicial context, referred to those in holy orders only. Certainly the *Leges Henrici Primi* had ordered trial in ecclesiastical court only for those who 'ad sacros ordines pertinent et eis qui sacris ordinibus promoti sunt'[1] and Henry II promised to maintain the customs of his grandfather's reign. As time went by there were more and more men who, when brought before a secular court for purpose of arraignment, claimed to be clerks, hoping thereby to be delivered into the hands of the diocesan. By Bracton's era clerks in both higher and lower orders were being tried in ecclesiastical courts and the word 'clericus' had, according to Lyndwood taken the meaning of one who had had the first tonsure.[2] Apparently a certificate by the bishop that the accused man had been so tonsured had come to be accepted as proof of clergy by the courts of common law.[3] There is some evidence that proof of clerkship could be made more positive by the prisoner wearing clerical dress in addition, or if he or someone on his behalf offered a certificate of his orders.[4] Whether these were alternatives to a certificate of tonsure or used simply as supplementary evidence is not entirely clear.[5]

What is very evident is that from the early fourteenth century a reading test came to be the standard method of determining if a prisoner should be eligible for benefit of clergy. At the outset this device was used only when difficult cases were involved, the other 'proofs' being unable to tilt the scales decisively in either direction, but by mid-century the results of this examination of literacy had become the sole criteria. Since by this time literacy was by no means the sole preserve of the church a large and ever increasing proportion of fourteenth century criminous clerks were laity pure and simple, despite the fact that the canon law only required the privilege for those in higher orders.[6] This did not mean that any member of the laity if he asked for benefit and showed the ordinary he was able to read, could gain exemption from secular trial. Women could not have it save for nuns. Nor could any man who had a physical disability which would prevent his becoming a priest.[7] Blindness was not held such an impediment as long, that is, as the prisoner could speak Latin congruously. There is no evidence that men whose religion was not Christianity were allowed the privilege.[8] For a time, before the passing of the act 9 Edward II st.1 c.16 (known as the *Articuli Cleri*), secular justices went as far as to deny benefit of clergy to those who admitted guilt when appealed of theft, robbery or murder, but this was probably stopped by the statute. The privilege was also denied to convicted clerks who, when incarcerated in the bishop's gaol, managed to effect their escape.[9] When a prisoner pleaded his clergy it was not unusual for a counterplea of bigamy to be entered in order to defeat it. Bigamy meant marrying a widow or marrying a second time whether or not the first wife was dead and from the mid-thirteenth century the church was quite ready to deliver a man, whose guilt of the same had been proven before his bishop, to the secular courts for trial. The validity of this practice was established for Christendom as a whole by the church council at Lyons in 1274 and the relevant constitution was then confirmed by the statutes 4 Edward I c.5[10] and 18 Edward III st.3 c.2, the latter stating more fully that where a prisoner took to his clergy but was then accused by a witness or informant of being bigamous he should be sent to the spiritual court, as in a case of bastardy.[11] If investigation there confirmed the bigamy then presumably this was reported to the secular court and clergy refused.

Although the laws of England did not state as much in so many words, benefit of clergy was never granted to those accused of an offence which was less than felony: the crime had to be one which carried the death penalty.[12] Even a perpetrator of homicide could not claim the privilege if he had acted in self-defence or killed by mischance. The nearest any early act came to formally limiting benefit of clergy to felony was probably the first statute of Westminster (3 Edward I c.2), which sought to ensure proper purgation on the part of those whom the lay courts delivered to the ordinary. Such a man, for the drafters of the statute, would be a clerk 'pris por ret de feloni'. The exception to the rule of allowing benefit of clergy when the prisoner's life was at stake was the crime of treason. Those convicted of high treason were never allowed the privilege, but in 1352, at the time when the most heinous of offences was receiving statutory definition, a distinction was made between treason against the king's person (high treason) and treason against one's immediate master. The latter was given the title 'petty treason' and by another statute (25 Edward III st.6 c.4) those clerks who committed such treasons or felonies 'touching other persons than the king or his royal majesty' were to enjoy 'the privilege of the holy church' as it was called and be delivered to the ordinary on demand. If we except high treason or put it in a category of its own then it is fair to say that the late medieval rule about which offence was clergyable and which not followed the accepted distinction between felony and trespass with, for example, larceny of any object worth more than twelve pence conferring the privilege, and petty larceny of anything worth less being outside it.

Central in the process of obtaining benefit of clergy was the entering of such a plea by the prisoner and the reaction to his claim by the ecclesiastical authorities. On arraignment some prisoners answered only to claim clergy or ask for the ordinary: they would plead neither guilty nor not guilty. Others pleaded not guilty and put themselves on the country; if they were convicted would they then claim the clerical privilege. A third group, so it has been argued, pleaded not guilty and put themselves on a jury adding that they reserved the right to claim benefit of clergy if they were convicted. If we judge from the records of gaol delivery sessions the first manner of response was the one most common in the period *circa* 1250–1350 after which the second type was predominant. The third way of responding seems to have been peculiar to the sessions at Newgate and may have been in essence the same as the first.[13]

There was no way the church could prevent clerks from being arrested by lay authorities in the first place, nor could it stop appeals or indictments being brought against them. Its strategy until the mid-fourteenth century was probably to restrain them from entering a plea at all in the lay court. The constitutions of Clarendon, which claimed to be accepted custom, stated clearly that accused clerks should answer before the king's justices 'what it shall seem to the king's court shall be answered there' but in 1176 Henry II conceded that in the future, for any crime or misdemeanour except a forest offence, clerks should not have to appear at all before secular judges.[14] Bracton sheds no light on what had become the practice a century later but the statute of Marlborough showed that in theory the church had lost little ground, since it contained the words 'although he (the clerk-prisoner) will not answer before them (the secular justices) nor cannot by reason of his ordinary'. The statute of Westminster I (1275) seems to have been drafted in a way designed to avoid direct reference to the matter of pleading: it spoke clumsily and vaguely of when a clerk 'est pris por ret de feloni' and is demanded by the ordinary, nothing more. Only in the reign of Edward II do we find evidence, in this case the statute *Articuli cleri*, which suggests practice may have altered. The act made a mention of clerks confessing their offences before 'non-lawful' (i.e. secular) judges and thus we may assume that at this time, since they were unlikely to confess without being arraigned, they must have been actually entering a plea and no longer merely requesting benefit and the presence of the ordinary.[15] Confirmation of this turn of events seems to be provided by the evidence of the gaol delivery rolls, where this 'lay plea', as it has been called,[16] begin to assume significant proportions from the end of the thirteenth century.[17]

Should the prisoner refuse to plead and simply claim his clergy the secular justices were wont to call for an *ex officio* inquest by jurors in order to ascertain in what condition he should be handed over to the eclesiastical arm. In fact, since if the inquest found him not guilty the prisoner was set free, this meant telling the ordinary that the man being handed over had been convicted in the secular court. The 'ex officio' inquest seems to have had its beginning before the middle of the thirteenth century. Bracton gives no description of it and indeed states quite clearly that those imprisoned for homicide should be delivered 'sine aliqua inquisitione inde facienda',[18] but there are instances of inquests of the *ex officio* type in the crown pleas of the Berkshire eyre of 1248.[19] At such inquests, since no plea was entered by the clerk-prisoner, no judgment could be given by the secular justices although the jurors could and did return a verdict.[20] Why the secular power should demand an inquest concerning the accused clerk before he was handed over to the ordinary demands an explanation. One obvious reason was a desire on the part of the crown to demonstrate that it had never yielded its right to enquire into a felony (as distinct from judging it) whoever the committer, even if the prisoner might eventually be transferred to another authority. Another and quite distinct reason is suggested by the author of the *Mirror of Justices*, which was probably written at the end of the thirteenth century. When a clerk is brought into a lay court 'en cause criminale e mortele', he says, the judge should immediately enquire *ex officio* of his guilt by means of a jury in order to give 'acciouns as actours vers les accessoires en appeax e enditementz'.[21] The common law rule was that there could be no suit against an accessary to a crime unless the prinicipal had been convicted first. The *ex officio* inquest, by giving a verdict, allowed an accuser to bring his charges against any accessary immediately, whether by appeal or bill of indictment. A third reason for the inquest must have been the confiscation of goods which was involved. A verdict of guilty by the jurors resulted in the forfeiture of the clerk's goods, movable and immovable, although it was not an irreversible loss for it was referred to by the clergy by the canon law term of confiscation.[22] This was because if on subsequent trial before an ecclesiastical court the clerk managed to clear himself by purgation he would, by the end of the thirteenth century, seek a royal writ ordering restitution of the king's special grace of the goods from the lay authorities.[23] He did not get his possessions back automatically as a result of the ecclesiastical trial, and it is possible that the writ was not always forthcoming, at least not without some payment or intervention.[24] Thus eventually the crown might draw financial benefit from the *ex officio* inquest if the clerk managed to clear himself in the court ecclesiastical, although it would be more profitable should he fail in his purgation: in that case the crown would retain the goods permanently.[25] Open admission by the crown that inquests as to the guilt of the accused clerk were normal practice does not seem to have occurred before the reign of Edward II. But by 1313 it was the dictum of the king's judges that a clerk who did not plead should not be handed over to the bishop unless he had already been found guilty in a secular court:[26] there was no suggestion that procedure there finished when the clerk demanded the benefit of his clergy. There was never, in fact, any statute which stated clearly that an inquest was compulsory.

The *ex officio* inquest concerned only clerks who refused to enter a plea and instead demanded the benefit of their clergy. From the early forteenth century a growing number did not mention initially their claim to clerical status but put themselves on the country and were tried like laymen. Only if and when they were convicted did they ask for their clergy. At this point, as was the case when the prisoner had asked for the privilege as soon as he was arraigned, an ecclesiastical official was expected to claim his delivery. The attendance of this ordinary, by the end of the thirteenth century at least, was compulsory[27]: if the prelate or his deputy was not present he could be fined as much as £100 by the king.[28] The letters patent of commission which the ordinary had to present to the secular justices gave the names of the latter and of the ecclesiastic who had issued it. This was usually a bishop, but there were others in the church hierarchy who also had the authority, as for example the abbot of Westminster.[29] The commission might give authority for the claiming of one or two particular offenders within a limited category of crimes or where there was a particular type of accusation involved; on the other hand it might cover any clerk whatsoever and all types of clergyable offence to be tried at a particular sessions.[30]

The task of the ordinary, when the arraigned prisoner asked for benefit of clergy, was to determine if in fact he was a *clericus* and so entitled. This involved tests of tonsure and dress and inspection of letters of ordination, which we have already noticed, but primarily, from the early fourteenth century at least, an assessment of the prisoner's literacy. Although only a handful of these have been found in the records of Edward I's reign and none in the gaol delivery rolls of Edward II's, they seem to have occurred freqently from the time of Edward III onwards.[31] The ordinary's commission, by the third decade of the fourteenth century, gave its holder the power to demand, claim, examine and receive imprisoned clerks, and it was the word 'examine' which signified that the literacy of the prisoner was to be tested.[32] The form which the earliest literacy tests took is not certain. In a case from the year 1326 the ordinary asked the prisoner if he could speak in Latin or French, but apparently did not ask him to read.[33] There is no direct evidence of prisoners being given a book and told to read aloud from it before the middle of the fourteenth century. Even then the literacy test was not always acceptable by itself: indeed it was ruled quite clearly in one case 'quod literatura non facit clericum nisi haberet sacram tonsuram'.[34]

Already at this point in time the decision by the ordinary as to whether he ought to claim a man as a clerk was fraught with difficulties for him, which suggests that in benefit of clergy procedure he was very much the junior partner of the lay power. In 1352 Sir William Shareshull, at that time chief justice of the king's bench, pronounced that if an ordinary claimed for the church a man who was not in fact a clerk then his prelate would stand to lose his temporalities.[35] If the prisoner could read or could prove his clergy in another way the ordinary was virtually obliged to claim him even if the church thought him particularly obnoxious. A complaint by the clergy in 1301 suggested that there should be no need for the ordinary to claim known recidivists, but the crown did not concede the point.[36] The only occasion when the ordinary might lawfully refuse was if the clerk could be shown to have broken out of an ecclesiastical prison. By the middle of the fourteenth century the secular judges had begun to make their own rules about benefit of clergy. In 1348 they appear to have stipulated that if a prisoner would not ask for his clergy yet it was known to the justices that he was in fact a clerk they might remand him until he changed his mind or they might grant it without any request on his part.[37]

From the mid-thirteenth century lay justices, even if they did not contravene any law, were frequently guilty of using deceitful practices against the ordinary. In 1257 the clergy had cause to complain at a council at London that when prelates claimed clerks who were held in secular gaols they were not delivered but kept incarcerated until the assize judges came to hear pleas once more, even if this took a matter of years.[38] Furthermore clerks, including those who had been arrested while wearing clerical habit, were being hanged before the ordinary could claim them for the church. If anything was done to remedy these abuses it must have been only temporary since in 1285, at the time of the Easter parliament, the clergy again complained about clerks being retained in gaol after the ordinary had made a claim for them. On this occasion the crown offered the belligerent statement that the clerks would be freed as the king and justices decided. The grievance about the lay arm delaying the release of clerks was rehearsed by the clergy once more in the Lent parliament of 1301.[39] In answer the king promised they should be freed, but after judgment by trial or inquest. This annoyed the ecclesiastics, who pointed out judgment was contrary to clerical liberties and asked for the levying of a £100 fine on any lay justice who tried to avoid handing a prisoner over. What the ecclesiastical authorities viewed as sharp practice by the laity occurred also in the fourteenth century and resulted in two remedial statutes. In the parliament of 1316 they drew attention to the way some temporal justices were not delivering to the ordinary clerks who had confessed to theft, robbery or murder but were admitting appeals (i.e. suit of party) against them. The concessions which the crown made in this instance were meagre. A statute produced by a parliament of 1352 admitted that lay justices were remanding men who had been arraigned, claimed their clergy and even been requested by the ordinary, back to gaol because they believed there were other charges yet to be brought against them. The proper practice, it stated, was for clerks to be put to answer to all charges against them at the same time, and this was ordered to be done in the future.[40]

As the representatives of the English clergy told the general church council at Vienne in 1311, in England any clerk who had been accused of felony would only be handed over by the lay arm to the ecclesiastical authorities as one who had been found guilty. It was then for the bishop to try him on the church's behalf.[41] In essence this ecclesiastical trial took the form of a compurgation with the swearing of oaths by the prisoner and others that he was innocent, but there were important preliminaries and addenda. Even if the lay authorities had no high opinion of an ecclesiastical trial they were determined to insist upon it as a means of preventing bishops from releasing prisoners soon after delivery. The statute of Westminster I probably put into permanent form what by the late thirteenth century had become standard practice, namely a convention there should be no setting an indicted clerk at liberty without due purgation. At the same time the crown may have felt that some bishops were too lax in their handling of criminous clerks, for there was a threat at the end of the statute that if the matter was not attended to voluntarily the king would provide some 'other remedy'.

In the fourteenth century it became not uncommon for clerks to be handed over by secular justices with instructions or advice to the bishop that the delivered man was to be held in prison 'absque purgatione'. There was no statute which regulated this procedure and indeed only a single year-book case commented upon it. Whether the instructions originated entirely with the justices, from their feeling that the felony was an exceptionally serious one, or that the prisoner was a persistent offender, is not clear. What evidence there is suggests that the crime or the situation of the miscreant was in some way different from what it was in the normal run of felonies: the accused might not have been arraigned in court but have been outlawed or have abjured the realm;[42] the crime might have been a 'manifest' one or the offender 'notorious' for his persistent misbehaviour. In February 1351 the clergy of the province of Canterbury fearing that the privilege of benefit of clergy was likely to be curtailed, agreed there should be no purgation for notorious malefactors or those who had confessed their offences:[43] however, no statute to this effect was ever promulgated. The year book case, which dated from Richard II, was one involving an appeal, that is to say it arose at the suit of a private party, not of the king.[44] Clearly any purgation could be viewed as depriving that party of his just rights. Apart from the proposals of the clergy of 1351 there is little evidence from the fourteenth century that confession barred purgation, yet it is quite likely that such was the case. As Staunford pointed out, a clerk convict might have purgation because he asked for benefit of clergy before judgment was given against him. A clerk attaint, on the other hand, might not because when he asked there was already a judgment of the secular court standing against him.[45] The other categories of offenders who were not permitted to have purgation comprised those who, although they had not been adjudged guilty before the justices, stood in law as men convicted nonetheless. The outlaw could be executed without further process, and the abjurer had perforce confessed to the coroner.

By the early fourteenth century the prisoner who successfully claimed his clergy was handed over to the ordinary as a man accused but, in the church's eyes, with little stigma of guilt attached to him. With him came a statement from the lay justices explaining the charges laid against him in the secular court.[46] He was placed in the bishop's prison until, so long as he was not in one of the classes which were barred, he was allowed to prove his innocence by compurgation. When the prisoner had petitioned for this opportunity in the proper form and a day had been set the bishop commanded a group of sworn and oathworthy men (probably including members of the local priesthood) who were acquainted with the prisoner, to provide information about his past life.[47] Then from a group similarly qualified he enquired whether the prisoner was in fact guilty of the charges. The results of this double enquiry into reputation and the facts of the case were to be certified back to the bishop.[48] Resort to an inquest in this manner had, towards the end of the thirteenth century, given rise to conflicting ecclesiastical regulations. One complaint by the clergy in July 1285 referred to the crown forbidding laity from appearing before ecclesiastical judges making investigation by sworn inquest, except in testamentary or matrimonial causes.[49] Mention was made of the fact that those defamed of a crime were wont to purge themselves by their oath or by subjecting themselves to the special inquest of others: the two methods were apparently alternatives, not complementary. Now, said the clergy, the latter alternative, demanding as it did the oaths of oathworthy persons, had been rendered impractical by the prohibition against laity.[50] A petition by the prelates to the king in 1295, on the other hand, implied that inquests utilizing laymen, far from being superseded, were in common use and even superseding purgation. The bishops requested that the accused should be able to purge himself or make his justification, and not be compelled to submit to inquest by laity as had been recently introduced.[51]

Whatever the position of the ecclesiastical inquest in the last decades of the thirteenth century, there can be no doubt that it continued to be used in dealing with criminous clerks for the next two centuries at least.[52] How the inquest functioned, on the other hand, is less certain. Commissions in bishops' registers show that in theory the inquest operated through a band of men 'fidedigni et iurati' who inquired 'de vita, moribus et gestu' of the prisoner prior to his arrest, and also through others who provided information about the circumstances of the offence, such as whether the original accusers were prompted by malice and how strong was their evidence.[53] In this way the accusatory process of the common law was inspected for deficiencies. Quite possibly the prisoner was himself present at the inquest in order to confront the enquirers and any evidence they had gathered, for there is a reference to clerks having access to legal counsel for their defence.[54] Should the findings of the inquest favour the prisoner he was allowed to advance to purgation. There was, however, another and important hurdle to surmount as the first part of the actual purgative process. Order was given for proclamations to be made 'in partibus illis ubi fama contra dictum clericum maxime dicitur laborare', which invited anyone who wanted, to accuse or prosecute the clerk. How frequently such opposers to purgation appeared we cannot at the present time say, but it would be wrong to argue that these invitations were empty ones and that opposition to purgation was only a sham with the church protecting its own without thought for society at large. What the ecclesiastical authorities were doing was handling a clerk who had been accused of felony like one who was charged with an offence which fell properly under the church's jurisdiction. The rule had always been that those defamed by public report of any crime and unable to vindicate themselves were to be warned as to their conduct on the first and second occasions but if they misbehaved a third time they were to confess and make satisfaction.[55] If they did not do this but stood firm in denying the reports then they would be ordered to purgate. Accusation of felony brought from a secular court were clearly considered as a serious matter which must be dealt with by purgation at the least.

The ritual of purgation took place before an ecclesiastical judge and a jury composed of clerks. It was supposed to be performed not perfunctorily but with all the solemnity of law so as not to offend the king. The prisoner, when the crime was put to him, swore to his innocence and a group of compurgators, whose number was set at ten or twelve for a 'horrible' crime, swore to the prisoner's credibility.[56] The compurgators were men of good character from the prisoner's own locality and frequently a large proportion of them were clerks.[57] A proclamation had to be made that any objections to the composition of the panel of compurgators should now be brought forward.[58] If there were no such opposers the prisoner and compurgators made their oath and the judge pronounced the former purged and restored to good fame. It was of course important that if the prisoner had been convicted of several felonies in the lay court he should make purgation for all.[59]

From the secular point of view the unsatisfactory aspect of purgation must have been the small proportion of those who failed. Aware of this weakness in the ecclesiastical system, bishops seem to have responded by keeping clerks in their prisons for an extended period before allowing them to attempt purgation. Examples of a delay of ten years are not uncommon and those of over twenty are not unknown.[60] Maybe it was this which made it less remarkable that purgation, which was being superseded in borough custom at this time, was the subject of few threats or suggested reforms on the part of the lay authorities. There may have been some pressure to stop purgation when a clerk committed another felony and sought it a second time but no act resulted.[61] In 1351 secular judges complained that criminous clerks were not being punished sufficently by imprisonment as they should be: escape was easy and so was purgation. In response, fearing for the future of the *privilegium fori* as a whole, the clergy, as we have seen, issued a provincial constitution which ordered *inter alia* the witholding of purgation from notorious malefactors and those who had confessed.[62] No parliament of that period turned the rule into a statute, indeed the act 25 Edward III st.6 c.4 seems to have deliberately avoided the issue since it talked only of prelates having to safely keep and duly punish those found guilty of petty treason and felony in the secular courts, not of purgation as such. However, half a century later the constitution of 1351 by the act 4 Henry IV c.3 was partly confirmed and partly amended. Notorious thieves were to be safely kept by the ordinary without purgation: and so also now were petty traitors. The reference to clerks who had confessed their crime on the other hand was omitted.

Apart from those restricting the type of offenders who could benefit from purgation the only rule operative in the fourteenth century which affected the future of a criminous clerk once he had been handed over to the ordinary was that which made the bishop liable to a fine of £100 should he allow the clerk to go free without purgation. To the secular judges it must have been only a small comfort. When, by failure to purge or the verdict of the inquest or other manner, the guilt of the clerk had been proven in ecclesiastical court he might be degraded from his clerical status. On several occasions the church argued that this together with any penance which was assigned, was punishment enough and that the additional loss to the lay power of his movable or immovable goods, as seems to have occurred from the thirteenth century, was to suffer for the crime twice (and thus against Christian teaching).[63] On the other hand it was asked as late as 1239, in the legatine council at London, that no clerk should be hanged unless convicted before his judge and first degraded, which suggests that delivery back to the lay arm and the infliction of the death penalty was by no means uncommon.[64] Yet the normal punishment for a clerk convicted in the spiritual court of a felonious offence was imprisonment and the loss of his goods.[65] One canon of the council of Lambeth of 1261 ordered that any clerk so malicious and incorrigible and so wont to commit shameful crimes that if he had been a layman he would suffer capital punishment, should be put in prison for life.[66] To the bishops the intention was both to protect society from the prisoner's criminal inclinations and to allow him time to become penitent and show contrition: 'ut commissa defleat et defleanda ulterius non committat'.[67]

The history of the benefit of clergy in the fifteenth century prior to the accession of Henry VII was marked by one clearly discernible feature. To outward appearances there were virtually no changes of importance or noteworthy discussions about it between 1403 and about the middle of the century, but thereafter the debate was considerable. The issue which at mid-century reawakened the controversy concerned what should be done with those who had successfully claimed benefit once and later committed a second felony. In a case in the exchequer chamber at Hilary term 1450 the discussion was concerned with a man taken for suspicion of felony who, it transpired, had already been arraigned, had confessed and secured benefit of clergy for an earlier crime.[68] The king had asked for process for putting the ordinary to answer why he had allowed purgation for the first offence and why he should not be held guilty of allowing escape. The comment of the justices was simply that there could be no legal purgation if the prisoner confessed his misdeed, had abjured the realm (which also involved a confession), was convicted by outlawry, or had become the king's approver. In this there was nothing new, for such had been the practice in the fourteenth century. The importance of the case was that it arose at a time when in parliament a petition had been offered which asked that a felon who had once claimed clergy and purged himself should on committing a second offence be put straight into perpetual imprisonment by the bishop, or the bishop pay a fine of £100.[69] The Exchequer chamber case suggests that the crown was seeking to put the blame for purged felons who later committed further misdeed onto the shoulders of the ecclesiastical authorities and punish them for it. In 1450 apparently the judges of the two benches could not find sufficient legal grounds for initiating this policy and their answer was probably obtuse for that reason; although in all fairness it was asking a great deal of them to find the committing of a new offence after purgation as the equivalent of escape from gaol. The notion broached in parliament of perpetual ecclesiastical imprisonment without another trial was quite alien to the common law, although the idea of a fine on the bishop was not. Nothing came of the parliamentary petition in that session or later, but in the parliament which met in July 1455 there was a petition to the effect that when a felon who had received benefit of clergy for his offence committed a second it ought to be held as high treason, which of course carried no such privilege but a gruesome death and a severer type of forfeiture.[70] Despite its severity the king agreed to the petition, but no statute ever resulted. It is difficult to decide what occasioned these petitions. Was it a high incidence of purged clerks as second offenders in these years, or one or two particular cases? A close examination of the ecclesiastical records in some northern dioceses suggests that there was an absence of such clerks who offended a second time; at least no clerk achieved a second purgation.[71] Yet the church may have refused purgation to such men or made sure they failed the test, we cannot tell. It is just as likely, bearing in mind other petitions to be found in the parliament rolls of this period that the cause of the petitions of 1449 and 1455 was not a wave of second offences but one or two cases of nefarious criminals seeking purgation a further time.

The parliament which met in February 1449 received a petition sponsored by the parliamentary commons asking that four chaplains should be pardoned because they had been indicted maliciously.[72] These four, apparently, were to be numbered among many priests, secular and regular, who were being pestered at that time for private profit rather than the benefit of the crown in divers parts of the kingdom. If the complaint was based on fact and there was in the mid-fifteenth century a tendency for the laity to harass those in holy orders, it helps to explain why in November 1462 Edward IV went so far as to grant them a charter affording protection from lay indictments and inquests. The letters patent claimed to be a confirmation that no secular justice or royal minster should have the right to enquire into felonies, treasons, excesses and rapes supposedly perpetrated by bishops, priests and whoever was in holy orders or a religious person. If however any jury should accuse such an ecclesiastic of these offences the lay official who received the indictment or findings was, without arresting the accused, to send a copy forthwith to the ordinary, who must then proceed against the accused according to the law of the church. As to those who on arrest by a secular justice claimed to be clerks, the justice should call the ecclesiastical judge to decide their 'spiritual pretence'. Any man who was found a clerk was to remain under ecclesiastical jurisdiction for judging; if he was not found a clerk he stayed with the temporal power.[73]

Why Edward IV thought it necessary to issue this charter is not at all obvious. It has been suggested that the instigator was Cardinal Coppini, whose political friendship had been so important to the Yorkists in their rise to power.[74] Another reason may well have been a desire to free ecclesiastics from the threat of judicial proceedings against them for their misdeeds during the political confrontations of 1459–61. The proceedings against Thomas Merks, bishop of Carlisle, in 1400–1 had shown that a late medieval king might be ready to try them for treason in a secular court notwithstanding their status.[75] Equally noteworthy were the distinctive procedures envisaged by the charter. There was to be no enquiry (presumably by examination) or arraignment of those in holy orders who were believed to have committed the felonies and treasons, no obtaining of a plea, no *ex officio* inquest to ascertain in what condition they were to be handed over to the ordinary. Furthermore the bishop or his officer in arriving through the ecclesiastical law at a final judgment was authorized, when he received the accused, to make enquiry about the offence and offender not only in the normal ecclesiastical manner but also by use of presentment and indictment,[76] the methods of the common law. It all amounted to a legal device unique in the fifteenth century and without parallel until the later years of Henry VIII's reign.[77] The judicial process was left entirely to the ecclesiastical power. Similar though not identical was the process stipulated in the charter for dealing with captured malefactors who claimed to be clerks. The question of whether the claimant was a clerk or not was to be answered by the ordinary, who had been summoned by the secular judge, before the case was heard. This must have meant that the ordinary gave his decision before the prisoner was arraigned or had entered a plea and thus that those found to be clerks were to go immediately under ecclesiastical jurisdiction, as had been the practice in the twelfth century. Since the spiritual authority entered the case so early and received immediate custody of genuine clerks it is unlikely that *ex officio* inquests by the lay justices were to be allowed although they were not specifically forbidden. It seems that the intention of this part of the 1462 charter was essentially to preserve ecclesiastics of fairly high rank from being indicted by laymen for recent offences (some of them of a political nature) and if indicted to save them from a secular trial. Criminous clerks benefited also because it was thought this procedure, where it forbade secular enquiry and arraignment in a secular court, should extend to them as well. Whether there was a deliberate policy, with an eye to the future, of separating those in holy orders who had committed felony from other clerks is not certain, but it is a possibility. The extension by the king of benefit of clergy to include offences of treason was not only novel but potentially political suicide. This must soon have been pointed out to Edward IV by the secular judges, who must also have heartily disliked the vastly increased jurisdiction of the ordinary and the ecclesiastical courts. Perhaps the charter's provisions were never put into practice: certainly there is little evidence of any effect by the section relevant to clerks in ecclesiastical records, which still show lay courts handing men over as *clerici convicti*.[78] One cannot be so sure about the result of the section which was intended to stop charges against those in holy orders since the design was essentially negative, but there seems to be no evidence of the novel type of inquest on the part of the ordinary.[79] Despite the recent civil war and political revolution it seems unlikely that such important changes in English law could be implemented on the king's *fiat* alone, for there was never any supporting statute, without arousing considerable opposition in the country at large.

Complaints made in convocation soon after the granting of the 1462 charter seem to support the view that it was never properly implemented. The prolocutor of the convocation which met at St. Paul's in July of the subsequent year sought the setting free from lay prisons of several clerks under its terms.[80] Apparently the clergy were trying to make the enforcement of the charter a condition of their granting a subsidy but were manoeuvred out of it. Eventually the taxes were granted and as a sop five lawyers were deputed to make a report to the ecclesiastical hierarchy before the time of the next parliament as to how the charter might be enforced. In 1471 there was another complaint by the clergy, this time one more specific. They asked that priests and curates who had been indicted before royal justices should have a remedy from the king; also that no priest so indicted should be seized or gaoled but rather the indictment be immediately dispatched to the ordinary.[81] This was an obvious attempt to draw attention to violations of the first section of the 1462 charter and to ask it should be enforced. The complaint may also have been an expression by higher ecclesiastics of a determination to preserve whatever distinction the charter had made between those in higher orders and other clerks. If there was any response to these grievances the improvement was only temporary for early in 1475 a supplication of a similar sort was made in a convocation at St. Paul's.[82] The clergy complained that priests and curates were still being charged with offences before secular justices and requested that in future the latter should, on assuming office, have to take an oath that no priest should be accused before them or arrested or imprisoned on their orders; rather any such charges or indictments they should send to the ordinary. However, to this petition the king would not give his consent.

The clergy at this point seem to have turned to another method of obtaining the enforcement of the charter. In May of the following year (1476) Pope Sixtus IV issued a bull which, reminiscent of the parliamentary petition of 1449, claimed that priests and clerks were being indicted by means of perjury, put in gaol, and only able to secure freedom by giving in to demands they should resign their incomes both spiritual and temporal.[83] If anyone should do such mischief in the future they were to be excommunicated or anathematized. Again the effect must have been negligible although the king made no effort to revoke or alter the charter. The matter emerged once more in the convocation of Canterbury province in March 1481, where there was a complaint to the archbishop that justices, sheriffs, bailiffs, and other temporal officials were causing and receiving indictments of clerics whom they then attached or imprisoned.[84] The remedy requested was that the prisoners should be delivered freely (i.e. without trial) to the bishop, which was as stipulated in the 1462 charter. We do not know what eventually happened to the request but very likely it failed, as previous ones had. The Yorkist kings carried on the charade to the end for in February 1484 Richard III, far from cancelling or amending the charter, thought fit to confirm it.[85] Presumably throughout the whole of the Yorkist era the church was pressing the crown to preserve those clerics who were in holy orders from harassment by the laity and ensure that for felony they were only justiciable in ecclesiastical court. It would have liked also to secure the exemption of other clerics who claimed benefit of clergy from having to plead in a lay court, but if the opposition to this was too strong then the church was ready to sacrifice it in order to secure the other privilege. After all, if the second privilege was lost the position was no worse than it had been in the fourteenth and earlier fifteenth centuries. Nor is it beyond the bounds of possibility that the church was planning for a time, remote from the windfall of 1462, when the laity would be even more hostile to its judicial privileges. By separating those in holy orders from other 'clerics' it was preparing itself for a crisis when benefit of clergy for the latter might have to be surrendered.

The church's pessimistic view of the future of clerical privilege may have derived in some degree from the comments on the subject made from the later years of Henry VI onwards by the judges of the two benches. Cases in the year-books reveal a notable determination on the part of the secular justices to show how their authority was paramount over that of the ordinary in cases involving benefit of clergy. The matter which elicited these pronouncements was chiefly the literacy test. As early as 1406 Chief Justice Gascoigne was prompted to say that the examination of a man's clergy was the duty of the court, not the ordinary. A report from Trinity term 1456 mentioned a case in which the ordinary, who was the archdeacon of the abbey of Westminster, refused to claim as a clerk one whom the secular justices thought had read well. Therefore they put the fact that he had read in their record and remanded him to prison until a new archdeacon assumed the duties of ordinary when the test was given again and the church finally claimed the prisoner. This case was raised by Chief Justice Fortescue because he wished to discover the opinion of the judges of the benches as to whether the ordinary, because of his earlier verdict, ought to be fined.[86] All the judges agreed that he should be. There was a similar case about eleven years later. Again the ordinary refused to claim as a clerk a prisoner who, in the eyes of the secular justices, read well enough. Therefore the justices, who in this instance were engaged in delivering a gaol, reprieved him and certified the case to the king's bench. The writer of the report tells us that he had heard that the ordinary was penalized by a fine as a consequence. He finished his comments on the case by saying that the role of the ordinary, when a prisoner claimed clergy, was not that of a judge but rather of a minister of the court: the judges were the secular justices.[87] At Trinity term in 1469 there occurred in the king's bench a case involving a claim to benefit of clergy which shed more light than almost any preceding one onto the relative roles and authority of the justices and the ordinary.[88] The prisoner, it was held, must read 'distincte et aperte'.[89] If the ordinary claimed one who, to the justices, did not do this he would be fined and the prisoner hanged: 'for we', said the judges in the king's bench, 'are the judges of his reading because we make our record read 'quod legit ut clericus ideo liberetur ordinario' '. The ordinary on the other hand, so it was pointed out, was there only to claim for benefit of clergy and must do so properly. He was to be punished by fine if in the eyes of the justices he claimed or refused a prisoner wrongly, such as refusing a man because he had no tonsure or did not wear clerical garb.[90] Clearly this was a very far cry from the case of Trinity term 1328 in which the ordinary, in refusing to receive a prisoner as one who was attainted (i.e. one who had confessed), argued that the secular justices could in no way be the prisoner's judges.[91]

The history of the benefit of clergy in the fifteenth century was not of course entirely a tale of confrontation between authorities secular and ecclesiastical. Some cases simply resulted in clarification of legal principles without, on the face of it at least, any state versus church argument. It was decided in 1469 that a man who had committed sacrilege and was then taken for another felony might have his clergy if the ordinary claimed him: but the ordinary with the lay justices' assent might refuse such an offender even if he could read.[92] A case which was heard in king's bench at Michaelmas term 1473 led to a declaration of the rule whereby when a principal in a felony confessed his offence and took to his clergy the accessary was put to arraignment despite the fact that technically there was no judgment against the principal. Seven years later the issue of forfeiture came to the fore and was clarified through Chief Justice Billing's pronouncement that a convicted clerk was entitled to have the profits of his land because in taking to his clergy he had refused the English common law; if, however, he had confessed his offence, and was therefore a 'clerk attaint', he lost all his possessions because he had submitted to that law.[93]

Quoting Fitzherbert's *Abridgment* Sir William Staunford in his *Les Plees del Coron* made mention of one further significant rule to do with benefit of clergy which was established in the mid-fifteenth century,[94] He believed that sometime in the reign of Henry VI, John Prisot, who must have been either a justice or chief justice of common pleas at the time, refused any more to allow prisoners to ask for their clergy on arraignment, making them instead plead simply guilty or not guilty with no addition and then permitting them to plead benefit if they were convicted. Staunford thought this rule, which was in operation in his own day, a sensible one since if the prisoner pleaded clergy on arraignment he was not able to challenge the *ex officio* inquest whose verdict could mean the forfeiture of his goods: the other way he was able to 'challenge' the inquest. If Staunford's story was accurate then Prisot was ending a tradition which was already at the point of exhaustion, for it has been clearly demonstrated that few prisoners indeed chose to plead their clergy on arraignment in the lay court after the end of the fourteenth century. Admittedly this trend is partly explained by the fact that gaol delivery records get sparser from the early fifteenth century, yet the proportion of such pleas as against lay pleas (i.e. those who pleaded guilty or not guilty and only took to their clergy later) declined markedly from Richard II's reign onwards. We may speculate that Prisot's practice, if it was taken up by other judges, may have been partly responsible for the section of the royal charter to the clergy of 1462 which granted that those claiming to be clerks should be examined for their clergy not merely on arraignment but on arrest, and precluded lay justices from holding any inquest into the offences of those in holy orders.

The reign of the first Tudor monarch, although it has been characterized as a period of relative unimportance where legislation affecting the church was concerned, proved in fact to be a time when several significant changes occurred in benefit of clergy. Some of these were accomplished by means of statutes, others through decisions of the king's judges. Two acts were passed for the purpose of amending two others already on the statute book by making the offences they dealt with non-clergyable. Thus by 7 Henry VII c.1 any soldier receiving wages, who departed from the king's service without licence of his captain, was committing a felony and one which did not allow the privilege of benefit of clergy. This was a simple addition to the statute 18 Henry VI c.19[95] The crime which was the subject of the second act, 12 Henry VII c.7, was the very distinct one of petty treason. It was one of the few felonies which in the middle ages had been defined by statute, in this case in the great statute of treasons 25 Edward III st.2, c.5. The new rule stipulated that in the future anyone who slew his master or immediate sovereign was not to be permitted the privilege of his clergy as had been provided by the statute *pro clero* (25 Edward III s.6, c.4) at virtually the same time as the treason statute. The act of 1497 is particularly interesting because it reveals an uncommon thing, the cause of its promulgation. A London yeoman named James Grame had plotted the murder of his master during the time of the parliament which passed the act. The statute stated Grame should be drawn and hanged 'any privilege of clergy notwithstanding', so serving as an act of attainder. As well as removing the obstacle of his clergy the intention must have been to provide for him to suffer the death penalty when the crime was not in fact a capital offence: he had not murdered his master but only plotted his death, which was not a crime carrying danger to life and member. The new rule for dealing with petty traitors as a whole was no doubt an afterthought, the lords and commons of parliament feeling that such behaviour, so perilous to their respective classes, must be more positively discouraged for the future. It may also have salved the consciences of the lawyers in parliament who realized how far beyond the normal tenets of the common law this attainder act had gone; they could feel assured there would be no similar case in the future. The act also had the distinction of being the only one concerned with privilege of clergy which stated openly that that institution was for the advantage of laymen, for the word 'clerk' was not included. There was incidentally no suggestion clerks should forfeit the privilege if they killed their prelate.

Significant change in the history of benefit of clergy of another sort was introduced by the act 4 Henry VII c.13. This, having lamented how 'divers persons lettred' relying on their privilege had become quite bold in the committing of murder, rape, robbery and theft, enacted that all those not in holy orders who had once benefited from their clergy should not do so again. To prevent a second successful claim it was stipulated that on their first arraignment murderers should be branded on the brawn of the left thumb with the letter 'M' and felons with a 'T'.[96] Those in orders who asked for their clergy a second time were to prove their status by presenting a certificate of their orders to the justices. Here at last the persistent problem of offenders who made use of their clergy on more than a single occasion was remedied by an act. Attempts to obtain a similar solution had proved fruitless on two earlier occasions, as we have seen. The 1489 act was a severe solution but one likely to be successful. Even more important was the clear distinction made between the fate of those in holy orders and others who claimed ecclesiastical privilege. It was the first time this had been done by a statute, although the charter of 1462 had differentiated between them and special treatment for criminous priests had been requested in 1471 and 1475. The argument has been offered that by referring to 'every persone not being within orders', although in the negative sense of depriving them of benefit of clergy on a second occasion, the statute was extending the literacy test to the laity the first time they were taken.[97] This is to overemphasize the phrase. Rather it was an overt, although involuntary and accidental, admission of recent judicial practice. Very likely the expressed desire of priests and curates to be treated differently from other literates was prompted by the number of laity now obtaining benefit.

Other important developments in benefit of clergy in this reign are to be found primarily in the year books. The position of an accessary when the principal took to his privilege was clearly stated for the first time although the judges had debated the issue in Edward IV's reign. He was to profit not at all from the principal's action but be arraigned and if found guilty hanged.[98] Equally noteworthy was a further extension of secular dominance over the ecclesiastical authorities in regard to authority over the prisoner after he had been delivered to the ordinary. In a case discussed at Trinity term 1500, Chief Justice Fineux stated that when a clerk convict or clerk attaint was committed to the ordinary the custody of him was temporal since the misdeed was temporal, as was the judge who committed him.[99] Thus it followed that the ordinary must obey secular rules in supervising the imprisonment: he must not allow the prisoner to have bail or to go at large, nor should he imprison him more grievously or more easily than proper, nor refuse to allow him to purgate or prevent the king from pardoning him without purgation.[100] The ordinary had also to act as junior partner when a clerk convict obtained a charter of pardon. In a case heard in the king's bench at Michaelmas term 1505 the judges decided a writ rehearsing all the matter and the pardon should be sent to the ordinary to summon him before the justices 'to have the pardon allowed', that is to say he was instructed to free the prisoner.[101]

The reign of Henry VIII before the time of the Reformation Parliament produced only a single statute which affected benefit of clergy, yet it saw a confrontation between church and state over that issue of the first magnitude, one which caused more overt debate over fundamentals than any other quarrel in the previous three centuries. The statute, which was passed in the parliament of 1512, was the prime cause of this conflict which erupted two years later.[102] In essence this act severely restricted the numbers of those who could obtain the clerical privilege. No one who committed murder or felony in church, chapel or hallowed place, or with malice aforethought robbed or murdered any person on the king's highway, or robbed or murdered any person in his house, the owner or dweller there, his wife, child or servant being present and put in fear, was to be admitted to his clergy unless he was in holy orders.[103] It meant that those in lesser clerical orders and literate laymen could not benefit from their clergy if they committed in certain places robbery, burglary, sacrilege or murder. Here was a further extension of the principle of separating, for purposes of restriction, the various types of potential beneficiaries of clergy, a notion which had become noticeable in the reign of Edward IV and had first been incorporated in a statute in Henry VII's time (4 Henry VII c.13). The statute of 1512 was intended to last only until the next parliament, which suggests that its designers and sponsors had been forced to compromise to obtain a successful passage through the two houses. The end of the session did not close the matter as the government must have hoped, for a debate over the merits of the act continued outside parliament in the following years as supporters and antagonists got ready for new or renewed legislation in the next parliament. In convocation in June 1514 the prolocutor of the lower house, Dr. John Taylor, in an address attacked the misdeeds of the lower ranks of the clergy which had led to the 1512 statute, but whether there was a substantial party within the church in favour of the act seems doubtful.[104] Fuel had been added to the flames of controversy by a decree of the Lateran council of 5 May 1514 whereby Pope Leo X, to emphasize that human and divine law gave the laity no authority over ecclesiastics, renewed the constitutions *Felicis* of Boniface VIII and *Si quis suadente* of Clement V and all other apostolic decrees aimed against those who should seek to destroy the liberties of the church.[105] Whether this was done as a result of supplication from England is not known. The four ecclesiastical ambassadors the king originally intended to send to the council were recalled before they left the realm, but it is clear they were men conservative in their attitude to state-church relations, and sympathetic to the papacy.[106] Even if they never reached Rome it cannot have escaped the notice of Leo X that there was a conflict with the state approaching in England and that conservatives within the church there would welcome a decree against inroads by secular justice into areas of ecclesiastical jurisdiction.

Amidst this acrimony there arose the celebrated Richard Hunne case. The story is well known and does not need extensive rehearsal here. Hunne, who had lost in eccesiastical court a suit over the payment of a mortuary, brought an action of *praemunire* in the king's bench in retaliation, hoping thereby, according to Sir Thomas More, to make a name for himself in legal records.[107] Certainly, from other evidence, he appears to have been an eager litigant but this, if we accept that his heretical tendencies have now been proven, very likely stemmed from a desire to embarrass the church, not from his being the spokesman of a pro-common law party fighting to overthrow ecclesiastical jurisdiction, as was once thought.[108] The case is important in the history of benefit of clergy because it created a climate in London strongly hostile to ecclesiastical courts and the fees they enforced, and thus against the church as a whole. Writing at the beginning of March 1515, soon after the coroner's inquest had returned its verdict on Hunne's death, Polydore Vergil noted that the people were exceedingly vexed with the clergy.[109]

In this period of resentment, at the time of the opening of the parliament in which the renewal of the act of 1512 would obviously be sought, the church mounted a counter-attack. Richard Kidderminster, abbot of Winchcombe,[110] selected by Bishop Fitzjames of London, whose prisoner Hunne had been, gave a sermon at St. Paul's Cross on the text 'touch not mine anointed'. He argued that the statute 4 Henry VIII c.2 was contrary to God's laws and the liberty of the church, and further that all those who had contributed to its drafting and promulgation should be subjected to ecclesiastical censure. He pointed out that by a decree, presumably that of the Lateran council of 5 May 1514, criminous clerks were exempt from temporal punishment by secular justices if in minor as well as major orders, since both were sacred. Since the decree of 1514 was no more than a rehearsal of constitutions of Boniface VIII and Clement V, neither of which had had any effect on the operation of benefit of clergy in England in their day, it seems that the novelty was in Kidderminster's interpretation or because the clergy were now receiving two decrees they had ignored before. Here undoubtedly was a dramatic attempt to reverse the church's policy, operative since 1462, of concentrating on the preservation of benefit of clergy for those of the rank of subdeacon and above while doing little to prevent its withdrawal from those in lesser orders.

Little wonder then that in response the king, at the request of the temporal lords and commons of parliament, took the novel step of causing the issue to be debated at Blackfriars, the monastery in the city of London, before the judges and his temporal legal advisers by the spiritual counsel of the clergy and his own. There the argument broadened to take in benefit of clergy as a whole rather than the merits of a single statute.[111] It was at this meeting that the warden of the mendicant friars in London, Dr. Henry Standish, gained notoriety when, as one of the king's spiritual counsel, he argued that bringing criminous clerks before temporal judges was both hallowed by custom and concordant with divine law and ecclesiastical liberties. Furthermore, said Standish, it was a successful legal device which benefited the public weal. When counsel for the clergy in answer pleaded a decree expressly to the contrary (viz which made convening clerks before a temporal judge for criminal causes a sin) Standish said such decrees were frequently ignored and that anyway this one had not been received in England and therefore was not binding. He made a sound case, one which, where it involved history, was quite correct. According to the author of the law report which provides nearly all our information about the incident, Standish then confounded his opponent's argument that Christ himself had insisted 'Nolite tangere Christos meos' and thereupon some of the knights of the lower house tried to persuade certain bishops that they should make Kidderminster openly renounce what he had said in his sermon. The prelates however firmly refused to do this.

Although at this point there must have been much activity, the seeking of new arguments and allies and the like, we have no factual knowledge of developments before the subsequent law term when Standish was summoned before a 'court of general convocation' and put to answer a number of articles offered against him by word of mouth. These interrogatories, which went to the heart of the differences between the two sides, asked whether a secular justice might summon clerks into his court, whether lower orders were sacred, whether a constitution ordained by the pope and clergy was binding in a region where usage was to the contrary, and fourthly whether a temporal prince could call bishops to account if they failed to castigate those they should.[112] Later the archbishop of Canterbury in the full court of convocation gave Standish some articles in written form naming a day he should make his answer. Realising the prelates had made a dead set at him, Standish complained to the king he was being persecuted because he had maintained the royal cause in the earlier debate. The clergy in reply said Standish was being put to answer because of some lectures he had given, not because of what he had said as one of the king's spiritual counsel. At this point, through the prompting of the house of commons, Standish obtained the intervention of the temporal lords and the judges. They asked the king to maintain his temporal jurisdiction in accord with his coronation oath and protect Standish, in his quarrel over the exemption of clerks, from the hostility of the clergy, King Henry thereupon asked the dean of his chapel, Dr. Vaisey, whether convening clerks before temporal judges was against the law of God and the liberties of the church as the bishops said. Vaisey answered that it was not.

Next the judges and the king's spiritual and temporal counsel, together with some members of the parliamentary lords and commons, assembled on the king's instructions at Blackfriars house once more. There the bill of conclusions, the articles laid against him by the archbishop of Canterbury, were read out and Standish was asked to answer. The gist of the charges was that he had said that minor orders were not holy, that exemption of the clergy from appearance before temporal judges was not supported by divine law, that ecclesiastical laws did not bind other than the recipients, and that laymen might punish clerks if bishops neglected to do so.[113] In reply Standish said he thought the last three articles were untrue. As to minor orders, he believed they were sacred in one respect in one respect but not in another; what he meant by this is not reported. On the crucial question of whether clerks might be called before temporal justices he said it was not against the divine law positive. On the very important issue of reception of decrees he argued that the law ecclesiastical had not been binding except where it was received; he did not explain what constituted proper reception. There was also some argument over the summoning of spiritual fathers before secular justices. Standish held that a temporal judge could call anyone before him, although he admitted that the citing of one's spiritual father was difficult to justify. Then Dr. Vaisey spoke in support of Standish's arguments, and in particular concerning the matter of reception of decrees.[114] He demonstrated how at one time secular priests had had wives. Later a decree had been made against it, one which had been received in England. But it had not been received in the east and such marriage was still practised there. He also offered two other arguments reminiscent of Standish's at the Blackfriars debate, neither being drawn from ecclesiastical law. The English custom of benefit of clergy was of continuous usage and secondly it was a practice necessary for the 'weal' of the realm. Finally he tried to define the relative authority of the secular justices and their ecclesiastical counterparts.

By this time the debate had become a head-on collision between church and state, the most crucial conflict for well over a century and probably the most important since the reign of Henry II. At issue was not only how criminous clerks should be tried but the authority of ecclesiastical courts and their judicial officers, and whether England should be exempt from parts of the Roman canon law. According to Keilway's report the judges, when Vaisey had finished, considered the arguments advanced by the two sides and 'made a full decision' that those who had cited Standish before convocation were liable to proceedings under the statute of praemunire.[115] They did not define the offence exactly but we may take it they thought the clergy had been guilty under 16 Richard II c.5 through obtaining or receiving from Rome bulls or instruments which harmed the king's regality. If this weapon was not powerful enough to obtain the clergy's submission the judges had one other. They said that the presence of the spiritual lords was not essential in parliament: their place there was not by reason of their spirituality but only because of their temporal possessions. The making of this threat reveals how the opposition to the renewal of the statute 4 Henry VIII c.2 must have stemmed from the prelates in the upper house of parliament. Very likely they had also been responsible for the defeat of a bill to restore the property of Richard Hunne to his children, a responsibility which would have increased episcopal unpopularity in the country at large.[116]

There then followed the final scene of the crisis, set by royal command at Baynard's Castle. At this assembly almost all the parliamentary lords were present, several members of the lower house, and all the judges and the king's spiritual and temporal counsel. This time the king presided so as 'to deal with the said cause'. The clergy made a last effort to win the day and used their most influential spokesman, the archbishop of York, Cardinal Wolsey. He assured the king that the clergy would never do anything in derogation of the king's prerogative, but then reaffirmed that all the clergy thought the convening of clerks before temporal justices was against the laws of God and the liberties of the church, which they were sworn to maintain. Realising, no doubt, that by now the voicing of the claims of the clergy had aroused the implacable hostility of the judges and those who provided legal counsel to the king, he attempted to capitalize on any sympathy Henry might have for the spirituality by requesting the issued be taken to the court of Rome for a decision by the pope. The king answered that he had been convinced by the arguments of Standish and his own spiritual counsel. Even at this stage the clergy, although on the defensive, were still ready to argue. William Warham, the archbishop of Canterbury, thinking no doubt of Becket, pointed out how the fathers of the church had opposed the usage of the law of the land in regard to clerical privilege and been willing to suffer martyrdom for so doing.[117] This implied that he at least would not be cowed into surrender. His statement was well countered by Chief Justice Fineux, who pointed out that the convening of clerks before temporal courts had had the support of both holy kings and holy fathers of the church, which they would not have given if they had believed it was contrary to the law of God. These words of Fineux demonstrate quite clearly that the stand the church was taking under Henry VIII was a volte-face from its attitude under earlier kings. The chief justice then turned to the very practical matter of how the church would deal with felons and murderers if, as the clergy wished, the secular justices handed over men taken for such offences on arrest. He pointed out that the canon law did not make provision for the trial of felons by the clergy. Why therefore should they claim them? 'To which', says the report, 'no answer was made'. Certainly it was a telling point. The time had come at last for the king to make a decision and he did so. It was one very much against the clergy. The English monarch, he said, had never had any superior but God and thus he, Henry, would yield nothing of his temporal jurisdiction. As for the authority of decrees, he said he had noticed how the spirituality themselves sometimes ignored them if they felt so inclined and thus they could not be held as binding. Pursuing the last glimmer of a chance, the archbishop of Canterbury asked that the king should not make his final decision until the clergy, at their own cost, had taken the issue (presumably the validity of the statute 4 Henry VIII c.2) to the Roman curia. To this the king gave no answer, but before the assembly was dismissed he extracted a promise from the bishops to dismiss Standish's case from the court of convocation.

While the assembly at Blackfriars was engaged in argument the clergy and their allies were fighting strongly in the second session of the 1515 parliament. The commons, who in the first session had passed a bill to renew the 1512 act on benefit of clergy, passed it a second time when progress was delayed. This duplicate bill reached the lords on 14 December 1515, to be given a first reading there three days later. However, on 22 December, before anything further was done, parliament was dissolved. The battle had ended roughly in a draw: neither the judges and their allies in parliament nor the ecclesiastics could claim a victory. There was no renewal of the act 4 Henry VIII c.2, neither was there to be exemption for all clerks from answering before secular justices initially, which notion the clergy at the end claimed was only a test question to determine if Standish was heretical, although in fact it had been first advocated by the spiritual counsel for the clergy at Blackfriars.[118] In so much as the church, by asking once more the old and fundamental question of whether clerics could properly be convented before a secular court, and thus questioning the whole development of benefit of clergy in the later middle ages had temporarily halted the steady erosion of clerical privilege, it could perhaps claim the struggle had ended slightly in its favour. Yet the clergy were treading a dangerous path, particularly when they asked if a constitution ordained by pope and clergy was binding in a country whose use was to the contrary, since the English kings throughout the middle ages had maintained their right to control the reception of all ecclesiastical decrees originating outside the realm when non-spiritual matters were involved. Furthermore, English usage on benefit of clergy was partly based on statute and there had never been any suggestion that anything could override a statute except another statute.

The church was challenging what may be called one of the fundamentals of the English constitution and by so doing, and refusing to play the moderate and acquiescent game it had in previous centuries, it was in danger of provoking a strong counter attack by the state. This threat the church may have been able to obviate by means of a papal decree issued in February 1516.[119] Noting that in England many men were receiving the first tonsure and minor orders not for the purpose of ascending to superior orders but so that they might commit crimes and avoid having to appear before secular justices, the pope stipulated that for the next five years no man was to be held a clerk in England unless he was promoted to all minor orders and the order of subdeacon at the same time or provided to an ecclesiastical benefice.[120] This meant that in the future there would be no one who became a clerk in minor orders only; all would of necessity be in holy orders. Thus that part of the clergy which the secular power blamed for so much crime and whose benefit from the clerical privilege it sought to erode would in time disappear, after, that is, those already in minor orders had taken higher ones or died. Very sensibly the church was intending to cut off the diseased limb so as to preserve the clerical privilege for the priesthood, an aim largely in accord with the demands of the clergy in the reign of Edward IV, although there was no renewal of the request for those in holy orders to be exempt from answering before temporal justices. What we do not know is whether the English government and the clergy accepted ('received') this decree: whether it was part of a compromise entered into by Henry's advisers and the papacy quite deliberately, or whether it was a sop offered to the former by the church because it had prevented the renewal of the statute 4 Henry VIII c.2. The results of the decree are equally unclear. It has been argued that the effects were negligible since episcopal registers show no increase in those ordained subdeacon in the period 1516-21, and furthermore clerks in minor orders continued to be convicted in secular courts and then delivered to the ordinary.[121] The thesis may be plausible but it does contain certain weaknesses. Such clerks may have been in minor orders already at the time of the 1516 decree, and there is no irrefutable reason why there should be an increase in those seeking entry to the rank of subdeacon if the former holders of minor orders were in fact as worthless and unspiritual as the prologue to the decree suggested. To argue that the decree was applied thoroughly would also be erroneous. Very likely the situation at the beginning of the 1520's was as Palsgrave, in his summary of Wolsey's proceedings, said it was: 'We have begun to send commandment to all ordinaries that they should give the lesser orders and subdeacon all at once'.[122]

The only other aspect of this church-state confrontation, so important in the history of benefit of clergy, which calls for comment, is the role of King Henry and his minister Wolsey. The crisis was caused by an attempt by the clergy to capitalize on Leo X's decree of 5 May 1514. Whether this was initiated by

Wolsey or by conservative members of the clergy on their own account cannot at the moment be determined. It is even possible that the decree was the result of lobbying by English ecclesiastics, but neither this nor whether it was done with Wolsey's blessing is clear either. The appearances are that the Hunne case accelerated some endeavour to seek redress for church grievances and made the protest take a more extreme form; further that ecclesiastics of a 'no compromise' disposition directed this assault with Wolsey only taking up the role of spokesman for the clergy when the king, stirred by the temporal lords to action, decided eventually in favour of the judges' arguments. Until the meeting at Baynard's Castle the king's role was a quiescent one, Henry not seemingly aware or very interested in what was at stake. To all outward appearances he had to be propelled into calling the two debates at Blackfriars. These conferences and the meeting at Baynard's Castle also pose a problem: what exactly was their nature? The first assembly at Blackfriars was called in order to have a debate between spiritual counsel of the king and that of the clergy in front of the judges of the two benches. It was a novelty, for although meetings of the judges to discuss knotty points of law and to agree on a policy for the handling of similar cases in the future were by no means unknown, to set the professional judges to decide an argument between experts in the canon law was new. Probably they were only there to discover ecclesiastical views on benefit of clergy in order to help them in dealing with such cases in the future. Even this, however, was new. Hitherto the king's temporal counsel, in whose ranks the judges naturally were, had interpreted the rules governing benefit of clergy very much as they liked. The second assembly at Blackfriars seems to have been a meeting of the judges and the king's other legal advisers to decide if the clergy, in making Standish appear and answer before convocation, had contravened the statutes of praemunire. There was no new principle involved here but there was when the judges decided the king could hold parliament without the lords spiritual. So important a constitutional decision had not been seen since the fourteenth century. The assembly at Baynard's Castle seems to have been summoned in order that the king could give his verdict in the case. The fact that most of the parliamentary lords were there as well as some of the commons, the judges, and the king's other legal advisers, suggests it was a meeting of the council afforced so that all sections of the community might see the submission of the clergy which was the desired conclusion of the whole episode. But the clergy did not act with humility at all. Instead they sought to reopen the argument and had to be answered harshly by the chief justice of the king's bench. Even when the king had delivered his decision the primate still tried to bargain; if Henry preserved his prerogative he certainly lost something in the way of majesty.

One of the last powers Cardinal Wolsey acquired in his capacity as legate was through a bull which gave him authority to arrange a more efficient way to degrade criminous priests. A number of the latter, so it appears, had been guilty in the period immediately preceding the issuing of the bull in May 1528, of committing atrocious crimes. For this, the church admitted, they ought to be degraded by ecclesiastical judges and delivered to their secular counterparts. However, because it had not been possible to muster the number of bishops required for degradation at the place where the crime was committed there had been no such procedure, and the laity had been highly critical of what they took to be the preservation of criminous priests from a duly deserved penalty of death. The bull permitted Wolsey henceforth to utilize, for the purpose of degrading, a single bishop together with two abbots or two 'worthy' seculars from cathedrals or colleges.[123] We do not possess any additional information about this wave of priestly felony or the circumstances leading to the request for the privilege but that it was Wolsey's emissaries in Rome who brought the matter to Pope Clement VII's attention is not in doubt.[124] That the offences were attributed to priests alone and not to men in minor orders is perhaps explained by the papal decree of February 1516, which had been intended to abolish the ranks below subdeacon unless concurrently held with those above.

Despite degradation from clerical status being an accepted method since the time of Glanvill of dealing with those clerks who failed in their attempt to purgate, it was a part of the laws governing benefit of clergy which had drawn little attention since the thirteenth century. The church clearly did not relish handing over those who failed in purgation to what was certain death and, judging by the contents of bishops' registers very few were delivered to the lay arm in the fifteenth and early sixteenth centuries. Wolsey seems to have intended to placate hostility towards his government by introducing procedures which would remove one ecclesiastical excuse for failing to degrade. How effective the reform was we cannot tell. Very likely the issue was lost sight of in the welter of ecclesiastical change brought about by the Reformation Parliament. Yet degradation of clerks did make two appearances in the subsequent decade. In a case in king's bench at Michaelmas term 1532 mention was made that certain gentlemen had criticized the conviction of a priest for treason and his subsequent execution because there had been no degradation. Then in 1536 the clergy of the northern convocation, answering a number of articles which had been addressed to them, said that in their opinion no clerk ought to be put to death without degradation by the laws of the church.[125] The similarity between the two instances is clear. In neither case was the king or his lawyers involved; both concerned the feeling at large that no priest should be executed without being degraded from his order, a popular tradition which reflected accurately what the clergy had claimed from the thirteenth century.

Whatever the effect of the bull of 12 February 1516, the privilege of benefit of clergy suffered no other diminution during the period that Wolsey was in power, but from the time of his fall to the end of the reign there were a good number of alterations all of which restricted its effects. The acts which made these amendments, despite the omens of 1514–16, were not at the heart of the redefinition of church-state relationships. There was no one statute which revamped benefit of clergy in all its aspects, no attempt to settle the favoured position of the clerk, either beneficially or detrimentally, once and for all. Alteration was piecemeal and *ad hoc*, suggesting beliefs in governmental circles, in parliament and in the country at large, that there were elements of the system which should be preserved. Most easily distinguished among the changes which legislation accomplished was the creation of new felonies which permitted no benefit for those who would be found guilty of their commission, and the removal of clerical privilege from certain established felonies. Secondly there was the group of three statutes which made clear distinction in their provisions between the procedure to be followed if the offender was in holy orders and if he was only in minor orders. Thirdly there was the taking away of benefit of clergy from those in minor orders in regard to murder and certain types of robbery, the extension of branding of those who took to their clergy to men in holy orders,[126] and the establishing of a procedure whereby the records of a convicted clerk were to be certified into the king's bench and to the ordinary to whom he was committed.

Perhaps the most important single statute was 23 Henry VIII c.1. One reason for its importance was that it restored 4 Henry VIII c.2, which the prelates had prevented being renewed in the parliament of 1515. It stipulated that for those who committed petty treason, wilful murder, highway robbery, stole from churches or holy places or dwelling houses where the owner or members of his household were present, burned houses or barns where grain was stored, were not to have benefit of clergy if they were below the rank of sub-deacon; nor were accessaries before or after the fact. The only real differences from the earlier act in regard to offences covered lay in the inclusion of petty treason and the burning of barns; the latter was no doubt prompted by notorious cases which had just occurred, although petty treason was probably there because of the form of medieval legislation on the subject.[127] It came at a time when Christopher St. German was noticing much criticism by ecclesiastics in sermons and elsewhere of the putting of priests to answer before laymen.[128] In several ways relating to procedure the statute went far beyond its precursor of 1512. Its second and third sections took up the theme of the extensive preamble to the act, where the first had in fact dealt with something quite different. This notion was that as yet, despite efforts made in 1275 and 1403,[129] there existed no law which prevented bishops from freeing clerks convict or allowing them to make purgation improperly; and that as a result they were speedily setting at large manifest thieves and murderers despite 'proveable evidence' against them. The second section stipulated therefore that sub-deacons and above who were convicted of the crimes mentioned in the first were only to be allowed to purgate if they found sureties, presumably for their future good behaviour: these, with the prisoner, were bound in a total sum of £80. The third section of the act was intended to deny purgation in future to those who sought to plead their clergy after they had been convicted, outlawed or had confessed the offence. This, it can be seen, was very likely to end the common late medieval practice of pleading of clergy after a jury had returned a verdict of guilty. In its fourth section the statute achieved something equally novel. It became the first piece of legislation to make a pronouncement on degradation, allowing the ordinary by himself to degrade a clerk convict. If this was done then the clerk was to be sent with a certificate of his degrading into the king's bench, where the judges were to repeat the original judgment and the prisoner executed. All in all, one of the most noteworthy legal features of the act was the way it continued and extended the notion first mooted in the late fifteenth century of restricting benefit of clergy to those in holy orders only. Viewed politically, of course, the legislating of a more powerful version of the statute whose renewal had been opposed so bitterly by the church nearly two decades before catches the eye. The second aspect which should take our attention was the sensible way the vexed problem of purgation was handled. It was not forbidden, but the size of the sums demanded as surety were likely to restrict purgation to a much smaller number than heretofore. Also, making clerks plead their clergy early on in their appearances before lay courts was more likely to result in convictions by inquests made hostile by that very plea. All this would mean great increase in the number of clerks who were subjected to an extended period of imprisonment in the ordinary's gaol, particularly since the act failed to put any pressure on the ordinary to use the sanction of degradation.

However well intentioned it was, the act revealed within the space of two years a disastrous weakness in its wording which had to be corrected by further legislation. The chief deficiency was in its first section, where the statute, in referring to the various types of offence it was intended to combat, spoke only of those who were found guilty of the same. The result was that offenders quickly discovered they could not be deprived of benefit of clergy, as one who was found guilty could, if on arraignment they stood mute and refused to plead or would make no direct answer or challenged peremptorily more than twenty of the jurors. Presumably having adopted these modes of defence they waited until the justices summarily declared them convicted, and then they claimed their clergy. Offenders against 23 Henry VIII c.1 could apparently also obtain benefit of clergy if they were tried in a county other than the one where their misdeed had been committed. The closure of this fortuitous loophole and the one connected with pleading were thus effected by the statute 25 Henry VIII c.3. There was another act besides the latter which had several close connections in ideas and terminology with 23 Henry VIII c.1. This was 23 Henry VIII c.11, 'an acte for breking of prison by Clerkes convicte', which in order to discourage escapes from the bishop's prison made such behaviour felonious. Those who contravened the act were to be denied benefit of clergy unless they held the ecclesiastical rank of subdeacon, deacon or priest. However, even these offenders, when convicted and delivered to the ordinary, were to be denied purgation. Another connection with the act 23 Henry VIII c.1 was the provision for the degrading of such clerks. Again the ordinary was given authority to 'disgrade' offenders as he thought fit and then to send them into king's bench 'with letters witnessing his disgrading'. Clearly the aim was to give support to the scheme of favouring imprisonment in bishops' prisons as visualized in the earlier act.

The statute 23 Henry VIII c.11 created a new felony and at the same time prevented all those who were not in holy orders and who offended against it from gaining benefit from their clergy. Three other Henrician acts put new felonies into the statute book but these denied the clerical privilege not merely to the majority of clerks but to all.[130] By 25 Henry VIII c.6 buggery 'with mankind or beast', because as yet there was no sufficient or 'condigne' punishment for it, was made a felony and one without benefit of clergy for offenders.[131] This act was apparently drafted by the judges and may therefore reflect their opinion that the clerical privilege should be denied to all.[132] This sin 'contra naturam' as the ecclesiastical law called it, had in theory been dealt with by church courts, although in practice it seems very few offenders had ever been put on trial.[133] A second act in the category was 31 Henry VIII c.14, designed for 'abolishing diversity in Opynions'. It forbade benefit of clergy for those who contravened any of its first three sections: these concerned denying transubstantiation, affirming or teaching things which contradicted the other five articles of faith, or simply being discovered a second time to hold an opinion which was contrary. Such offences were viewed by the crown as being the equivalent of heresy before the break with Rome, and indeed were referred to as such elsewhere in the act. Because medieval heretics were dealt with in ecclesiastical courts there had been no former use of benefit of clergy in this regard, but now such errant beliefs were classified as felony, and authority over the matter was vested in both bishops and laity, and their powers as commissioners enabled them to proceed as for felony under the common law. Thus the question of benefit naturally arose and had to be decided. The act was not entirely concerned with matters of dogma. Its twentieth section dealt with priests who kept concubines. One who offended in this way a second time was to be held a felon and be deprived of the benefit of his clergy. This was a traditional offence among the priesthood and was dealt with as such; there was no general distinction made in the act between offenders who might be in holy orders and those who were not. The third Henrician statute which created a novel felony and barred any benefit of clergy was 33 Henry VIII c.8 'against conjuracions and witchcraftes and sorcery and enchantments'. It was directed against those who by such methods sought to provoke 'unlawful love', discover where stolen goods had been hidden, destroy a person in body or goods 'or for any other unlawfull intente or purpose'. To be an accessary before or after the fact was also made felonious. It is quite possible the act arose out of the practising of 'astronomye and necromancie' by John Heron, bastard brother of Giles Heron, which was investigated in September 1540. The council believed he had contravened the 'prohibition of the late Erle of Essex'. If this was so then Thomas Cromwell deserves some small credit for the act of 1542, but there may have been another contributory factor. In July 1540 Lord Hungerford was thought to have been guilty both of incest and of practising magic and invoking devils.[134] Again the crimes covered by the act were those which in previous centuries had been left for the church to deal with,[135] unless, that is, the attempt to destroy a person had been directed against the king, when it was regarded as felony or treason.[136] Coke argued that the medieval writers of legal treatises said the penalty for sorcery was death by burning, thereby implying it was a form of heresy, and he quoted the Margery Jourdemain case of 1442 in their support. There is evidence from the earlier fourteenth century to substantiate this viewpoint.[137]

The growing practice of restricting the use of benefit of clergy was further strengthened in this period by statutes which denied it to those who committed three types of existing felonies. In one case an administrative change was obviously responsible. By the act 27 Henry VIII c.4 those suspected of committing robberies, murders or other felonies at sea, who hitherto had been tried before the admiral or his lieutenant under the civil laws, were ordered to be tried under the common law but without benefit of clergy. Since its establishment in the mid-fourteenth century, trial of criminal cases in the admiral's court had been according to the civil law, under which there was no common law system of claiming privilege. The new regulation, therefore, cannot have seemed at the time to be introducing a more severe climate. A statute passed in the same session, 27 Henry VIII c.17, removed the clerical privilege from any servant who should steal, feloniously take away without his master's assent or convert to his own use, goods entrusted to his care worth more than forty shillings. The parliamentary bill in its original version had allowed benefit to those in higher orders; its removal may have been the work of the parliamentary commons[138] The third type of felon who lost his benefit was the horse stealer. The second section of the act 37 Henry VIII c.8 took it away from those who had judgment against them for this offence. The drafters, remembering how the act 25 Henry VIII c.3 had been necessary to supplement 23 Henry VIII c.1, constructed the statute so it would apply to those whose guilt had been proven by confession, by their standing mute or by their challenging peremptorily more than 20 jurors, as well as those convicted by jury. The only feature of the statute in its relation to benefit of clergy which stands out as quite novel is the final phrase. Those who had judgment against them were not only to forgo benefit of clergy but were to 'suffer death as if not a clerk', a statement so forthright as to the penalty to be inflicted that it had no earlier parallel.

There were three statutes promulgated in the later Henrician period which were not concerned with particular felonies either old or new, but which made important modifications in the general operation of benefit of clergy. The earliest was 28 Henry VIII c.1 which, having extended to the end of the next parliament the life of three esisting statutes touching benefit (23 Henry VIII c.1, 25 Henry VIII c.3 and 25 Henry VIII c.6), went on to introduce changes of great consequence namely that offenders against them who were in holy orders were in future to be liable to the same penalties and dangers for their offences as other persons admitted to their clergy, which meant they would not be able to claim their privilege if they committed petty treason, wilful murder, robbery of churches, highway robbery, robbery in houses when the owner was at home, the burning of barns containing grain, or sodomy. Nor would they if, when arraigned in a county other than where the offence was committed for larceny of goods, they stood mute, would not answer directly or challenged peremptorily over twenty jurors. The statute 32 Henry VIII c.3, which made 28 Henry VIII c.1 perpetual, ordered those in holy orders should be branded as others who had their clergy were. They were to suffer pains, dangers and forfeitures as did lay persons. This probably meant they lost the right to have purgation, not that they were to be treated in every way like claimants of clergy who were not in holy orders. Perhaps in the years since special treatment for subdeacons and above had first been mooted it had become the practice to give them more gentle treatment than others. The third statute in the category was concerned with legal records. The fact that no convicted clerk could thenceforward have his clergy a second time made it doubly imperative for records of those claiming and being granted benefit to be kept carefully and the information be made available to justices before whom privilege of clergy was sought on a subsequent occasion. The act 34/5 Henry VIII c.14 was clearly drafted for this purpose. Its preamble made mention of the records of outlawed and convicted clerks being 'embecyled' and 'not certified into any place certain'; the act therefore stipulated that clerks of the crown, peace or assize should, as soon as the prisoner had been convicted, certify a brief transcript concerning the tenor of the offence, the effect of any outlawry, indictment or conviction 'and the certeyntie of the saide felonye or other offence',[139] the day and place of outlawry, conviction or attaint, and the day and place of the felony, to the king's bench within forty days. Another transcript of the indictment was to be delivered to the ordinary who had received custody of the prisoner after conviction. By this arrangement the clerk of the crown in the king's bench would, as the act stated, be able to certify the names of previously convicted or outlawed clerks and the type of felony to the justices of the peace or gaol delivery who now had before them felons suspected of taking to their clergy on a previous occasion.[140] The value of this act in ensuring courts were not made to look foolish is obvious. The crown's intention, or rather the design of the drafter, was not simply that, however. A basic reason for the act was to prevent offenders obtaining their benefit a second time and thereby depriving the king of his proper escheats, which was the first occasion in the history of clerical privilege that a relevant act had made reference to such a mundane matter.[141]

Did any new principles in the handling of benefit of clergy emerge in the later Henrician years? The evidence suggests they did. Turning, by statute, felonies which had formerly carried benefit into ones that did not, had been practised since the early years of Henry VII. Preventing by statute clerks from pleading and obtaining clergy for a second felony (i.e subsequently to obtaining it for an earlier one) had started with the act 4 Henry VII c.13. On the other hand the attempts to restrict purgation and discourage escape from the gaol of ordinaries (23 Henry VIII cc.1 and 11) were the first statutory measures in that field, and acts which in creating new felonies specifically banned benefit of clergy were unknown before the 1530s. So also were laws aimed at removing the special position of those in holy orders. Such beneficial status was granted in regard to certain felonies by the acts 23 Henry VIII cc.1 and 11, but only five years later policy changed and the privilege was removed by 28 Henry VIII c.1. Then in 1540 by 32 Henry VIII c.3 it was stipulated those in holy orders who were admitted to their clergy were to be burned in the hand as lay clerks were. They may even have lost the right to have purgation, but it seems unlikely they were to be treated for all felonies exactly as literate laymen and those in minor orders, otherwise there would be no purpose in making acts like 23 Henry VIII c.1 and 25 Henry VIII c.3 perpetual as they were at this time. Another novelty of the period was a reduction of the clerical privilege by means of a proclamation. This was issued on 18 April 1538 and designed *inter alia* to deprive those (and their accessaries) who hurt, maimed, slew or murdered any royal officer seeking to arrest them, or slew or murdered 'by reason of sudden foins with swords'.[142] Most other substantial changes hitherto, or at least since the fourteenth century, in the operation of benefit of clergy had been by means of statute, but since no life or limb was threatened (rather the reverse) there was no rule forbidding the policy. Murderers, whoever their victim, had been excluded from benefit of clergy by 23 Henry VIII c.1, although nothing was said in that act about accessaries. Those who hurt or maimed a royal official were by this proclamation held to be committing the equivalent of a felony in that they were to forfeit all lands, goods and chattels, but were to suffer perpetual imprisonment, not death. Those who committed manslaughter through their 'sudden foins' together with the murderers of royal officials were to be executed. Possibly the key to the proclamation is to be found in one further phrase: the killers were not to be allowed pardon. The granting of the latter was always held by the king to be central element of his prerogative and therefore a suitable subject for the crown to proclaim about. Thus the exclusion of such privileges as sanctuary and clergy may therefore have been uncalculatingly incidental. On the other hand the forbidding of pardon may have been included not simply to bar a way by which troublesome criminals could avoid their just deserts, but as a precedent for some future royal policy. If so it was never implemented. Finally in regard to new instruments there was the scheme to provide justices, having before them men claiming clergy whom they suspected might have successfully obtained it for an earlier offence, with the means to discover if their suspicions were correct. Whether the act (34/5 Henry VIII c.14) simply gave formal approval to a system which had developed piecemeal over the years or whether it was the new brainchild of some legal adviser to the crown we cannot tell. Whatever its nature the statute was a well designed and very necessary piece of reform, bringing all justices closer to the king's bench and thus correcting other weaknesses as well as abuse of benefit of clergy. It is surprising Thomas Cromwell had not instituted something similar.

The change in political climate occasioned by the accession of Edward VI resulted in a wholesale alteration of the laws designed to enforce the religious changes of the two previous decades. One of the most striking of these changes was accomplished in the first parliamentary session of the reign by the celebrated 'Acte for the Repeale of certaine statutes concerninge Treasons, Felonyes etc.' (1 Edward VI c.12). The design of the bill, so it has been argued, was essentially the work of Protector Somerset himself, who was keen to provide a greater degree of liberty for the populace, believing, if we accept the preamble to the statute as reflecting his own political philosophy, that the times were more suited to laws mild enough to move the subject to obedience out of love rather than fear.[143] The act had not one but several sections relevant to the history of benefit of clergy. The ninth paragraph stipulated there should be no benefit of clergy for those convicted of murder, poisoning, breaking into houses with residents within, highway robbery, stealing horses or thieving from churches or chapels; nor if they confessed, would not answer directly, stood mute, or challenged too many jurors peremptorily. For all other felonies benefit of clergy was to be allowed as it had been at the outset of the reign of Henry VIII. In essence this 'act of repeals', as it has been called,[144] confirmed the major part of the statute 23 Henry VIII c.1 and of 28 Henry VIII c.1 which continued it, and excluded from benefit those in holy orders as well. Petty treason and the burning of houses or of barns containing grain and the rule which forbade clergy if a bishop thought any offender was a heretic, a committer of sacrilege or apostate, were all omitted in 1547. So also was the section of 23 Henry VIII c.1 which excepted from clergy for the listed offences accessaries before the fact as well as principals.[145] For all felonies other than those we have mentioned the statute 1 Edward VI c.12 stipulated benefit of clergy should be permitted as it had been in 1509.[146] Such a rule would not have affected the four felonies newly created in Henry VIII's reign because they did not allow the privilege but in any case the third section of the act repealed all new felonies created by statute since 1509. Then a later section of the act, the eighteenth, made an exception to this last rule by confirming 27 Henry VIII c.17, the law about servants who embezzled their masters' property. Old offences from which statutes of the previous reign removed the privilege had numbered two: 37 Henry VIII c.8 removed it from horse thieves and 27 Henry VIII c.4 deprived pirates. While the privilege was made available once more for stealers of horses, pirates may not have been so lucky. Hale argued that 1 Edward VI c.12 did not restore benefit in trials of piracy because the crime was not known to the common law as a felony.[147]

Deciding which felonies should be clergyable in the future may have been the most important pronouncement which the Edwardian 'act of repeals' made, but there were two other major and very different alterations to the granting of clerical privilege. One made the concession that a peer of the realm sitting in parliament might, on a request by the house of lords alleging he was in fact a peer, claim benefit of clergy for any felony save murder or poisoning.[148] This privilege was to be awarded even if the peer could not read, and conviction with benefit was not to result in the loss of inheritance or corruption of the blood. It was to be allowed once only and the recipients were to be branded on the hand and used 'as clerks convict which may make purgation'. Trial of a peer, according to another section of the act, was to be held before other peers. Those responsible for suggesting this act and obtaining its promulgation can only have been the members of the house of lords themselves. Why they felt the need to protect themselves from the penalties for felony by means of benefit of clergy cannot be determined from direct evidence. The concession does not seem to have had any close connection with any particular type of crime mentioned elsewhere in the act. Perhaps for the first time the nobility felt exposed to punishment for its felonies. Although the trial of a peer for felony had been of great rarity in the later middle ages at least two had occurred in Henry VIII's later years.[149] At that time the peers must have been much perturbed, but they took no action; in 1547 on the other hand, they had the weight because of the changing political and religious circumstances to do something about the danger, something in fact very drastic. Very noticeable was the proviso that in claiming their newly acquired clergy the peers should suffer no loss of inheritance or corruption of blood, reminding us that these concessions would be considered quite as valuable as the protection of life itself. In regard to the history of benefit of clergy, the most striking part of this section of the act was the way the privilege might be obtained even though the peer had no claim at all to clerical status. A new principle was established, or rather the earlier carefully guarded rule of demanding literacy was coolly breached without any semblance of an excuse. How any lawyer, if such was involved in the drafting of the bill, could justify this novelty from legal precedent is difficult to imagine. Presumably the numbers of laity who were seen to escape their death through a small knowledge of letters had made men cynical about the religious nature of the privilege.

Another major break with tradition was in allowing benefit of clergy to the bigamous. The act stated the privilege should be permitted to those who had been married 'divers and sondry times' to single women or widows and even to those married to two wives or more, that is to say were bigamous in the twentieth century sense. The medieval rule, as we have seen, had been that marrying a widow or marrying a second time subsequent to the death of his first wife deprived a man of his clergy. Now marriage even more than twice was not to jeopardize the clerical privilege, nor was being married to more than one woman at a time.[150] Probably the designers of the act were influenced by a reform proposed in convocation at this time (December 1547), namely that canons, laws, statutes and decrees forbidding or condemning matrimony because of any vow of priesthood, widowhood or chastity, should be void.[151] Beneficiaries and perhaps instigators of this part of the statute were likely to have included those who in rescent years had been in exile because of their religious beliefs and although married had taken new wives while abroad.[152]

The wideness of the act 1 Edward VI c.12, taking in as it did what were reckoned to be over-severities in many parts of the criminal law, was likely to lead to some confusion and need for clarification. This indeed was what happened with benefit of clergy. The section which denied the privilege to those who had committed murder and highway robbery had also refused it to those who feloniously stole horses, mares and geldings. The original act on horse stealing, 37 Henry VIII c.8, had sensibly referred to 'stealing an horse' but in 1 Edward VI c.12 this tightness had given way to a much slacker draft which spoke of horses, geldings or mares in the plural. According to Hale the judges, apparently very keen to keep to the exact letter of the law wherever possible, soon took the opportunity to allow benefit to a man who had stolen only a single horse. This strict interpretation of the statute led to an amendment of the law. The act 2/3 Edward VI c.33, pointing out how unclear the matter was, stipulated clergy should not be available in future to the stealer of one horse any more than it was to he who had taken two. There were two other deficiencies in the 'act of repeals' which also gave rise to supplementary statutes. Doubt arose as to whether clergy should be allowed to those robbing from a dwelling house when the owner or occupier, his family and his servants, were either asleep or not in the room where the offence occurred.[153] There was also the question of whether those who robbed from booths or tents at markets, the owner and his family being within, were subject to the same law as those who robbed from houses. The act 5/6 Edward VI c.9 therefore declared that offenders in such cases should lose benefit of clergy, ensuring they should be treated as those who infringed in a similar way the act of the first year of Edward's reign. The second weakness in the latter act for which remedy had to be found later was where it made void the Henrician statute 25 Henry VIII c.3,[154] which ensured there should be no benefit of clergy for murderers, highway robbers, burglars, horse thieves and the rest, even if they were taken and convicted outside the county where the crime was committed. Many miscreants were taking advantage of this loophole, presumably through moving soon after the commission of the offence into another shire. The deficiency was therefore remedied by a statute (5/6 Edward VI c.10), which revived and confirmed 25 Henry VIII c.3.

Three other Edwardian statutes also made significant changes in benefit of clergy. The act 2/3 Edward VI c.2 took it away from any soldier who quit his captain without the licence of his military superiors when in enemy country or on garrison duty or with booty: this was really a clarification of the act 7 Henry VII c.1 which had refused clergy simply to soldiers who quit the king's service without the licence of their captain. The statute 2/3 Edward VI c.29, which replaced the repealed statute 25 Henry VIII c.6 in making buggery punishable by death once more (although this time without the loss of goods or lands), denied the benefit of their clergy to all such offenders. Worthy of our notice was how the drafters of the act refused to call the crime felony: miscreants were to be executed like felons and justices of the peace were to hear and determine such cases 'as in felony'. Presumably there was still some reluctance to treat the crime as a secular one. The third statute was one concerned with the persistent and dangerous problem of riot. This was 3/4 Edward VI c.5, which stipulated that should a band of twelve or more persons try to destroy park enclosures, fishponds, dovecotes, houses, barns, stacks of corn, or deer, and when commanded by authority to retire stay together for an hour or more, they should be held felons and be deprived of benefit of clergy; so should those who summoned such assemblies or incited groups of men numbering from two to twelve to kill others or smash down enclosures. This was a new felony and it followed in the tradition of the previous reign when all statutes creating new felonies, after 1530 at least, had excluded offenders from having benefit of clergy.

One of the more important issues in sixteenth century criminal law, although it has received scant attention from historians, was the position of accessaries. For our purpose it is important to notice that the relationship between accessaries to felony and benefit of clergy came to the forefront in the early 1550s. The judges of the two benches, who as we have seen were probably eager to restrict benefit of clergy where they could, in this case set the words of a statute above their desire to punish criminals. The instance concerned the act 1 Edward VI c.12 and although it occurred at Lent term 1554 it probably reflected the judicial attitude of the previous reign as well.[155] There was a discussion in the king's bench as to whether the justices had been correct in allowing benefit to an accessary in a case of horse-stealing. It was agreed they were because the statute was to be taken strictly and in denying the privilege to those committing the specified offences it was intended to refer only to principals since counsellors, abettors or receivers received no mention. Of course if the principal in any other felonious offence asked for and received his clergy it did not save the accessary from arraignment. This was a rule of long standing and it was confirmed in a case discussed in the king's bench in 4 Edward VI.[156]

Two other aspects of Edwardian legislation also demand consideration. One is the statutory general pardon. If we consider those dating from the later years of Henry VIII together with those of his son's reign a changing attitude to benefit of clergy becomes apparent. Thus 26 Henry VIII c.18 actually excepted convicted or attainted persons in the custody of the ordinary from pardon. Those of 1539 (32 Henry VIII c.49), 1545 (35 Henry VIII c.18) and 1547 (1 Edward VI c.15) on the other hand allowed the privilege to such offenders. The general pardon of 1549 (2/3 Edward c.39) went further still and actually gave preferential treatment to those who had claimed benefit, stipulating bishops should release convicted or attainted clerks in their custody without the prisoner being put to the trouble of sueing out his pardon. At this point the trend stopped. The final general pardon of the reign, 7 Edward VI c.14, did not exclude convicted clerks unless they were guilty of escape but neither did it favour them especially. The other law which had an apparent bearing on benefit of clergy affected it in fact very little. This was 2/3 Edward VI c.1 which gave approval to the new ordinal and thereby to the elimination of minor ecclesiastical orders. It did not alter the law of benefit because by this time the privilege went either to those in holy orders only or to all who could pass the test of literacy. No statute allowed those in minor orders alone to claim clergy, nor was there one which restricted it to those in holy or minor orders together.

The reign of Queen Mary was a period of relatively little change in matters pertaining to clerical privilege. There were four relevant statutes enacted. One annulled a section of the Edwardian 'act of repeals', one created a new felony which did not carry benefit of clergy; a third statute was concerned with denying clergy to a single named miscreant and was thus quite distinct, and a fourth extended benefit to cover accessaries to offences whose principals were already dealt with in an existing act. The first of these was 1/2 Philip and Mary c.8, which was intended to repeal 'all statutes articles and provisions made against the Apostolic See since 20 Henry VIII'. It abrogated the fifth and sixth sections of 1 Edward VI c.12 about challenging the king's title as supreme head of the English church and 'all other clauses tending to the derogation of the supremacy of the Pope's holiness or see of Rome'. Sir William Staunford, who should have known, stated two years after the event that the Marian act had abrogated thereby the section of the Edwardian act which dealt with bigamy because the latter was derogatory to the church council of Lyons, where Pope Boniface VIII had issued the decretal which had become the basis of English common law practice on bigamy in regard to claims of benefit of clergy: thus it was derogatory to papel supremacy.[157] There is no suggestion the act repealed any other part of 1 Edward VI c.12, such as the permitting of peers to claim benefit.

In the same session of parliament was also passed an act (1/2 Philip and Mary c.4) which was intended to punish those calling themselves Egyptians, who after being banished by Henry VIII were now returning and taking up once more their livelihood of palmistry. It was decided that if they remained in England for more than one month or in some cases 40 days they were to be deemed felons and were not to be allowed privilege of clergy. There was nothing really novel in this; it was simply the creation of a new felony and making it non-clergyable at the same time. Another part of the statute on the other hand was designed to clarify the position of accessaries. It deliberately excluded accessaries from any legal guilt and thus from any necessity of seeking the privilege of their clergy. The third statute of the reign which concerned benefit of clergy, 2/3 Philip and Mary c.17, was very different from the others. It took the form of a petition by a private party. The petitioner, Margery Rufford, complained that one Benedict

Smith had maliciously obtained the indictment of her husband, Giles, for robbery. When Rufford had been acquitted Smith had brought a writ of appeal against him and then hired men who had murdered him. Margery Rufford's petition begged further that Smith, if he was indicted or appealed as an accessary to the murder and was found guilty or the equivalent, should not be allowed benefit of clergy. Rather remarkably the petition was turned into an act as it stood. Clearly it had revealed what was considered a grave weakness in the law. The result was the promulgation in the next session of parliament of an act deliberately designed to deprive all such accessaries before the fact of their clergy and for offences other than murder as well. This was the statute 4/5 Philip and Mary c.4 which was intended to restore a section of 23 Henry VIII c.1 (omitted by 1 Edward VI c.12) by specifically stipulating that accessaries before the fact (commanding or counselling the offence) in crimes of petty treason, wilful murder, highway robbery, robbery from dwelling houses, and the burning of any house or barn containing grain, who were found guilty, were outlawed, stood mute at arraignment, challenged over twenty jurors peremptorily or refused to answer directly, should not be permitted benefit of clergy.

The reign of Elizabeth cannot be said to have been a time of crucial importance in the history of benefit of clergy. The big issues were by now mostly settled and the story of the clerical privilege in the last four decades of the sixteenth century was largely one of benefit being denied in statutes which brought into being new felonies or redefined old ones. Nonetheless there were three statutory alterations in the law of clerical benefit of more than average importance in the first half of the reign. These were contained in the acts 1 Elizabeth c.1, (the act of supremacy) 8 Elizabeth c.4, and 18 Elizabeth c.7. Essentially the 1559 statute was one of repeal and its prime object was 1/2 Philip and Mary c.8. On the face of it we would therefore expect benefit of clergy to be permitted once more to the bigamous, as provided by 1 Edward VI c.12, but that this was in fact achieved is by no means clear. Although in its first section 1 Elizabeth c.1 restored those statutes directed against the holy see since 20 Henry VIII which 1/2 Philip and Mary c.8 had annulled, it stated in a later section that if the acts repealed by the Marian act were not revived specificallly (i.e. by name) then they were still annulled. 1 Edward VI c.12 was in fact not mentioned by name and was in theory therefore still void. However, Ferdinando Pulton in his *De Pace Regis et Regni* commenting on the repeal of the Marian act by 1 Elizabeth c.1 added somewhat cryptically 'for the which and some other causes it is agreed and holden for lawe, that the before rehearsed statute of 1 Edward VI doth stand and remaine in force, and Bigamus shall have his Clergie'.[158] Pulton's 'it is agreed and holden for lawe' suggests that there was more than one interpretation of the Elizabeth act and that there had at some point been considerable debate on the matter. What the arguments and who the protagonists were we do not know, but that the legislation had been imprecise and badly drafted cannot be denied. Sir Matthew Hale in the seventeenth century, noting Staunford's doubts as to whether 1/2 Philip and Mary c.8 repealed 1 Edward VI c.12 on bigamy and benefit of clergy, claimed that 'the law hath been sufficiently settled in this point', that 1 Elizabeth c.1 did repeal the relevant section of 1/2 Philip and Mary c.8 and that therefore 1 Edward VI c.12 from 1559 stood renewed.[159] He then introduced a note of uncertainty and confusion once more by adding the words 'if at all impeached (i.e. 1 Edward VI c.12) or repealed by 1/2 Philip and Mary'. What seems to have brought Hale to the view that the Edwardian act was restored was in fact less his interpretation of the meaning of the statutes than a case in Dyer's reports.[160] This concerned an appeal of rape brought at Trinity term 1561 by Ellen Lambe against one R.P.. The accused was convicted but, being known to be a clerk and a bigamist, was found entitled to have his clergy 'as the law is now'.[161]

The next statute with an important bearing on the clerical privilege was 8 Elizabeth c.4, whose second section established the position of those who obtained benefit for one felony having also committed other non-clergyable felonies. It was clearly set forth that for the latter offences they should be indicted (or appealed) and arraigned regardless of their gaining benefit for the other offence. Of course in practice this put great power into the hands of the secular justices, for they might now arrange to have a man suspected of many felonies, of which some were clergyable and some not, indicted and arraigned on separate occasions for the two different types so that one claim for benefit would not serve for all.[162] Thus the statute repealed 25 Edward III st.6 c.5, which had insisted men should be put to answer all charges outstanding against them on a single occasion.

The third Elizabethan statute concerned with ecclesiastical benefit which affected procedure in a general way rather than in regard to a particular felony was the relatively well known 18 Elizabeth c.7. In its second clause this act stipulated that those who in future were permitted benefit of clergy and burned in the hand should not thereupon be delivered to the ordinary but set at liberty, although the secular justices before whom they had been tried might, if they wished, first keep them in gaol for up to a year.[163] The reason for this, as avowed in the preamble to the act, was to avoid perjury and 'other Abuses' in the purgation of clerks convict. Imprisoning under secular jurisdiction those who were allowed their clergy or setting them free was a crucial alteration in the operation of the clerical privilege, diminishing to a very minor level the role of the ordinary in such cases. All that was now left to the bishop and his representative was the giving of an opinion in the lay court as to the accused's literacy. The fifth section of the act dealt with the multiple offender again. It decreed that persons who had been allowed their clergy for one offence might then be tried for any other felony of which they were indicted or appealed and if found guilty punished as though they were clerks convict who had been delivered to the ordinary and made their purgation. The intention of this part of the statute was apparently to clarify what had been said in 8 Elizabeth c.4 about those who had committed both clergyable and non-clergyable felonies. The principal alteration concerned what should happen to them when subsequently put to answer for the non-clergyable felonies. By 8 Elizabeth c.4 they were, after arraignment, to be 'ordered and used in all things according to the laws and statutes of this realm in such manner and form as though no such admission to clergy had been made' i.e. treated as laymen, but by 18 Elizabeth c.7 they were to suffer execution as they should have done 'if as a clerk or clerks convict they had been delivered to the ordinary, and there had made his or their due purgation' i.e. be treated as purged clergy. The latter formula acknowledged to some degree the obtaining of benefit for an earlier felony, while the former ignored the event entirely. Perhaps the ecclesiastics had made some protest at the way their role had been slighted in 8 Elizabeth c.4, or perhaps having so severely reduced the involvement of the bishop in section two of 18 Elizabeth c.7 the drafters felt obliged to make some deferential reference to delivery to the ordinary and to purgation in section five. More likely the judges had been concerned by the way in which the wording of the act of 1566 seemed to give the crown no title to the goods of the felon for the crime of which he was originally accused and for which he had had his clergy, should on subsequent trial for non-clergyable offences he be acquitted.

While there were three statutes which affected the mechanism of benefit of clergy in a general way there were as many as fourteen which removed the privilege from separate classes of felonies. Eleven of these types of felony were novel, being created by the statute which at the same time forbade benefit of clergy for them, although at least three and probably four, could be regarded also as slight emendations or extensions of existing felonies. What these eleven categories of crime had in common was, as we might expect, a close connection with areas of contemporary and major governmental concern. 14 Elizabeth c.5 made non-clergyable felons of erstwhile beggars who quit service a second time; 39 Elizabeth c.17 did the same for wandering men calling themselves soldiers and assembling in highways who offended a second time, and to soldiers and sailors found lacking a proper testimonial from a justice of the peace or who failed to reach their home or birth-place within a regulated time; 43 Elizabeth c.13 made felons without benefit of clergy out of those who abducted persons, ransomed them, extorted from them or burned barns in the four northern counties. Two other statutes in this category were concerned with offences not very far from treason: 23 Elizabeth c.2 made felony without benefit of clergy out of repeating slanderous tales about the queen (if it was the second time the offender had erred in this way), printing, writing or publishing a seditious book,[164] or 'casting nativities' and 'prophesying' as to how long the queen would live and who should succeed her; 27 Elizabeth c.2 classified as felons who should not have the clerical privilege wilful receivers and comforters of Jesuits and seminary priests. Two acts of 1593, 35 Elizabeth cc.1 and 2, were concerned with recusants. The first, aimed at sectaries, made non-clergyable felony out of refusing to attend divine service or persuading others not to attend and then when convicted refusing to abjure the realm or doing so only to return without permission. The second, entitled an act for restraining Popish recusants worth less than 20 marks a year, provided similarly for catholics who refused to confess their conformity and then would not abjure the realm, or who did so and returned without royal licence.

The four statutes which extended or slightly altered existing felonies were concerned with more mundane offences than religion or sedition. Two which were passed in the parliament of 1563 concerned forging evidence and being an 'Egyptian' or consorting with the same. 5 Elizabeth c.14 stipulated that forgers of evidences in regard to land or those who offered such forgeries in court, if they committed such a crime a second time, should be held as felons and be deprived of advantage of their clergy. 5 Elizabeth c.20 was aimed at those who consorted with Egyptians. It was thought necessary because the original act against those wanderers, 1/2 Philip and Mary c.4, was being interpreted by some justices as not relevant to the native English who were living with them.[165] The Elizabethan act therefore, having confirmed the Marian, made felons out of all those who were found to have been in the disguise or in the company of vagabond Egyptians for more than a month, and forbade them benefit of clergy. Of the other two statutes 18 Elizabeth c.7, which as we have seen also altered the mechanisms of benefit of clergy in a general way, abolished the clerical privilege for any manner of 'Rapes, Ravishementes of Women, Maydes, Wieves and Damsells and of felonious Burglaries', adding for good measure that those found guilty (or the technical equivalent) of these crimes should suffer death and forfeiture as for felony. In addition the fourth section of the act extended the laws on rape to make felony of having carnal knowledge of girls under the age of ten.[166] The second act to be noticed here was 31 Elizabeth c.12. It extended 2/3 Edward VI c.33, which was concerned with the theft of horses. It altered the law concerning benefit of clergy by taking the privilege away from all accessaries to horse-stealing whether they were involved before or after the fact.

The three established felonies for which in future the perpetrators were to be denied benefit can be listed in similar short order. The act 8 Elizabeth c.4 denied clergy to any who cut or picked purses 'subtly or privily', thus making a distinction with common larceny. The statute 39 Elizabeth c.9 provided for what was considered the insufficiency of 3 Henry VII c.2, which had made felony out of abducting heiresses. This act, in defending its own necessity, explained why all these exclusions of benefit had come about,[167] and then it deprived principals and all accessaries before the fact. Lastly there was 39 Elizabeth c.15, the third statute denying clergy passed in the parliamentary session of 1597. It was concerned with the robbing of houses and stipulated there should be no clergy for those stealing in daytime, with no one being therein, goods of five shillings or more in value. Miscreants, it pointed out, realizing that robbing houses by daylight when no one was at home carried a less severe penalty, had turned increasingly to this crime.

The legislation on the matter of benefit of clergy was thus extended and substantial, demonstrating that the privilege, its use and abuse, gave the government a frequently recurring cause for concern. To reduce the periphery of the benefit seemed an obvious way, so the king and his advisers thought, to cut down the level of crime and satisfy the persistent complaints about the latter emanating from parliament. Yet they could not do so easily, for the church fought long and hard to preserve the privilege and by the middle of the sixteenth century it may well have been that there was some resistance to abolition among the middle and higher ranks of lay society. Apart from the frequency of remedial legislation (and instructive as is the provence of the legal notions contained therein) and the sparse comments of medieval and Tudor legal writers, do we have any evidence of how frequent the claiming of *privilegium fori* was? The answer is that we do, both from the middle ages and the sixteenth century, although in neither case is it so extensive as to be conclusive.

Thus the extant Wiltshire gaol delivery rolls of the period May 1275 to January 1304 show that of a total of 560 persons charged only twenty (3.57 per cent) requested the privilege. Records of trailbaston trials in London in 1305 and 1306 yield a ratio slightly higher: there were 30 cases where clergy was claimed, in a total of 350.[168] An examination of the surviving gaol delivery rolls for Norfolk, Northamptonshire, and Yorkshire for the period 1300 to 1348 has been held to show that benefit of clergy was claimed in 'from 5 to 16 per cent' of the cases with some sizeable but not persistent differences of incidence between county and county and from decade to decade, the Yorkshire average being distinctly lower than the other two shires'.[169] Other samples from this period, substantially smaller in the number of cases they contain, give an incidence of privilege claiming even lower, as does one from the mid-fifteenth century where the figure is only 2.22 per cent.[170] Such evidence suggests that into the fifteenth century complaints about benefit of clergy must have been occasioned rather by the notoriety of the claimants than the incidence of the claims, which was never great. Of course not all seekers of the privilege were successful. The Wiltshire gaol delivery rolls mentioned above show 20 per cent of claimants were refused, but the London trailbaston records reveal only two out of 30 cases where clergy was pleaded unsuccessfully. The extant gaol delivery rolls for Cambridgeshire for the years 1332–4, admittedly a smaller sample, do not provide a single example of failure.[171]

Although it is not possible to discover with any degree of accuracy how many accused persons took to their clergy under the earlier Tudors a fairly clear picture can be obtained for the reign of Elizabeth, or at least for a large part of it. The so called 'assize files' for Essex reveal a relatively high percentage of convicted felons pleaded their clergy and did so successfully.[172] In the period 1566–70 the percentage was 34.5, in 1571–5 it was 25.0 and in 1576–80 30.8. The high years were the 1580s: in 1581–5 it was 51.3 and in 1586–90 53.1. Thereafter there was a modest decline: in 1591–5 it was 47.3 and in 1596–1600 41.7. Literacy may well have been relatively common in south-eastern England for if we look at the north west, at the comparable sessions of the palatinate of Chester, we discover benefit of clergy was allowed much less frequently in these years.[173] The records, which unfortunately do not provide satisfactory figures for the period 1558–65, show that in 1566–70 the percentage was 14.75, in 1571–5 17.6, and in 1576–80 20.7. Thereafter there was an increase, but not a steady one: in 1581–5 the percentage was 28.3, in 1586–90 it was 27.5, while in 1591–5 a peak of 38.7 was reached. In the closing years of the century, 1596–9, the percentage declined to 25.7. The assize records for Sussex provide figures which, as we might expect, lie somewhere between those for Essex and Cheshire. In that county in the years 1566–70 felons obtained the clerical benefit in 18.7 per cent of cases tried, and the figure remained virtually the same in the subsequent quinquennium (18.6 per cent). In contrast with the other two counties there was a decline in the period 1576–80 to 15.7 per cent, but there then followed a sharp rise to 35.1 per cent for the years 1581–5, the statistics for 1582–3 being particularly high. This was the peak in incidence, for the period 1586–90 showed a decline to 29.9 per cent and 1591–5 a further one to 23.7 per cent. The last five years of the decade, in Sussex as elsewhere, also demonstrated a decline, this time a very marginal one, to 23.6 per cent.[174]

One possible factor which springs to mind when we are seeking to account for this decrease in benefit cases is a more severe application of the reading test by the judiciary. It has been stated that from 1559 to 1589 the assize files are lacking any instances where clergy was refused because the claimant failed the reading test but that from the latter date onward failures became a 'regular feature'.[175] This is not strictly accurate. There were some examples before 1589, though few; and there were some after, but again few. The Sussex assize records provide one case where the clergy claimant failed the test at the delivery sessions of June 1589 and five more at those of 1590. Thenceforward there were but two others (one each at the deliveries of February and July 1595) in the 23 sessions for which we have records to the end of the reign. In Hertfordshire the first examples appeared in July 1590, when there were two. In the deliveries of July 1591, February 1592, and July 1592 there was a total of eight cases where it occurred but thereafter only three more (all in February 1595) in fifteen deliveries before Elizabeth's death.[176] The incidence of *non legit* cases in Sussex between 1585 and 1603 was 4.94 per cent of all cases where clergy was claimed, and 1.10 per cent of cases of every sort. The figures for Essex were even smaller. There was one case at the gaol delivery of July 1589, two at that of July 1590, and one each at those in the summer of 1591, March 1594, and March 1595. There were thus only six such cases in that period in a total of 314 where clerical benefit was claimed, a percentage of 1.91. This hardly looks like 'the re–emergence of benefit of clergy as a meaningful test of literacy' nor yet an 'abrupt hardening of judicial attitudes';[177] it is much more like an *ad hoc* response to spasmodic exhortation by the privy council to limit the allowance of the clerical privilege if there was any reasonable opportunity.

One other cause of the decline in the incidence of clerical benefit cases in the last dozen or so years of the reign of Elizabeth is perhaps to be found in the increasing frequency with which juries found those who had stolen goods to be guilty only of petty larceny (i.e. of articles worth less than one shilling) and therefore not capable of being condemned to death or able to have their clergy. Certainly the percentage of those arraigned who came within the category increased noticeably from 1590 and particularly markedly in the last seven years of the reign. In the Essex assize files of the period 1581–90 393 persons were found guilty and only in 41 cases (10.4 per cent) was the value of the goods set at less than a shilling and the crime rated as trespass. In the period 1591–5 by comparison there were 203 convictions as felons and 30 cases in which the crime was found to be only trespass (14.7 per cent), and in 1596–1602 308 convictions and 75 cases giving a percentage of 24.3. The palatinate of Chester pleas tell a story that is not much dissimilar. In 1571–5 the percentage of those found guilty whose theft was rated at less than twelve pence was 16.6. In 1581–5 there was a rise to 21.1 per cent, a proportion which stayed fairly constant until the last years of the century when there was a further increase to 24.0 per cent. The finding of theft as amounting only to petty larceny may have been a reaction on the part of petty juries against judicial reluctance to allow the clerical privilege. However, we cannot be certain these decisions were not reached without the approval or indeed at the prompting of the bench, who were likely to prefer a whipping to an acquittal.

The attitudes of the judiciary have also to be considered in regard to matters of greater moment. To what degree, we may ask, was the letter of the many and varied new regulations concerning benefit of clergy properly observed and operated by those who administered justice? Did the justices of the benches make their own distinctive interpretations of the new laws; did they implement new statutes only when it suited them? Was there not, as has been recently suggested, a considerable difference, perhaps for the purpose of equity and moral justice, between the theory and the application of the criminal law?

As part of this thesis it has been implied that the part of the act 18 Elizabeth c.6 which referred to benefit of clergy in regard to those convicted of burglary was totally ignored by the judiciary until after a conference at Serjeants' Inn at Trinity term 1594.[178] On that occasion, so it was reported, the judges and the barons of the exchequer decided that breaking into a house at night with intent to commit a felony was burglary even if there was no one present in the house at the time. This decision was apparently to counter the nefarious practice of inserting, quite untruly, in burglary indictments that there had been occupants in the house burgled at the time of the offence. The report tells us the judges were influenced in reaching their conclusion by two factors: there was in existence 'the statute of 18 Elizabeth' which took away clergy 'in every case of burglary'; there were also 'ancient presidents' which demonstrated conclusively that it had not been the practice of yore to mention that anyone was in the house.[179] No exception can be taken to the second argument; such an effort to keep the criminal law in harmony with its past was entirely praiseworthy, but the first was distinctly odd. What notice had been taken of the 1576 statute between its promulgation and 1594? Had it been interpreted in that period as forbidding clergy only when the house broken into had occupants; was it in fact (since such had apparently been the practice in the period before 1576) totally ignored?

The wording of the act was that those found guilty of felonious ravishment, rape, or burglary, were to suffer death and forfeiture without benefit of clergy. This juxtaposition of burglary and rape suggests one possible cause of the new law. It may have been that the statute was originally designed to deal with burglary in the course of ravishment for it was common for the assailant during the abduction (which is what many sixteenth century rapes really were) to take some of the woman's personal possessions with him, which was then charged as burglary by the irate husband.[180] However, this theory rests on the assumption that some words in the act showing a greater connection between rape, ravishment, and burglary, were lost through amendment in passage through parliament, and such evidence we do not have. Another possibility is that the statute was designed to remove doubt about the word 'burglary', whose relationship with benefit of clergy had not been clearly stated in parliamentary acts. Indeed it had been persistently confused there with robbery. Thus the act 4 Henry VIII c.2 and its reviver 23 Henry VIII c.1 had denied the clerical privilege where there was robbery perpetrated in houses, the dwellers in which were present and put in dread. Neither of these statutes mentioned burglary *per se* at all, although the subsequent 25 Henry VIII c.3 clearly stated that 23 Henry VIII c.1 referred to 'robbers, murderers and burglaries'. The latter act was reaffirmed in fact though not by name a second time by the statute 1 Edward VI c.12, but this did not use the word 'burglary' either, even if it spoke of the breaking of houses by day or night when the person within was put it fear or dread. The designers of this statute were obviously attempting to ensure that by speaking of house-breaking 'by night' burglary was specifically included for the essence of that crime, at least according to Marowe and the *Boke of Justyces of Peas*, was nocturnal breaking into a dwelling place and the committing of a felony or breaking in with intent to murder (according to Marowe) or rob (according to the *Boke*).[181] Two later Edwardian acts, 5/6 Edward VI cc.9 and 10, the first extending 23 Henry VIII c.1 the second reviving 25 Henry VIII c.3, although dealing *inter alia* with the crime which was in fact burglary did not use the word save in one place where it had figured in a general way in the 1534 statute. Neither did the Marian act 4/5 Philip and Mary c.4 which withdrew benefit from pre-facto accessaries; this, like the Henrician and Edwardian acts, preferred 'robbery from houses' to 'burglary'.

By the beginning of Elizabeth's reign, as Staunford shows, burglary was an accepted category of offence among lawyers even if it had not yet become part of the vocabulary of the statutes. Thus when in 1576 it was felt the recipients of clerical privilege should be reduced further it was not unnatural to use the word. Yet there was a distinct danger in this course because, to judge by Staunford's definition, the debate as to what the essential elements were had not, in his time at least, been concluded. Could burglary be committed by day as well as by night? Staunford certainly thought so but he found it necessary to add that all burglary indictments should say nevertheless 'quod noctanter fregit'.[182] In 1576 burglars lost benefit of clergy, but what exactly was burglary? The statute gave no indication. Was it burglary if there was no one in the home broken into who might be put in fear or, as just mentioned, if the crime was committed in the daytime? We can see therefore that in the years following 1576 it is quite possible the judges might have been inclined to allow benefit where such circumstances were established.

Even so there do not seem overall to have been many such burglary cases between 1576 and 1594. In Sussex there were at first sight six, yet one was concerned with breaking into a granary while another was in regard to a close. In a third case the accused was an accessary, probably a receiver, whom the law clearly allowed to have benefit. There were in fact only three cases of burglary, in a total of 121 felony cases of all types between February 1577 and February 1595, in which benefit of clergy was successfully claimed, where there can be any suspicion that the justices allowed benefit against the tenor of the law. The 115 cases which were not burglary, we may note incidentally, involved largely felonious larceny for which, of course, benefit was quite permissible as well as eleven cases of non-murderous and therefore clergyable homicide and a single instance of arson. In Hertfordshire between March 1576 and the summer of 1595 there were 99 out of a total of 381 cases of felony in which the clerical privilege was claimed successfully. Not one was burglary on the part of a principal; indeed there was only one such case in the whole of the Hertfordshire assize records for Elizabeth's reign. In Cheshire between July 1576 and October 1595 71 men successfully claimed clergy but only one of these had been indicted of burglary, virtually all the others being charged with larceny. Only in Essex do we find there was a sizeable proportion of burglars who achieved the clerical privilege. The assize records for that county show 172 cases of burglary tried between March 1576 and August 1594 with the clerical benefit being successfully claimed in 55 of them, a percentage of 31.9. The two gaol deliveries of July 1580 and March 1581 provided a combined total of ten cases and that of July 1587 a similar number, which were a high proportion of the total number of burglaries tried at those times, the percentages for the three different years being 100.0, 60.0, and 83.3 respectively. These figures stand in contrast with the low percentages for the similar sessions of April 1579 (7.14), July 1586 (12.3), and March 1587 (10.0), and particularly with those of March 1576, July 1576, July 1578, August 1579, March 1582, and March 1584 where there were no instances at all. From 1588 to 1594 there were never more than three cases in which the accused was allowed the privilege in any gaol delivery and the average was only one per sessions. When the judges held their conference at Serjeants' Inn in 1594 there had only been one instance in Essex of burglary for which benefit of clergy had been allowed in the last four gaol deliveries.

This uneven pattern in the incidence of clerical benefit for burglary in Essex is particularly difficult to explain since in the period 1576 to 1594 the commissions of gaol delivery contained the same names year after year and there cannot have been sudden changes of judicial policy through the introduction of new justices. Perhaps the cause was direction from the centre. Before the commissioners set out for Chelmsford or whatever, they may have been instructed by means of a circuit charge that for this turn benefit of clergy for burglary was to be eschewed; on another occasion they may have been advised that it was permissible or more likely, failure to advise was taken as permission to allow it. Against this thesis is the extremely small number of burglary cases where benefit was claimed successfully which appear in the records for Hertfordshire and Sussex, counties in the same judicial circuit. One other possible explanation is that perhaps Essex, a shire which seems to have had a fairly high standard of literacy, had established a local tradition of allowing the clerical privilege to a sizeable percentage of burglars but that this was sometimes overridden or curtailed by the orders of the crown.

Perhaps from 1512, certainly from the reign of Edward VI, it had been an occasional practice to reinforce burglary indictments with a statement to the effect that at the time of the offence the owner, his family, or his servants were present within the house burgled; sometimes it was stated they had been put in fear or dread.[183] The intention was to profit from those statutes which forbade benefit of clergy to men who committed burglary in such circumstances. In the Essex assize files the first instance of this sort of afforcement dates from March 1561. The next occurred in the gaol delivery of March 1575, there was one in March 1576, a fourth in July 1578, and then five appear in the records of April 1579. There were another 23 examples in the 1580s after which, to the middle of the subsequent decade, each gaol delivery shows three or four instances. From 1597 the number per sessions increased sharply, there being as many as eleven in the assizes of June 1597, ten in February 1598, and eleven in July 1601. Did the inclusion in indictments of a reference to the owners or the members of his household being present when the crime was committed, prevent, or at least hinder, the obtaining of clerical privilege? The answer seems to be that it did. In the period March 1575 to August 1594 there was only one such case in Essex where clergy was allowed (2.7 per cent) and indeed there was only one other between 1594 and the end of the reign.

Very probably these phrases of afforcement also increased the chances of a conviction. Petty juries were seemingly very eager to find the accused guilty. The Essex assize records show that in these cases, as long as the crime remained burglary and was not commuted into a lesser offence and as long as the accused was actually put on trial, the percentage of 'guilty' verdicts was 93.1 while acquittals amounted to only 6.9. This contrasts with the whole class of burglary cases in this period (1576–94) where convictions amounted to only 72.9 per cent and acquittals 27.1.

Recently the argument has been advanced that criminal process underwent notable changes at the end of the 1580s and that benefit of clergy figured prominently in this 'mini-revolution'.[184] What arose at this time, we are told, was what is now known as 'plea-bargaining', a general and self-explanatory term which covers three types of procedural development. There was in certain cases of theft an increase in pleas of guilty with the value of the goods stolen found by the jury to be under twelvepence, not a greater sum as stated in the indictment originally; in a few of these cases, apparently, the confession was followed by a request for the clerical benefit which was allowed even if the convicted man was unable to read. There was also a rise in the number of cases where the court decided the claimant of clergy could not read and therefore could not have the benefit. Thirdly, there appear in the assize files a number of cases where the clerical privilege was permitted although the offence was burglary. These cases demonstrate, so the thesis runs, that the bench was not following the normal procedures of the common law but striking bargains with the accused, waiving penalties in some cases but taking a sterner line than had been customary in others; they were behaving in this unfettered and discretionary manner in order to deal with a considerable rise in felony and also, for purposes of equity, to moderate the unfairness of the common law's anomalies. Whether this argument is true or false is not at the moment to be determined; we need more evidence of the gaol delivery variety from parts of the country other than the south-east and this is scant. The files for Essex, Sussex, and Hertfordshire, as we have seen, do not provide unqualified support. Certainly we cannot accept without reservation the view that 'it seems very unlikely that in practice assize judges respected the technical distinction between clergyable and non-clergyable felonies.[185] The evidence outlined above suggests that, although there must have been times of remissness, the judges, in a high percentage of cases, were careful to follow the law, and their zeal to do so was apparently stimulated by a watchful eye on high.

Perhaps the most remarkable thing about benefit of clergy in the last years of the sixteenth century was its continued survival when there was no longer delivery of the successful claimant to the custody of the bishop. For this we must credit not so much the judges or the lawyers as society as a whole. The literate ranks of society do not seem to have been at all hostile to the institution, wondering perhaps if they themselves might not have need of it someday. The petty juries must also have been witnesses to its usefulness. Because of the existence of benefit of clergy the jurors may have felt more free to return verdicts of guilty, for they knew the convicted man still had at least one opportunity of saving his neck. The criminals themselves, even if not vocal on the matter, cannot have been blind as to the value of clerical benefit and may have planned and committed for preference crimes which would provide them if taken with the protection of the privilege. Indeed, it has been calculated that following the promulgation of the statute 39 Elizabeth c.15, which removed benefit of clergy from the reach of those who stole goods or cattle worth over five shillings from houses or out-houses in the day time, thefts of the breaking in variety diminished from 25 per cent of property offences to a meagre seven per cent.[186] In the fifteenth century there were moves to restrict benefit of clergy by limiting it to those who were in holy orders. In the sixteenth the policy changed to restriction through the exclusion of those who had committed offences of a particular type. By Elizabeth's reign the only crimes of importance where the privilege was allowed were felonious killing of the non-murderous variety and felonious larceny. It is by no means impossible that the much criticized institution of benefit of clergy helped to change the pattern of crime so that criminals learned to eschew violence to persons and make do with furtive theft.

The history of benefit of clergy in the fifteenth and sixteenth centuries was therefore, as we have seen above, a complex one, but the main features are not, I think, in doubt. Throughout the later middle ages and into the Tudor period the judges of the two benches, who were in essence the interpreters of the secular law (common or statute), generally showed an eagerness to diminish the role and authority of the ecclesiastics in regard to the privilege. They constantly whittled away at the position of the ordinary in regard to the examination of clerks and criticised such not uncommon occurrences as easy purgation, failure to degrade, escapes from bishops' prisons, and the committing of new offences by those who had been allowed benefit for an earlier one. There was, we may suspect, a clandestine struggle over the ex-officio inquest and possibly one over clerical offenders having to offer any plea at all in the secular courts. The latter issue surfaced in 1462 when the church in theory won the immediate delivery of arrested clerics to the ordinary and an ecclesiastical trial for them instead of one before lay justices. Although there is little indication the stipulations of the charter were ever put into operation, the episode revealed the church had hopes, indeed intentions, either of trying to regain ground lost in the twelfth and thirteenth centuries or of making a pre-emptive strike, as the modern term is, to confound any further attempts at aggrandizement by the secular judges and their governmental masters. The showdown came in 1515. Although on the surface the quarrel between the clergy, and their ally the pope, and the secular authorities was over the exclusion of those in lesser orders and literate laity when they committed robbery, burglary, sacrilege or murder in certain places, the underlying issue was whether clerks should be convened before secular judges at all. The result was a draw, but one slightly more favourable to the church than its opponents. To prevent future conflict the ecclesiastics seem subsequently to have made some effort to do away with lesser orders, but to no great effect.

In the 1530s the church's secular opponents took the offensive. The statute which had led to the confrontation in 1515 was renewed, and benefit of clergy was removed from some existing felonies and limited in regard to other new ones. In addition, the administration of the common law in regard to the privilege was improved so that record could be kept of those who had received it. Edward VI's short reign in contrast, even if some of the restrictive statutes of Henry VIII were renewed, saw benefit made more available. This was in part because of the removal of the rule denying it to bigamists and partly through its being allowed to secular peers, whether they could read or not, which was the biggest anomaly in the history of the privilege. Mary's reign, somewhat surprisingly, saw no significant extension but rather a contraction. It appears to have been in the time of Edward VI and Mary, and particularly through the Edwardian repeals and confirmations which did not cover the full extent of the statutes they were repealing or renewing, that confusion about the scope of benefit started. This was not just among the public. Even judges appear to have been in doubt at times and they seem to have decided to follow the letter of the law exactly, even where the intent of any act was different.

In Elizabeth's reign there was legislation which was reminiscent of that of her father's, namely the removal of the privilege from certain felonies where it was still permitted and its forbiddance in statutes creating new ones. There were however two changes to the benefit which cannot be regarded as other than major, and affecting fundamentally the operation of the criminal law. A statute of 1566 stipulated, *contra* the rule dating from 1352, that allowance of the privilege in regard to a clergyable felony could not henceforward take in any non-clergyable one for which the accused was being arraigned at the same time. An act of 1576 ended the delivery of successful claimants of the benefit to the ordinary and allowed them their freedom after a short time in a secular gaol. Thus the church and its officers no longer figured in the post-trial process of the criminal law.

The statistics we have in regard to the successful claiming of benefit of clergy are by their nature more reliable than those based on other workings of the criminal law. They show a persistent increase in the percentage of such claims from the end of the thirteenth century to the end of the sixteenth. The fact that in the last few years of the latter there may have been a decline in some localities brings us to the important questions of whether by then the justices followed the letter of the law and allowed benefit only where justified, or whether on some occasions they were wont to demand such a high standard of literacy in the reading test that a good percentage of claimants failed, and on others to grant it where not deserved because of 'plea-bargains' struck with the accused. Although the evidence is not unequivocal it seems quite likely that some of the decline in successful claims is attributable to instructions by the queen's legal advisers and to local legal traditions being superseded rather than to judicial bargaining with the accused. In the main, it seems fair to say, the substantial body of law relating to benefit of clergy was interpreted strictly to the late sixteenth century at least.

NOTES

1. *Leges Henrici Primi*, ed. L.J. Downer (Oxford, 1972), p. 178.
2. *Henrici de Bracton de Legibus et Consuetudinibus Angliae*, ed. G.E. Woodbine, translated and revised by S.E. Thorne (Cambridge, Mass., 1968), ii, 348; W. Lyndwood, *Provinciale* (Oxford, 1679), pp. 92–4.
3. A statute of the diocese of Worcester of 1229 mentions clerks as being 'coronati et tonsorati': *Synods and Councils, II*, ed. F.M. Powicke and C.R. Cheney (Oxford, 1964), p. 180.
4. It was held at the end of Edward I's reign that if a man claiming clergy had been taken in lay clothing he ought not to be delivered to the ordinary without proof of his orders 'according to a constitution of the Roman curia': *Select Cases in the King's Bench, I*, ed. G.O. Sayles (Selden Society, 55, 1936), p. 171.
5. See *Year Books, Liber Assisarum*, 26 Edward III no.19.
6. F. Pulton, *De Pace Regis et Regni* (London, 1607), f.207v.
7. *Ibid.*
8. English Reports, 11 Coke 296.
9. M. Hale, *Historia Placitorum Coronae*, ed. Sollom Emlyn (London, 1736), ii, 372. Sir John Spelman, a justice of the king's bench, writing in the reign of Henry VIII, said that any clerk convict who killed a gaoler could not have his clergy; he based this on a case of the eyre of Kent, 1313–14: British Museum, MS. Hargrave 388 f.182v.
10. The canon was not intended to have retrospective force, although the statute of Edward I attributed it with such: see C.R. Cheney, 'The Punishment of Felonous Clerks', *Eng. Hist. Rev.*, li (1936), 217. See also Pollock and Maitland, *History of English Law before the time of Edward I*, i, 445.
11. If, however, the prisoner answered that the bigamy was the 'premier espousals' whilst he was not yet fourteen years of age and that when he reached that age he refused to marry, then the issue of bigamy was to be tried by an inquest of the country: W. Staunford, *Les Plees del Coron* (London, 1557) f.135.
12. *The Mirror of Justices*, ed. W.J. Whittaker (Selden Society, 7, 1895), p. 92.
13. Gabel, pp. 35–51; R.B. Pugh, 'Some Reflections of a Medieval Criminologist', *Proceedings of the British Academy*, lix (1973) 90.
14. 'Videlicet quod clericus de caetero non trahetur ante judicem secularem in persona sua de aliquo criminali . . .': Radulfi de Diceto, *Opera Historica*, ed. W. Stubbs (Rolls Series, 1876), i, 410.
15. A London trailbaston case of July 1306 shows a suspect with no tonsure refusing at first to plead at all save to claim clergy. He was then put to the *peine forte et dure*, which must have made him change his mind, for when brought back to court later he pleaded not guilty: *Calendar of Trailbaston Trials under Commissions of 1305 and 1306*, ed. R.B. Pugh (London, 1975), no. 289.
16. i.e. plead like any lay prisoner would.
17. See Gabel, p. 41 and appendix A.
18. Bracton, ii, 348.
19. *The Roll and Writ File of the Berkshire Eyre of 1248*, ed. M.T. Clanchy (Selden Soc., 90, 1973), pp. 311, 338, 351, 383.
20. This despite what the clergy of Coventry and Lichfield diocese believed in 1256: Powicke and Cheney, p. 508. The royal answer to the complaints of the clergy in the Lent parliament of 1301 about this matter was that the lay justices might pronounce guilt or innocence on the testimony of the laity according to custom; this pronouncement was the announcing of the jury's verdict, not the giving of judgment: *ibid.*, p. 1211.
21. *The Mirror of Justices*, p. 92.
22. Powicke and Cheney, p. 1353. There is evidence of at least one clerk arguing, quite logically, that he could not forfeit because in refusing to plead except to demand benefit of clergy he

had not put himself on the country: *Year Books of Edward II. The Eyre of Kent, 6 and 7 Edward II, A.D. 1313–1314,* ii, ed, W.C. Bolland, F.W. Maitland and L.W. Vernon Harcourt (Selden Soc., 27, 1912) p. 106.

23. The first mention of the crown arguing that restitution of goods was 'of the king's special grace' was in a memorandum about royal responses to the prelates' articles of grievances at the time of the Easter parliament of 1285: see Powicke and Cheney, p. 963. In 1313 the church claimed that the writ so ordering restitution was a new addition: *ibid.,* p. 1353.

24. *Ibid.,* p. 1212.

25. *Ibid.,* p. 1354.

26. *Year Books of Edward II. The Eyre of Kent, 6 and 7 Edward II,* p. 106. 'Ingham. He was sent to the Bishop's prison because he would not put himself [upon a jury] in accordance with the law of the land; and he was claimed by the Ordinary, and so was delivered to him'. *Staunton J.* 'You must say that he was delivered after being found guilty by this Court, for otherwise he would never have been delivered'.

27. Although Staunford, from a case in Richard II's reign, argued that the ordinary's presence was not essential so long as the clerk, if delivered, might be received into his custody: Staunford, *Les Plees del Coron,* f.133.

28. There was a case in the fourteenth century where the ordinary was not ready 'but was not punished': *Year Books, Liber Assisarum,* 12 Edward III no.15.

29. The officers of the abbot of Westminster were referred to as 'attornatos et procuratores nostros speciales': *Select Cases in the King's Bench, IV,* ed. G.O. Sayles (Selden Soc., 74, 1955), p. 52. But see also *ibid.,* p. 103.

30. C.f. *ibid.,* pp. 52, 160.

31. See Gabel, pp. 66–7.

32. Lay plea rolls never said 'the ordinary examined the prisoner'; they said the prisoner 'was examined' or 'after he had been examined' and implied it was an examination by the court, not by the ordinary alone.

33. *Select Cases in the King's Bench, IV,* p. 163.

34. See *Year Books, Liber Assisarum,* 12 Edward III no.15. The first example in *Select Cases in the King's Bench* is from Michaelmas term 1402.

35. *Year Books, Liber Assisarum,* 26 Edward III no.19. In a case of 1331 the ordinary said he would not claim the clerk who had been examined as he did not wish to put his lord in peril: *Select Cases in the King's Bench, V,* ed. G.O. Sayles (Selden Soc., 76, 1957), p. 58.

36. *Year Books, Liber Assisarum,* 12 Edward III no.39; Powicke and Cheney, p. 1212.

37. Staunford, *Les Plees del Coron,* f. 131v.

38. *Mathaei Parisiensis Chronica Majora,* ed. H.R. Luard (Rolls Series, 1872–84) vi, 355–6.

39. Powicke and Cheney, pp. 957, 1211.

40. See *Statutes of the Realm* (Record Commission, 1810–28), i, 174, 326.

41. Powicke and Cheney, p. 1353.

42. However 'fugitives' (presumably those in flight not yet outlawed) might have purgation: Powicke and Cheney, p. 963.

43. *Concilia Magnae Britanniae et Hiberniae,* ed. D. Wilkins (London, 1737), iii, 13–14.

44. *Year Book, 12 Richard II, 1388–9,* ed. G.F. Deiser (Cambridge, Mass., 1914) p. 40.

45. Staunford, *Les Plees del Coron,* f. 138v.

46. The church talked of *de facto* conviction by the laity.

47. Powicke and Cheney, p. 971.

48. *Registrum Johannis de Trillek, A.D. MCCCXLIV–MCCCLXI,* ed. J.H. Parry (Canterbury and York Society, 8, 1912), p. 81.

49. Powicke and Cheney, p. 971.

50. This may be why the members of inquests were often rectors and vicars.

51. Powicke and Cheney, p. 1139.

52. In 1351 the clergy of Canterbury province recommended that there should be inquests taken

at the place of the crime as to the life, fame, and conversation of the clerks, which should be signified to the ordinary.

53. *Registrum Johannis de Trillek*, p. 81; *The Register of Ralph of Shrewsbury, bishop of Bath and Wells, 1329–1363*, ed. T.S. Holmes (Somerset Record Society, 9, 1896), pp. 470–1.

54. *The Register of Walter de Stapleton, Bishop of Exeter, A.D. 1307–1326*, ed. F.C. Hingeston-Randolph (London, 1892), p. 477.

55. See the statutes of Canterbury, I (1213–14), and of Salisbury, I (1217–19): Powicke and Cheney, pp. 37, 73.

56. Powicke and Cheney, p. 719. Five compurgators were suggested for a light crime.

57. As demonstrated by Gabel, p. 103.

58. Staunford, from a case at Michaelmas term 2 Edward III, argued this was only done with the crown's approval since a royal writ to the sheriff was necessary for the effecting of the proclamation: Staunford, *Les Plees del Coron*, f.138.

59. *Ibid.*, f.142.

60. *The Register of Bishop Philip Repingdon, 1405–1419*, ed. Margaret Archer (Lincoln Record Society, 47, 1963), p. xxxiv.

61. Powicke and Cheney, p. 1212.

62. Wilkins, *Concilia*, iii, 13–14.

63. Canon law doctrine of the late twelfth and early thirteenth century concerning the privilege is well explained in C.R. Cheney, *Eng. Hist. Rev.* li (1936), 218–21.

64. Powicke and Cheney, pp. 282, 462, 534, 542. For another view see C.R. Cheney, *Eng. Hist. Rev.*, li (1936), 222, 234–5, where it is pointed out that Bracton stated that if a man failed to purgate he should be degraded but not suffer futher punishment except in cases of apostasy.

65. There is no mention of a clerk losing the temporal lands he held until the later fifteenth century: see *Year Books*, Trin.20 Edward IV no.3. Hale argued that a clerk who made purgation received his lands back; he did not however if he was a clerk attaint, i.e. had confessed the offence: Hale, *Placitorum Coronae*, ii, 383.

66. Powicke and Cheney, p. 684.

67. *Register of Waltter de Stapleton*, i, 477–8.

68. *Year Books* Hil., 28 Henry VI no.4.

69. *Rot. Parl.*, v, 151b.

70. *Ibid.*, v, 333a–334b.

71. P. Heath, *The English Clergy on the Eve of the Reformation* (London, 1969), p. 124.

72. *Calendar of Patent Rolls, 1446–52*, p. 302.

73. Wilkins, *Concilia*, iii, 583–4. The letters patent did not state what earlier grant they were confirming.

74. Heath, *English Clergy*, p. 120.

75. Merks had been indicted for treason and felony although at the trial the justices referred only to treasons: *Select Cases in the King's Bench, VII*, p. 104.

76. Presumably those sent by the lay authority.

77. *Vide infra*. It is most remarkable how the charter has failed to draw the attention and the comments of historians.

78. As Gabel points out (p. 123).

79. It is possible the charter of 1462 accounts for the absence of higher clergy from Yorkist attainder acts.

80. *Registrum Thome Bourgchier, Cantuariensis archiepiscopi, A.D. 1454–1486*, ed. F.R.H. Du Boulay (Canterbury and York Society, 54, 1957), p. 98.

81. See C.B. Firth, 'Benefit of Clergy in the time of Edward IV', *Eng. Hist. Rev.*, xxxii (1917), 180.

82. Wilkins, *Concilia*, iii, 609.

83. *Ibid.*

84. *Ibid.*, iii, 612–13.

85. *Ibid.*, iii, 616.
86. *Year Books*, Pasch. 7 Henry IV no. 6, Trin. 34 Henry VI no. 16. Thomas Marowe, however, writing in 1503–4, stated justices of the peace ought not to fine an ordinary who claimed a clerk unable to read: see B.H. Putnam, *Early Treatises*, p. 411.
87. *Year Books*, Hil. 7 Edward IV no. 12.
88. *Year Books*, Trin. 9 Edward IV no. 41.
89. It was acceptable for the prisoner to spell the words out slowly.
90. Although another case of this time (*Year Books*, Pasch. 21 Edward IV no. 1) can be read as showing ordinaries did have the right to refuse a clerk for not having habit or tonsure.
91. Staunford, *Les Plees del Coron*, f.133.
92. Poulton, *De Pace Regis et Regni*, f.207v; *Year Books*, Trin. 9 Edward IV no. 41.
93. *Year Books*, Mich.13 Edward IV no. 6; *ibid.*, 20 Edward IV no. 3.
94. Staunford, *Les Plees del Coron*, f.131.
95. 18 Henry VII c.19 also made felons of soldiers who returned from beyond the seas without licence.
96. This was the first statute to stipulate branding as a punishment.
97. Gabel, p. 123.
98. *Year Books*, Mich.3 Henry VII nos. 1 and 10.
99. *Year Books*, Trin. 15 Henry VII no. 8.
100. One other matter made more clear in Henry VII's time concerned a prisoner claiming clergy who challenged more than the permissible number of jurors. It was decided in 3 Henry VII he should be committed to the ordinary as a clerk convict, not as a clerk attaint: *Year Books*, Mich.3 Henry VII no. 8. Another clarification was the exclusion from purgation of those outlawed: *Year Books*, Mich.3 Henry VII no. 5.
101. *Year Books*, Trin.15 Henry VII no. 8.
102. The act was 4 Henry VIII c.2.
103. The government had been greatly disturbed by what it took to be a high incidence of serious crime and had issued a proclamation in July 1511 calling for the putting into execution of the statute of Winchester and all 'behaufull' laws: P.R.O. SP 1/231/174 (*Calendar of Letters and Papers, Foreign and Domestic, Henry VIII, Addenda*, i (1), no.97).
104. C.f. A.F. Pollard, *Wolsey* (London, 1953), p. 31.
105. *Disciplinary Decrees of the General Councils*, ed. H.J. Schroeder (London, 1937), p. 498.
106. They were Silvester de Giglis, bishop of Worcester, John Fisher, bishop of Rochester, Thomas Dokwra, prior of the order of St. John of Jerusalem, and Richard Kidderminster, abbot of Winchcombe: *Letters and Papers, Henry VIII*, I (1), nos.1048, 1067.
107. See S.F.C. Milsom, 'Richard Hunne's Praemunire', *Eng. Hist. Rev.*, lxxvi (1961), 80–2. Hunne also brought an action of slander against Henry Marshal, parish priest of Whitechapel and chaplain to the rector, who began the trouble by demanding the mortuary.
108. J. Fines, 'The Post Mortem Condemnation for Heresy of Richard Hunne', *Eng. Hist. Rev.*, lxxviii (1963), 529–31; Pollard, *Wolsey*, p. 33.
109. *The Anglica Historica of Polydore Vergil, A.D. 1485–1537*, ed. D. Hay (Camden Society, 3rd Ser. 74, 1950), p. 229.
110. See note 106.
111. English Reports, Keilway 180–5, is where the only detailed description of the episode is to be found. It has been suggested the reporter was in fact John Carrell: L.W. Abbott, *Law Reporting in England, 1485–1585*, (London, 1973), p. 39.
112. According to Wolsey's secretary Tuke, the clergy in convocation later denied they ever put articles to Standish so as to help maintain a position that clerks should not be convented before lay judges; nor had words to that effect ever been uttered in the convocation house. Nonetheless the very way the articles were phrased shows what the clergy were thinking and what, when Standish was dealt with, they hoped to achieve. In seeking the exemption of clerks from being summoned before temporal justices the clergy had shifted from the position

they had been seeking in Edward IV's reign. The constant element in the charter of 1462, the complaint of 1471, the supplications of 1475 and 1481, was that no man in holy orders should be put to answer in a secular court, not all clerks: P.R.O. SP 1/ 12/ 18–21 (*Letters and Papers, Henry VIII*, ii, no.1314).

113. Standish was also accused of saying knowledge of the sacred canons jeopardized theology, of which it was really the servant.

114. English Reports, Keilway 184.

115. The way this statement is put in Keilway suggests at first sight the judges were not at Blackfriars to hear a debate but to serve in a judicial capacity and actually give judgment on the proposers of the bill of conclusions and on Standish for his answers. Yet it is possible the judges hesitated to act in this role, realizing their inadequacies where common and statute law did not reach, and resolved to condemn the whole proceedings by pointing out how the very raising of the issues fell within the bounds of the statute of praemunire. This might perhaps have been through the clergy's acceptance of the Lateran council decree of 5 May 1514.

116. Pollard, *Wolsey*, p. 40.

117. Warham again hinted he was willing to suffer for his support of clerical privilege when he was accused in the house of lords of consecrating the bishop of St. Asaph illegally: *Letters and Papers, Henry VIII*, v, no.1247.

118. P.R.O. SP 1/12/18–21. (*Letters and Papers, Henry VIII*, ii, no. 1314).

119. Demanded and obtained by Wolsey, according to Pollard: 'Wolsey had wanted authority not only to make it, but to extend it if no scandal arose, and even to make it perpetual. To this the pope demurred saying it was much against the laws of the church to grant an elastic faculty of that nature': Pollard, *Wolsey*, p. 54.

120. *Foedera*, ed. T. Rymer (The Hague, 1741), VI, Pt. i, 111.

121. Heath, *English Clergy*, p. 125.

122. *Letters and Papers, Henry VIII*, iv, 2555–8.

123. Wilkins, *Concilia*, iii, 713.

124. *Letters and Papers, Henry VIII*, iv (2), no. 4120.

125. B.M. MS. Hargrave. 388 f.108; Wilkins, *Concilia*, iii, 812.

126. And indeed treating them in every way like those in lesser orders or as laity were.

127. The statute 4 Henry IV c.3, which was mentioned in the preamble to this act, was concerned with petty treason and notorious thieves.

128. Christopher St. German, *A Treatise concerninge the division betwene the spirytualtie and temporaltie* (1532) f.30v. He commented that judges did not make priests read if they could show their letters of ordination: *ibid.*, f.32v. He thought that perhaps the act 23 Henry VIII c.1 gave priests even greater privileges, but was not certain: 'never the lesse I leve that matter to the determination of other' (f.33v).

129. 3 Edward I c.1 and 4 Henry IV c.3.

130. The act 21 Henry VII c.7 made a felon out of a servant who embezzled his master's goods, and 27 Henry VIII c.17 took away from such the privilege of his clergy.

131. The act may well have been drafted with the 'impending visitation of the monasteries' in mind, as Lehmberg says (S.E. Lehmberg, *The Reformation Parliament 1529–1536*, (Cambridge, 1970), p. 185), but to suggest it mush have been aimed at the church because it denied benefit of clergy to offenders is doubtful logic. The considerable number of other statutes denying benefit of clergy at this time shows that such provision was frequently made where any type of literate person was thought to be involved.

132. *Journals of the House of Lords* (n.d.), i, 59b (as pointed out by G.R. Elton, *Reform and Renewal* (Cambridge, 1973), p. 148).

133. For example of the strictures against it see Powicke and Cheney, pp. 219, 632, 1068–9.

134. Nicolas, vii, 30; *Letters and Papers, Henry VIII*, xv, no. 926.

135. See for example Powicke and Cheney, pp. 1062, 1073.

136. In the early fourteenth century it looked for a time as if necromancy was going to become a felony. There was a case in 1324 where a necromancer was appealed of feloniously attempting to compass the death of Edward II, the earl of Winchester, and the prior of Coventry. The principal died before trial and the accessaries were acquitted: *Select Cases in the King's Bench, IV*, pp. 154–7. In a case of 1331 it was decided that although an attempt had been made to kill a minister of the king 'per artem ymagicam et karactas' because it had been unsuccessful there was nothing to justify proceedings which might endanger life and limb (i.e. put the suspect to answer for felony): *ibid.*, *V*, 56. For an example from 1457 of necromancy being tried at the same time as heresy see *Lincoln Diocese Documents, 1450–1544*, ed. A. Clark (Early English Text Society, Original Series, 149, 1914), p. 111.

137. Coke, *The Third Part of the Institutes of the Laws of England*, p. 44; *Select Cases in the King's Bench, V*, p. 56.

138. See Elton, *Reform and Renewal*, p. 136n.

139. Presumably the crown wanted to have this information to hand when the question of a pardon arose.

140. The act has not always been noticed by historians; c.f. Cockburn, *A History of English Assizes*, p. 129n.

141. Perhaps the potential financial profit to the king had always been present in the minds of those who designed, on the crown's behalf, statutes limiting benefit of clergy.

142. *Tudor Royal Proclamations I*, ed. P.L. Hughes and J.F. Larkin (New Haven, 1964) no.179.

143. W.K. Jordan, *Edward VI: The Young King* (London, 1968), p. 172. However, Bush sees Somerset as 'undoubtedly a firm supporter' of the act but not acting alone or prompted by liberal principles: M.L. Bush, *The Government Policy of Protector Somerset* (London, 1975), pp. 135–6.

144. Jordan, *Edward VI: The Young King*, p. 175.

145. Because of this omission the judges, interpreting 1 Edward VI c.12 strictly, decided at Easter term 1 Mary that for the listed crimes accessaries before the fact might have their clergy: *English Reports*, 1 Dyer 99a.

146. Whether the Edwardian act annulled 32 Henry VIII c.3, which ordered those in holy orders claiming benefit to be burned in the hand and treated as laity, is not clear. Furthermore, setting practice as it was in 1509–10 would allow those in orders to have the privilege several times (i.e. by repealing 28 Henry VIII c.1): see Pulton, *De Pace Regis et Regni*, f.205.

147. Hale, *Placitorum Coronae*, ii, 370.

148. Hale did not believe the words 'shall be in case of a clerk convict that may make purgation' were to be interpreted as excluding a peer who confessed the charge: *Placitorum Coronae*, ii, 377.

149. Thomas Fynes, Lord Dacre 'of the south' was tried for murder in June 1541: P.R.O. KB 8/12/8; Lord Hungerford was attainted of buggery in 1540.

150. One wonders if a notable case of bigamy amongst the secular nobility like that involving the Marquis of Northampton (January 1548) played any part in creating the statute's clauses on bigamy and on benefit for peers: see *Acts of the Privy Council*, ed. J.R. Dasent (London, 1890–1907), ii, 164.

151. Wilkins, *Concilia*, iv, 16.

152. Perhaps their zealous study of the scriptures, especially the Old Testament, made the exiles sympathetic to polygamy (as it seems to have done in regard to slavery). It is worth reminding ourselves that ecclesiastics were formally permitted to marry only by 2/3 Edward VI c.21. The law of men, said the statute, had wrongly forbidden marriage whereas God's law permitted it.

153. And thus not able to be 'put in dread'.

154. 25 Henry VIII c.3 was, as we have seen, a necessary supplement to 23 Henry VIII c.1.

155. *English Reports*, 1 Dyer 99a.

156. *English Reports*, Brooks New Cases, 50.

157. Staunford, *Les Plees del Coron*, f.134v.
158. Pulton, *De Pace Regis et Regni*, f.204v.
159. Hale, *Placitorum Coronae*, ii, 372.
160. Confusion probably came about because men, in 1559, did not know if 1/2 Philip and Mary c.8 had repealed 1 Edward VI c.12. The legislators felt they were in danger of repealing a confirmation, not a repeal.
161. English Reports, 2 Dyer 201b–202a.
162. The statute probably had its origins in Stone's case (English Reports, 2 Dyer 214b–215a). Stone had committed both burglary and larceny on the lord treasurer on the same day. On arraignment for the latter he was convicted, pleaded his clergy, and found 'non legit ut clericus'. He was then reprieved without judgment to another sessions, where he was arraigned for the burglary (which was not clergyable) and found guilty. Mysteriously he was then allowed to take literacy test again and was found a clerk. The judges who debated the case in Serjeants' Inn at Trinity term 4 Elizabeth found him discharged of the clergyable offence but were equally divided on whether he should be executed for the non-clergyable. Those who favoured execution did so because no judgment of clerk convict had been given against him and because the second offence was committed after the arraignment for the first, or at least it could be argued so for the queen's benefit. Presumably once a prisoner was officially designated clerk convict in the court records he could not be arraigned for another offence. Those who favoured discharge did so apparently because it was the court's fault for omitting the words 'tradatur ordinario'; furthermore the two offences were committed the same day 'without priority of time'. They believed being adjudged a clerk convict for the one offence protected the miscreant from the consequences of the other since by such he was discharged of all other felonies done by him before conviction. They pointed out that Staunford (*Les Plees del Coron*, f.108) clearly stated such an offender should be charged with all crimes imputed to him before he was allowed clergy or allowed to depart from the bar. The situation was further complicated according to Sir Matthew Hale (*Placitorum Coronae*, ii, 386) by Stone, on 28 May 1566, being indicted for a murder committed in April 1559 i.e. before the burglary and the larceny. Since he was convicted and executed, said Hale, 'it seems the former opinion obtained', meaning Stone ought not to be saved from a deserved death for the burglary because of having clergy for the larceny, otherwise he would have been saved from execution for murder also.
163. The assize judges made rolls of those convicted of felony who had read, been branded and then delivered. P.R.O. KB 9/150 is one such for the Midland circuit.
164. Or promoting the same.
165. The lawyers were apparently arguing as early as September 1559 that since the Egyptians had come to England from Scotland they could not be charged with felony under the Marian act: P.R.O. SP 12/ 6/ 39 and 51.
166. See English Reports, 2 Dyer 304a.
167. Allowing the privilege emboldened offenders, it was as simple as that.
168. *Wiltshire Gaol Delivery and Trailbaston Trials, 1275–1306*, ed. R.B. Pugh (Wiltshire Record Society, xxxiii, 1978), pp. 34–101; *Calendar of London Trailbaston Trials*, pp. 49–129.
169. B.H. Westman, *A Study of Crime in Norfolk, Yorkshire and Northamptonshire, 1300–1348* (Ph.D. dissertation, University of Michigan, 1970), p. 151.
170. P.R.O. JI 3/213 mm 1–12d. The cases are from Yorkshire.
171. *A Cambridgeshire Gaol Delivery Roll, 1332–1334*, pp. 32–78.
172. The statistics for Essex used here and below are my own computation.
173. These and the subsequent statistics relating to Cheshire are drawn from P.R.O. Chester 21/1 fos.29–199v.
174. See *Calendar of Asssize Records, Sussex Indictments, Elizabeth I*, ed. J.S. Cockburn (London, 1975), pp. 112–384 for these and subsequent Sussex statistics.
175. Cockburn, 'Trial by the Book?', p. 77.

176. These and the subsequent statistics relating to Hertfordshire are calculated from the *Calendar of Assize Records, Hertfordshire Indictments, Elizabeth I*, ed. J.S. Cockburn (London, 1975).
177. Cockburn, 'Trial by the Book?', pp. 77, 79.
178. *Ibid.*, p. 76.
179. English Reports, Popham 42–3, 52–3; Moore K.B. 660 pl. 903.
180. The same is true of the later middle ages.
181. Putnam, *Early Treatises*, pp. 377–8; *The Boke of Justyces of Peas*, B i.
182. W. Staunford, *Les Plees del Coron* f.30.
183. Surely this was done by the proferring of the bill of indictment rather than by the justices: c.f. Cockburn, 'Trial by the Book?', p. 76.
184. Cockburn, 'Trial by the Book?', pp. 72–9.
185. Cockburn, *A History of English Assizes*, p. 128.
186. J.S. Cockburn, 'The Nature and Incidence of Crime in England 1559–1625: A Preliminary Survey', *Crime in England 1550–1800* (London, 1977) ed. J.S. Cockburn, p. 51.

INDEX